VOX DAY

The New
Economy

The Return of
THE
GREAT
DEPRESSION

WND Books

The Return of the Great Depression

WND Books
Published by WorldNetDaily
Los Angeles, CA
Copyright © 2009 by Vox Day

Jacket design by Linda Daly

Interior design and layout by Genesis Group (www.genesis-group.net)

WND Books are distributed to the trade by:
Midpoint Trade Books
27 West 20th Street, Suite 1102
New York, NY 10011

WND Books are available at special discounts for bulk purchases. WND Books, Inc. also publishes books in electronic formats. For more information call (310) 961-4170 or visit www.wndbooks.com.

First Edition

ISBN 10-Digit: 1935071181
ISBN 13-Digit: 9781935071181
E-Book ISBN 10-Digit: 1935071726
E-Book ISBN 13-Digit: 9781935071723

Library of Congress Control Number: 2009936827

Printed in the United States of America

10 9 8 7 6 5 4 3 2 1

CONTENTS

List of Tables and Figures

All Tables and Figures appear courtesy of Vox Day, with the exception of Figure 4.3, which is credited to David E. Runkle and was published in the *Federal Reserve Bank of Minneapolis Quarterly Review*, Vol. 22, No. 4, Fall 1998.

ACKNOWLEDGMENTS

Thanks to Eric Jackson and Joseph Farah for their confidence and Ami Naramor for her editorial labors. Many thanks to Spacebunny for her constant encouragement and support. Thanks to Mark Neuman, Michael Moohr, and Robert Chernomas for the independent studies. An appreciative thanks to Scott Jamison, Peter Magee, Russ Lemley, Larry Diffey, Donald Owen, Don Reynolds, Chris Pousset, Char Live, Ryan Olberding, Tim Peterson, and Mark Niwot, intrepid Vox Popoli readers whose generous assistance with proofreading and content verification was most helpful. And special thanks to The Prisoner, whose Milton Friedman collection proved to be rather useful after all these years.

This book is dedicated to my boys Big Chilly, White Buffalo, and Friedrich der Große, without whom I would not have survived to finish an economics degree.

INTRODUCTION

A SIDE FROM biology and physics, economics is the science that is probably the most relevant to your daily life. But unlike those two sciences, which don't require a conscious knowledge of their principles in order to make effective use of them, an inability to understand basic economic principles is quite likely to have a negative effect on various aspects of your life, especially in the present economic environment. In referring to these principles, I do not mean the colossal clashes of aggregate macroeconomic forces that occupy the headlines; while their interactions will have an effect on your employment, your bank account, and perhaps even your mood, there is no one who truly understands those great forces. In fact, the complexity of their abstract interactions is such that it may not even be possible for anyone to fully comprehend them. I am referring instead to the fact that whether you recognize it or not, you are an economic actor and most of your decisions, conscious and unconscious, have an economic aspect to them. Furthermore, even the smallest of your decisions will inevitably make an impact on the world around you.

At its core, economics is the study of value. The major differences between very different economic theories such as socialism and monetarism can be ultimately traced back to their competing definitions of what value is. This is admittedly not the usual definition of economics, but upon sufficient reflection, it will soon become apparent that every conventional definition of the science can eventually be factored down to a consideration of value. It does not matter if you consider economics to be the study of "the production, distribution, and consumption of goods and services"; "an agglomeration of ill-coordinated and overlapping fields of research" involving history, statistics, theory, sociology, and political economy; or even, as Xenophon defined it, "a branch of knowledge whereby men are enabled to increase the value of their estates." All economics ultimately rests on the basis of a single question: What is value?

The great challenge of economics, as well as the ultimate source of its tremendous complexity, stems from the fact that value is a variable. Even worse, it is an extraordinarily complex variable that can be assigned a different valuation by every single *potential* actor who has the capability of interacting with a particular object or action assigned economic value by someone. Even a series of actions as simple as getting out of bed, taking a shower, and eating breakfast necessarily involves thousands of intertwined economic decisions made by a literally incalculable number of economic actors, each of whom are affected, in turn, by the decisions you made in the fifteen minutes it took you to shave, shower, and drink your coffee. The seemingly insignificant decision to hit the snooze alarm and sleep for an additional five minutes is an action of distinct economic impact with the potential to affect everything from the net consumption of domestic agricultural products to the amount of crude oil imported from Saudi Arabia.

In 1958, Leonard Read of the Foundation for Economic Education wrote "I, Pencil," a story subsequently made famous by Milton Friedman in *Free to Choose*, in order to explain the power of the free market. He told of the amazing way the division of labor and international free trade combined graphite from South America with rubber from Malaysia and wood from Oregon in order to produce something as mundane as a yellow No. 2 pencil. The incredible thing, of course, is that all these diverse elements are produced by the cooperation of people without any central direction. And yet, this classic tale only told half the story, the half related to the supply side. The story on the demand side is arguably even more amazing, as the myriad assignments of personal value for a pencil made by the millions of people who buy pencils and by the tens of millions who elect not to buy them are all factored into an incredibly massive, but ever-changing, computation that always manages to produce a definite price for every single transaction that takes place at millions of different points in the space-time continuum.

Of course, it is impossible to consider the potential economic aspect of all your daily actions; that way lies madness. And yet, there are many decisions that are well worth contemplating from an economic perspective even though they are not usually considered to have much to do with economics. Decisions about attending college, renting, dating, marrying, home-buying, selecting a career, and propagating the species are all life-defining decisions. Each of these decisions has an economic aspect to it, and these economic aspects will often have a significant impact on the shape your life will subsequently take as well as the sort of economic decisions that you will face in the future. Unfortunately, few individuals ever take these economic aspects into account because they are seldom aware that they exist. This means they are also unaware of the probable ramifications of those decisions, to their probable detriment.

This lack of awareness is especially true of politicians, whom the economist Adam Smith described as "assuming, arrogant, and presumptuous" and "great admirers of themselves," a perceptive description that is as relevant in the age of Obama as it was in the age of Pitt the Younger more than two centuries ago. It is doubtful that Jimmy Carter and the Ninety-fifth Congress had any idea that the Housing and Community Development Act of 1977 might eventually play a role in the great tremors that shook the American banking system in 2008, while 25 years later George W. Bush similarly failed to grasp the consequences of his efforts to increase minority homeownership. And yet, despite the complex nature of most economic interactions, they are seldom quite as mysterious or as unpredictable as the financial media leads one to believe with their references to "black swans" and "unforeseeable events." As evidence in support of this assertion, consider the words of one armchair economist written seven years ago.

> "There can be little doubt that the implosion of the equity markets will soon be followed by the pricking of the credit and real estate bubbles. As great financial houses such as Citigroup

and JP Morgan Chase teeter on the edge of bankruptcy, it is well within the realm of possibility that the triple whammy of the equity, credit and real estate implosions will lead to the collapse of the entire global financial system."
—Vox Day, "My Hero, Alan Greenspan," September 23, 2002

The financial crisis was not unforeseeable, it was entirely predictable for those equipped with the correct theoretical models. In retrospect, it is now obvious to everyone that the bipartisan push for increased homeownership through low interest rates and relaxed lending standards did not create wealth in the American economy, but destroyed it instead. But what is less well known is that long before the subprime lending market erupted in 2004, it was already apparent to a few clear-eyed and contrarian economists that the housing market was possessed of the same irrational exuberance that had propelled the 1999 technology stock bubble to such gravity-defying extremes. Even before economic prophets of doom such as Marc Faber, Nouriel Roubini, and Peter Schiff became famous for their correct warnings of imminent crisis, Edward Gramlich, a governor at the Federal Reserve, told Fed Chairman Alan Greenspan that making home mortgages available to low-income borrowers would lead to widespread loan defaults having extremely negative effects on the national economy. This extraordinarily specific warning was given in 2000, amidst the wreckage of the dot-com bomb and before the housing bubble even began. Those possessed of a mordant sense of humor may appreciate how Greenspan rejected Gramlich's recommendation to audit consumer finance companies on the basis of his fear that it might undermine the availability of subprime credit.

Since you are reading this book it has probably not escaped your attention that many of the same individuals who did not see the crisis coming are now loudly assuring the public that the worst is already past, whereas those who correctly anticipated it tend to be somewhat less optimistic about the future. Wall Street televangelist Jim Cramer boldly announced on April 2, 2009 the end of what would be in historical terms a remarkably short depression.

This was less than a year after he was recommending aggressive purchases of stocks with the Dow industrial index priced at 14,280. In early 2008, the current Federal Reserve chairman, Ben Bernanke, told the U.S. Senate Committee on Banking, Housing, and Urban Affairs to expect "a somewhat stronger pace of growth starting later this year." It is perhaps worth noting, then, that the Bureau of Economic Analysis reported a year later that the American economy contracted at a rate of 6.3 percent in the fourth quarter of 2008, a strong pace of *negative* growth equivalent to the evaporation of $908 billion on an annual basis. That was hardly the Fed chairman's first errant forecast; in October 2005 he told Congress there was no housing boom, and that a 25 percent price increase in 24 months simply reflected strong economic fundamentals.[1]

Of course, the credibility of these and many other famous mainstream figures is more than a little uncertain these days. The present crisis was not supposed to be possible in a world without a gold monetary standard. To paraphrase Franklin Allen, professor of finance and economics at The Wharton School, the problem is not so much that the experts missed the crisis as that they absolutely denied it would happen.

> "We believe that the failure to even envisage the current problems of the worldwide financial system and the inability of standard macro and finance models to provide any insight into ongoing events make a strong case for a major reorientation in these areas and a reconsideration of their basic premises."
> —*The Financial Crisis and the Systemic Failure of Academic Economics*, February 2009[2]

This book is not intended as a literary victory lap for a single obscure prediction made by a minor political columnist seven years ago. It is not a get-rich book, a survive-the-post-apocalypse

---

1. Neil Henderson, "Bernanke: There's No Housing Bubble to Go Bust." *The Washington Post*, October 27, 2005.
2. David Colander, Hans Föllmer, Armin Haas, Michael Goldberg, Katarina Juselius, Alan Kirman, Thomas Lux, and Brigitte Sloth, "The Financial Crisis and the Systemic Failure of Academic Economics," Kiel Institute for the World Economy, February 2009.

book, or a thinly disguised marketing tool for a financial services company. Its purpose is merely to consider how, after more than two hundred years of refining the science of political economy, we arrived in the present situation, and to reflect upon where we are likely to go next. My hope is that it will provide you with a rational and educated context to help you make more informed decisions as you face the difficult challenges that lie ahead. It will also help you put the economic news reported by the financial media in a more historical perspective. Neither markets nor economies go straight up or straight down; adding to the degree of difficulty in understanding where they are headed is that the mainstream media from which we receive most of our information has an institutional memory that is measured in days, if not hours. Due to the sizeable bear market rally that began in March 2009, many, if not most, economic observers are presently convinced that the global economic difficulties of last autumn are largely behind us now, courtesy of the aggressive, expansionary actions of the monetary and political authorities.

They are wrong. It is not over. It has only begun.

I believe that what we have witnessed to date is merely the first act in what will eventually be recognized as another Great Depression. The primary questions at this point do not concern *if* it will occur, but rather, the full extent of the economic contraction and how long it will take for the economy to return to its pre-contraction levels of wealth and employment *once it is finally recognized* to be taking place. In the historical case of America's Great Depression, it was 1941 before the economy again reached its nominal 1929 GDP; it was not until 1954 that the stock market returned to its previous levels. It does not require a doctorate in advanced mathematics to realize that if the present contraction is of similar scale to the one that began eighty years ago on Black Tuesday, it may well be 2032 before this second Great Depression comes to a similarly comprehensive end.

For all that it is an important science, it must be kept in mind that economics is a relatively young one. The chaotic nature of its inherent complexity means that economics is almost as much art and intuition as reason and scientific method. While one can use economics to identify trends that enable one to predict the general course of events, one can seldom hope to correctly anticipate either their timing or their scope with any degree of accuracy. Throughout this book, I have made a number of projections about the future based on historical patterns, government-reported data,[3] and economic models that I believe to be the best that economic theorists have made available to us. Because both the data and the models are known to be imperfect, and in some cases even intrinsically flawed, the specific details of these projections will almost certainly turn out to be wrong, although I hope they will hit reasonably near the target. Nevertheless, I have elected not to present these calculated conclusions in the usual Delphic manner favored by economists so as to cover all possible eventualities. To do so would be to destroy the clarity and usefulness of this book. Ergo, the ancient rule applies: *Caveat emptor!*

I have attempted to keep the use of technical terms to a minimum in the text, but because a certain amount of jargon is inescapable, a glossary of important concepts and oft-used abbreviations is available for reference in the appendices. While it is full of numbers, percentages, graphs, and tables, in the interest of clarity I have entirely omitted the algebraic equations so beloved of economic theorists as well as the calculus favored by econometricians. I have also presented the statistical references in the simplest possible terms, so there are no references to logarithms, regressions, or any other statistical methods that the untrained reader would be unlikely to understand. This is a book for economic actors, not the economists who study them.

I should also note that historical events have been largely described according to the conventional terms and measures utilized by mainstream macroeconomists. It is my intention that the reader first understand the present economic circumstances in the same

---

3. Except where otherwise noted, statistics for the various charts and tables in this book are taken from the published reports of the International Monetary Fund, the Federal Reserve, the Bureau of Economic Analysis, and the Bureau of Labor Statistics. Due to the frequent revisions of data performed by these organizations, some statistical figures will likely vary from more recently published numbers.

manner they are presented to him by the media before he is confronted with any unorthodox perspectives. In other words, the fact that I may refer to the size of a national economy in terms of Gross Domestic Product should not be interpreted as contradicting any subsequent doubts expressed about the accuracy or the utility of the statistic reported on a quarterly basis by the U.S. Department of Labor's Bureau of Economic Analysis.

Given its stark message, I do not expect that many readers will find this book to make for enjoyable reading, but I do hope that it will nevertheless prove to be worth the investment of time and money involved. And perhaps it will help to keep in mind that the old maxim about the value of keeping one's head when everyone else is losing theirs applies as well to economics as it does to the field of battle.

June 29, 2009
Geneva, Switzerland

Chapter 1

1988

*The whole world, as we know it, is subject to the law of cause
and effect; no effect can take place without sufficient cause.*
—EUGEN VON BÖHM-BAWERK,
The Positive Theory of Capital, 1891

O N AUGUST 31, 1988, Narita airport was invaded by thousands
of Japanese schoolgirls. Clad in matching navy jackets, white
socks, and plaid skirts, they were nearly rabid with excitement due
to the imminent arrival of the Norwegian electro-popsters *a-ha*,
who were scheduled to begin their Japanese tour at the Sun Palace
in Fukuoka four days later. Their high-pitched, high-speed chatter
that filled the terminal was all but incomprehensible to the executives from the great *keiretsu* who were returning home from business trips to Europe and the United States, and downright alarming
to the Western tourists who were disgorged from the murmuring
quiet of their 747s into the midst of what appeared to be a cross
between a swarming teenage hive and an anime clone army.

Fifty-three miles away from Narita, in the middle of Roppongi,
there was a bar with the name SUNTORY spelled out in large orange
letters across the front window glass. About thirty feet to the left of
the entrance to the bar was an unmarked door that opened to re-
veal a dark and narrow staircase leading down. This descent marked
the entrance to the Lexington Queen, a small and unassuming night-
club that in 1988 was as full of international models and MTV
music celebrities as it was devoid of décor. There was no parking
lot outside, only five or six spaces in front of the Suntory bar that
were invariably occupied by Ferraris or giant white Mercedes sport-

ing tinted windows and multiple cellular antennae. Every celebrity who happened to be passing through Tokyo always seemed to find the time to spend an evening or two in the VIP section at the Queen; on any given evening that autumn one might have encountered David Lee Roth, Dolph Lundgren, or Slash, Duff, and Steve from Guns N' Roses, just to drop a few names.

The celebrities were drawn there by the women, exceptionally tall and beautiful young women who were flown in from around the world by international agencies such as Elite, Yoshié, and John Casablancas. Then, too, there was a seemingly endless supply of less exceptionally beautiful girls of the pretty, fresh-faced sort that one used to see in Sears catalogs and Target newspaper ads. And then, there were the Disneyland dancers, the singers, the Snow Whites, and the Cinderellas. As the novelist Arturo Perez-Reverte once wrote of a sixteenth-century Spanish church, "the presence of so many ladies, genteel or otherwise, drew more males than lice to a muleteer's doublet." The men were at the Queen for the women, while the women were there because it was one of the few places where you could be sure that everyone spoke English. No one there of either sex had any serious interest in Japan or Japanese culture; they were all in Tokyo for the money. And there was a lot of money to be made in Tokyo back in 1988. No-name models could earn $225,000 per year for little more than occasional catalog shoots; the television ads proved that even famous American film stars couldn't resist the lure of the yen. Japan was simply awash with money. Real estate sold for as much as $140,000 per square *foot*, and it was calculated that the 843 acres of the Imperial Palace grounds were worth more than the 101 million acres that made up the entire state of California.

Only a year later, the Tokyo stock market reached such commanding heights that it accounted for 44 percent of the total value of every equity listed on every stock exchange around the world.[4] These stratospheric valuations marked the height of the Heisei Boom, as the Japanese economic expansion from November 1986

---

4. Edward Jay Epstein, "What Was Lost (and Found) in Japan's Lost Decade," *Vanity Fair*, February 17, 2009.

to July 1991 is known. *Gaijin* who were there and experienced it tend to remember different aspects of that crazy time. Since I had just turned twenty prior to my arrival in Tokyo, what I tend to remember most were the girls, the clubs, the cars, and the stars. It was a little bizarre to go from seeing "Sweet Child o' Mine" on MTV one week to trying to decide whether Izzy Stradlin merited a punch in the face or not the next.[5]

It may be difficult to imagine now, when it is China that has been at the forefront of the international news for more than a decade, but back in 1988 the intellectuals of the world were almost uniformly convinced that the future belonged to Japan. As early as 1970, *Time Magazine* had declared the Japanese to be "the heirs presumptive to the 21st century" and suggested that Japan was destined to become a superpower. The titles of the books from that era are telling. *The Emerging Japanese Superstate. Learning to Bow. The Enigma of Japanese Power.* Ezra Vogel's influential *Japan As Number One: Lessons for America* was published in 1979 and, combined with a series of favorable articles in magazines like *Time, Forbes,* and *The Economist,* helped spawn an enthusiasm for all things Japanese among ambitious American businessmen and college students. Everything from just-in-time manufacturing to sushi and karaoke was suddenly in vogue. Ten years after Vogel's book appeared on the scene, Sony Chairman Akio Morita co-published a controversial series of essays with a popular nationalist politician and author, Shintaro Ishihara,[6] entitled *The Japan That Can Say No,* just as Japan reached the very apex of its wealth and power.

Morita and Ishihara's essays were not intended for a foreign audience, and their unusually frank opinions about Japan and the United States were shocking to many in the West. Despite the fact that the Japanese publisher never authorized an English translation, the U.S. government arranged to unofficially translate the book and distributed it to Congress; rumor had it that the CIA was

---

5. He did. But I didn't.

6. Shintaro Ishihara is a fascinating and unusual public figure who won Japan's most prestigious literary award for his first novel in 1956 and had a long and successful career as one of the Liberal Democratic Party's most popular politicians. He has been the governor of Tokyo since 1999.

responsible for the bootleg text that was passed around Washington.[7] Morita's claims that America was unfair, shortsighted, and lacking in business creativity offended American pride, while Ishihara's tendency to blame all American criticism of Japan on racial prejudice bordered on the inflammatory. The book was a bestseller in Japan and reflected the growing Japanese confidence that the nation was ready to step forward into its rightful position of global leadership and that the eventual surpassing of the United States was all but inevitable.

As a visitor to Japan in 1988, it was not at all difficult for me to believe that Japan was the future. William Gibson's award-winning cyberpunk novel, *Neuromancer*, was set in Chiba City, and the neon-lit, technology-driven dystopia it described really didn't seem all that far off the possible mark. I was there to study for six months at Ôbirin Daigaku and lived with a family in Sagamihara-shi, which I was pleased to discover was only 43 miles away from Chiba City. However, the neon lights and flashy technology hadn't quite made it to Sagamihara at that point; in fact, one of the intriguing things about living in Japan at the time was the incredible contrast between the old country of peasants it had clearly been and the new economic powerhouse it was in the process of becoming. The family with whom I stayed was not poor, but they did not own a car, sharing instead a pair of rusty bicycles so ancient that they looked as if they predated Schwinn. The house, with its rice paper "walls," didn't have central heating but was kept warm with kerosene space heaters[8] instead, and the neighborhood houses were numbered *in the order they had been built*, which made it nearly impossible to find any place you hadn't been before.

There was a dramatic sense of change in the air, although the change that was to arrive within months was not of the sort that

---

7. The translator's note to the pirate text is most amusing. "*The material written by Mr. Morita is very straightforward; however, Mr. Ishihara tends to ramble, change from one subject to another without much transition, and uses a great deal of sayings and proverbs which when directly translated to English make no sense. What has been translated is the closest equivalent in English we could get.*"

8. This struck me as insanely dangerous. I was reassured, however, that the heaters were equipped with shutdown valves, so that when an earthquake struck and a heater fell over, you wouldn't actually be guaranteed to burn to death. Wait a minute…did you just say…WHEN an EARTHQUAKE strikes?

anyone was expecting. This was in part because throughout almost the entire course of my stay there, the 124th Emperor of Japan, Hirohito, was in the process of coming to an end. He was in poor health and no one knew what the problem was, except that it appeared to involve near-continuous internal bleeding. It was surreal; every night the evening news gave reports, complete with graphic charts, describing how much blood the Emperor had received in transfusions that day, and how much he had received since he collapsed at the imperial palace in mid-September. The 1988 Summer Olympics were also taking place in Seoul at the time, and although the Japanese aren't necessarily any fonder of *zainichi* than they are of any other group of *gaijin*, there was a definite spirit of Asian pride that added to the feeling of anticipation.

I should quite like to be able to inform you that I was an economic prodigy and had astutely observed that the Japanese economy was in the process of reaching unsustainable heights. The truth is that I was far too dazzled with the amazing wealth and glitter of Tokyo to notice that the nation was fast approaching an economic precipice. But I do recall one conversation that took place towards the end of my visit which serves as an apt reminder of the way that the nationalistic pride and glory on display was rapidly transformed into farce and indignity. By that time, my Japanese had improved to the point that I could understand most of the television news broadcasts, but there was one specific word which appeared in every evening report about the emperor that I did not understand. Try as I might, I simply could not figure it out. When I finally gave up and asked a Japanese friend what the word meant, he looked slightly puzzled before explaining that he didn't know the English word. Turning to a Japanese-English dictionary, he flipped through it before looking up and triumphantly exclaiming one of the very last words I expected to hear.

"Rectum!"

After reigning for sixty-three years, the Shôwa Emperor, who had survived a military dictatorship, two atomic bombs, charges of war crimes, the invention of tentacle porn, and the loss of his claim to incarnate divinity, was bleeding out his imperial backside. On

January 7, 1989, he finally died after having lost more than thirty gallons of blood.[9] Three hundred fifty-four days later, the Nikkei 225 began to hemorrhage, falling from 38,957.00 on December 28, 1989 to 7,693.46 on April 14, 2003. And twenty years later, little has changed; on March 10, 2009, the Japanese market closed at a twenty-seven-year low of 7,054.98. Despite the big summer rally that followed, the Nikkei is still down nearly 75 percent from its historic highs.

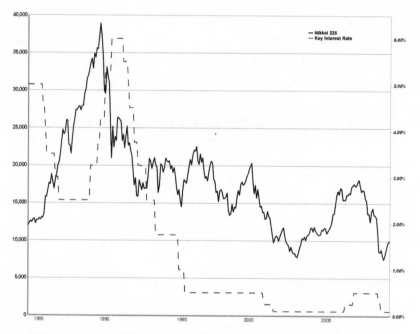

Figure 1.1. Nikkei 225 and key interest rates, 1985–2009

If Vogel's book had helped create the mystique of Japan as a global superpower in the making, Jon Woronoff's *Japan As Anything But Number One*, published in 1990, turned out to be the more prophetic tome. The idea that Japan was in the process of developing from a powerhouse into an economic superpower was based

---

9. After his death, the imperial household finally announced that the emperor had been suffering from duodenal cancer. The whole episode was unforgettable, as every day, the news reports would helpfully show yellow cartoon figures filling up with red in order to illustrate how many human bodies worth of blood the emperor had received to date. It was hilarious in a ghastly sort of way.

on a number of factors that included a homogenous population, devotion to the management philosophy of W. Edward Deming, the far-seeing guidance of the powerful Ministry for International Trade and Industry, a high personal savings rate, the long-term strategic perspective of the business groups known as *keiretsu*, and, as some ardent nationalists would have it, its unique racial characteristics. These factors came together to create the myth of the mighty Japan, Inc., and only the belief that Japan was fated to grow from global influence to global dominance could possibly have provided justification for the Nikkei's incredible average P/E multiple of 78[10] – more than twice as high as the 32.6 multiple of the 1929 Dow – a faith which in the end turned out to have no more substance than the seventeenth-century Dutch belief in the inherent value of tulip bulbs.

> *"Between 1986 and 1990, Japan experienced one of the great bubble economies in history. It began after the Japanese agreed, in the so-called Plaza Accord with the United States in 1985, to increase substantially the value of the yen (which doubled by 1988). Fearing the effects of the run-up on Japanese exports, the Japanese Ministry of Finance ordered the Bank of Japan to open the monetary floodgates while the ministry injected massive amounts of fresh spending into the economy via a series of fiscal packages and the expanded investment of postal savings funds. As the prime interest was lowered from 5 percent to a postwar low of 2.5 percent, asset markets predictably skyrocketed."*[11]

Unlike other industrialized economies, the Japanese economy was extremely susceptible to activity in the financial sector due to the unique corporate structure of the *keiretsu*. The six great business groups, which cumulatively controlled 55 percent of the total Japanese market capital from 1974-1995 and owned 39 percent of the total number of corporations, were each based around a major bank. The table below shows their pre-1990 structure as well as the

---

10. The Price to Earnings ratio. In other words, the average Japanese stock price was 78 times more than its after-tax profit per share for the previous year. It is now around 8.6.

11. David L. Asher, "What became of the Japanese 'miracle,'" *ORBIS*, Spring, 1996.

global ranking of the *keiretsu*'s central bank[12] and two of the group's most recognizable corporate affiliates.

Table 1.2. The Major Japanese Corporate Groups circa 1990

Keiretsu	Bank	Global Bank Rank	Affiliated Companies
Mitsubishi	Tokyo-Mitsubishi Bank	1	Mitsubishi, Nippon Oil
Mitsui	Mitsui/Sakura Bank	12	Toshiba, Sony
Sumitomo	Sumitomo Bank	3	Asahi, Mazda, NEC
Fuyo	Fuji Bank	9	Canon, Nissan
Dai-Ichi Kangyo	Dai-Ichi Kangyo Bank	6	Fujitsu, Hitachi
Sanwa	Sanwa Bank	7	Konica Minolta, Kobe Steel

By 1990, seventeen of the world's forty largest banks were Japanese, and each of the six *keiretsu* banks was four times larger than the biggest American bank, Citibank. Their massive size, combined with the tightly centralized structure of the Japanese economy, meant that whatever happened in the financial sector had tremendous ramifications in the nonfinancial sectors. In fact, it can quite reasonably be said that there was no significant distinction between the two. Not only did the *keiretsu* own many corporations directly, their core banks also provided the loans which were used to drive up the price of real estate and corporate stocks. The banks were able to do so because money was cheap; prime interest rates fell from 9.6 percent in 1976 to 4.9 percent in 1987. While a 4.9 prime rate may not seem remarkable now that the Federal Reserve has cut American interest rates so low that 30-year mortgages approached that figure earlier this year, it should be noted that in 1987, prime rates were 8.78 percent in the United States and over 10 percent in the United Kingdom. This meant that borrowing money was much less expensive in Japan than it was anywhere else in the industrialized world. The absolute price of borrowing money, which is what interest rates represent, usually has less of an impact on economic activity than the relative price, since leveraged inves-

---

12. "World's Largest Banking Companies," *American Banker*. August, 1998.

tors, like manufacturers, tend to migrate to where their costs are lowest.

Of course, the giant banks weren't merely loaning money to corporations and individuals who were buying land, erecting buildings, and purchasing equities, they were also buying vast quantities of real estate and corporate stocks themselves. Corporate cross-ownership, in which banks and corporations take minority interests in the companies with whom they do business in order to reinforce closer business relationships, had become an important aspect of the *keiretsu* industrial structure. By 1989, Japanese banks owned 42.3 percent of all Japanese corporate shares; another 24.8 percent were owned by corporations, many of whom were either affiliated with or directly owned by one of the six major business groups.[13]

The Heisei boom of the 1980s was not the first time that the Japanese economy had seen a period of great economic expansion. Twice before, Japan had enjoyed similar periods of rapid growth. The Iwato boom took place between 1958 and 1961, and the Izanagi boom occurred from October 1965 to July 1970. But the Heisei boom was an order of magnitude larger than its historical predecessors. Unfortunately, so too were the crash and recession that followed. In 1990, the Japanese government put policy measures into place limiting real estate-related loans; combined with the Bank of Japan's decision to raise interest rates, this brought the land price bubble to an abrupt end. However, neither the government nor the central bank appears to have had any idea what a profound effect this well-intentioned attempt to pop the real estate bubble would ultimately have on the stock market and other sectors of the economy, much less that the negative consequences would last so long.

The ten years following the end of the Heisei boom are known as Japan's "lost decade." During that time, which was characterized by a stagnant economy, monetary deflation, and rapidly declining asset prices, both the stock market and the real estate market gave up nearly all of their monstrous gains. The land price index for

---

13. Kenichi Miyashita and David Russell. *Keiretsu: Inside the Hidden Japanese Conglomerates* (New York: McGraw-Hill, 1994).

Japan's six major urban centers was 35.1 in 1985, rose to 105.1 in 1990, and was back at 34.6 in 2000.[14] The Nikkei took only until 1998 to fall below 14,000, within 400 points of its 1985 level. The bulk of the decline took place almost immediately; stock prices were already down 60 percent in 1992 and the decline in land prices was nearly as precipitate. Despite the aggressive efforts of the Bank of Japan on the monetary front and the Japanese government on the fiscal side, neither monetary policy nor fiscal policy proved effective in improving the economic situation.

In a paper which evaluated the effects of government spending and tax revenues on private consumption and investment, the economists Ihori, Nakazato, and Kawade concluded: "The overall policy implication is that the Keynesian fiscal policy in the 1990s was not effective." In another paper analyzing post-bubble Japan, Goyal and McKinnon wrote: "The government has resorted to expansionary monetary policy and has tried expansionary fiscal policy. However, these standard stabilisation tools have failed to stimulate the economy.... We believe that this emphasis on structural reform and further monetary (or fiscal) 'expansion' is misplaced."[15]

What was the cause of this epic economic disaster? Mitsuhiro Fukao summarized the origin of the problem in "Japan's Lost Decade and its Financial System," prepared for a symposium sponsored by the Japan Foundation at the University of Michigan in 2002:

> "The asset price bubble was created by the following three factors: loose monetary policy; tax distortions; and financial deregulation. In countries where those three factors were in place, asset price inflation was often observed. In this respect, the Japanese case was not an abnormal phenomenon. However, the magnitude of the asset price bubble in Japan was enormous and the impact of its collapse was extremely severe."

However, the macroeconomic policy prescriptions of Fukao and Ito, as well as those of a legion of Western economists eager to

---

14. Takatoshi Ito, "Respective on the Bubble Period and its Relationship to Developments in the 1990s." Japan's Lost Decade, 17-18.

15. Rishi Goyal and Ronald McKinnon, "Japan's Negative Risk Premium in Interest Rates: The Liquidity Trap and the Fall in Bank Lending," 2002, 73.

inform the Japanese of the proper way to end their economic nightmare, would ultimately prove futile, as it appears that economic historians will require a new appellation to describe what are now approaching two decades of economic stagnation in Japan. The Lost Decade was so called because annual economic growth during that time averaged only 1.48 percent, a steep reduction from the 3.96 percent average of the previous ten years. If the International Monetary Fund's projections for a -6.2 percent GDP decrease in 2009 are correct, this will bring the average economic growth down to 0.7 percent for the decade, less than half the average of the years described as lost.

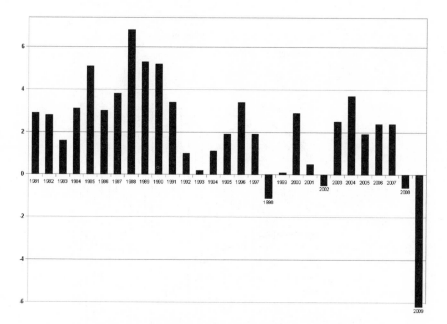

Figure 1.3. GDP Growth: Japan, 1981–2009

Nine years of concerted macroeconomic attempts to repair the Japanese economy have left it in worse shape than ever. The economic issues are complicated by the fact that the nation is aging, as the ratio of elderly to children is in the process of rising from 1.2 to an estimated 1.8 in 2010. It is also shrinking; Japan's population growth turned negative in 2006 and the population is expected to decline 4 percent to 123 million by 2020. The key interest rate is set at 0.1 percent and cannot be cut any lower. Whereas the government had a budget surplus of 1.9 percent of nominal GDP in 1990, the 2008 deficit amounted to 8 percent of GDP and in 2009 may rise to over 10 percent of the contracting Japanese economy. Due to these massive deficits, nearly 25 percent of government spending goes towards servicing the debt. And the last vestiges of the Japan, Inc. mythology were finally laid to rest with the government's shocking announcement this spring that Japan had run its first trade deficit since 1980.[16]

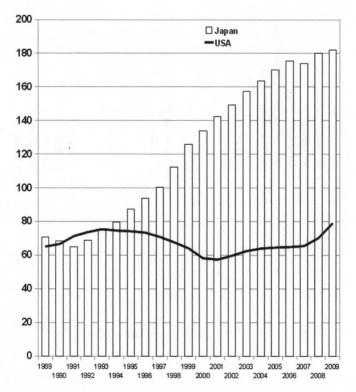

Figure 1.4. Government Debt-to-GDP: USA & Japan, 1989–2009

---

16. *"The finance ministry said the trade balance had plummeted to a deficit of ¥725.3bn (£5bn) in the year to the end of March - the first annual loss since 1980 when soaring oil prices ate into Japanese export earnings."* McCurry, Justin, "Japan suffers first trade deficit since 1980." *The Guardian.* April 22, 2009.

In nineteen years, neither monetary nor fiscal policy has managed to pull the Japanese economy out of the crater created by the Heisei boom. All they have done is to dig the hole even deeper, as the indebtedness of the Japanese government has increased to unprecedented levels. The Japanese debt-to-GDP level is now four times higher than it was in 1990 at the beginning of the post-bubble crash; the Japanese government now owes twice as many yen as the Japanese economy produces in a year. This means that Japanese policy options are significantly reduced, since there is no room for expansionary monetary policies and little more for the borrowing required to fund any additional increase in what is already an expansionary fiscal policy.

In the year 689, the Japanese imperial crown prince died at the age of 28. He had been expected to ascend to the Chrysanthemum Throne upon the death of his father, the Emperor Temmu, but died before his coronation. Of the poetic lamentations composed in his honor, twenty-three still remain. The dismay of the courtiers at the unexpected demise of Prince Kusakabe, also known as Equal-to-the-Sun, bears no small resemblance to the incredulity expressed by many Western observers at the astonishing decline of Japan.

> *My Prince's palace*
> *Would for truly a thousand years*
> *Be glorious;*
> *So thought I,*
> *Now sunk in grief.*[17]

---

17. Waka 221. Translated by Dr. Thomas E. McAuley, National Institute of Japanese Studies, Sheffield University. http://www.temcauley.staff.shef.ac.uk.

TWENTY YEARS AFTER

*I believe that, when all is said and done, the failure to end
deflation in Japan does not necessarily reflect any technical
infeasibility of achieving that goal.... I do not view the Japanese
experience as evidence against the general conclusion that U.S.
policymakers have the tools they need to prevent, and, if necessary,
to cure a deflationary recession in the United States.*

—BEN S. BERNANKE, 2002

IF THE PROSPECTS for the global economy were not spectacular
in 2008, neither were they particularly ominous. Japan was still
struggling in the long morass of its post-1989 crash, but other
Asian nations had weathered the disastrous 1997 currency crisis
that had seen their currencies and economies reduced in U.S. dollar value by nearly 50 percent in a single year. Even the country
that had been worst hit, Indonesia, had fully recovered; in 2007 its
GDP was twice what it had been prior to the crisis. The Chinese
economy was growing at an explosive rate thanks to a highly com-
petitive manufacturing sector and monetary unification. The expansion of the European Union had seen trade increasing throughout Eastern and Western Europe. Even the long-dormant Middle
East was home to the small but increasingly influential financial
center of Dubai in the United Arab Emirates.

The United States had survived its own series of challenges
towards the end of the millennium, which came first in the form
of a massive and unexpected worldwide stock meltdown in 1987
that caused U.S. stock markets to lose more than a quarter of their

value in a single day.[18] The crash hit stock markets around the world, beginning in Hong Kong and spreading through Europe before hitting the United States. The new chairman of the Federal Reserve, Alan Greenspan, had been appointed by President Reagan only two months before, but he reacted decisively by issuing a Federal Reserve statement that the central bank was prepared to keep the money flowing in order to support the markets, cutting the Federal Funds rate by 0.5 percent, and buying government securities.[19] These actions had the desired effect of increasing both investor confidence as well as the amount of credit that banks were willing to provide to the brokerage firms in order to allow them to make the required margin payments on the stocks they had purchased with borrowed money. While it took the markets more than a year to return to their previous valuations, it was soon clear that a slump of the sort in which Japan was enmeshed had been averted.

But no sooner had the markets recovered than the American economy was hit by a short but sharp recession that caused the American economy to shrink by 1.7 percent from late 1990 to mid-1991. Encouraged by his success in staving off the threat posed by the earlier market meltdown, Greenspan turned to the same monetary policies that had served him well before. Over the course of the next three years the Federal Reserve reduced its discount rate by more than half, from 7 percent to 3 percent. This had the desired effect of restoring an improved rate of GDP growth, but also helped trigger an investment boom in technology stocks that caused Greenspan himself to wonder if the United States was at risk of following the Japanese example as the NASDAQ technology index rose from 329.80 to 1291.03 in the nine years that followed Black Monday.

---

18. October 19, 1987 is known as Black Monday. The Dow Jones Industrial average fell from 2,246.73 to 1,677.55 at one point, a loss of 569.18 points.

19. "The Federal Reserve, consistent with its responsibilities as the Nation's central bank, affirmed today its readiness to serve as a source of liquidity to support the economic and financial system." Mark Carlson, "A Brief History of the 1987 Stock Market Crash with a Discussion of the Federal Reserve Response." Washington D.C.: Board of Governors of the Federal Reserve, 10.

"Clearly, sustained low inflation implies less uncertainty about the future, and lower risk premiums imply higher prices of stocks and other earning assets. We can see that in the inverse relationship exhibited by price/earnings ratios and the rate of inflation in the past. But how do we know when irrational exuberance has unduly escalated asset values, which then become subject to unexpected and prolonged contractions as they have in Japan over the past decade?"[20]

But the Fed chairman's concerns about asset prices weren't enough to convince him to reduce the money supply, and the discount rate was never permitted to reach the 7 percent it had been in 1991. In any event, it was clear that low interest rates and general economic growth weren't the only reason for the rising stock prices, as the increasing propensity of American households to invest in stocks caused great quantities of money to flow into the markets. Through the increased use of investment incentives such as Independent Retirement Accounts and 401(k) plans, the percentage of American families owning stocks, either directly or through mutual funds and retirement accounts, grew from less than a third to nearly half from 1989 to 1998. Compared to Japan, where the equity markets were still dominated by a small number of banks and corporations, American stock ownership was much more broadly distributed throughout the population.

The United States weathered the 1997 Asian crisis with comparatively little difficulty, except for a momentary scare when a large hedge fund, Long-Term Capital Management, ran into difficulties and lost close to $2 billion after the Russian government defaulted on its government bonds in 1998. Fearing that the fund's need to sell its securities to cover its debt would trigger a chain reaction taking down the entire market, the Federal Reserve quickly arranged for major financial institutions to fund what was then considered to be a massive $3.6 billion bailout that reassured institutional investors and stabilized the market. Stock prices continued to soar, until on March 10, 2000, a little more than a decade

20. Alan Greenspan, "The Challenge of Central Banking in a Democratic Society." December 5, 1996.

after the Nikkei had reached its historic high, the NASDAQ hit an all-time peak of 5132.52. Over the previous ten years, the technology index had increased in value by a factor of almost twelve, nearly twice as fast as Japanese stocks rose during the Heisei Boom. Unfortunately, not long after the final year of the second millennium began, the dot-com boom was rapidly transformed into the dot-com bomb.

The Federal Reserve had raised interest rates in a belated attempt to cool off both inflation and the overheated markets, but its attempt to bring the economy down with a soft landing proved impossible after the economic shock of 9/11. For the first time in history, the Federal Aviation Administration ordered all U.S. flights grounded, and the combination of travel restrictions and widespread fear of terrorist attack threatened to wreak serious havoc on Wall Street and the national economy. Once more, Greenspan was quick to act, restoring confidence by injecting liquidity into the financial system, and lowering the discount rate from 6 percent to 0.75 percent in two years. And once more, the chairman's decisiveness proved successful, as the economy fell into recession for only a single quarter before hitting its stride again.

The U.S. survived these challenges thanks to the bold decisiveness of Federal Reserve Chairman Alan Greenspan, who reacted to each disaster by immediately flooding the markets with immense sums of money from the central bank. On the chart below, which shows the effective Federal Funds rate from January 1987 to July 2009, one can clearly see how quickly the chairman was to react to these events by slashing interest rates and acting to increase the amount of financial liquidity made available to the investment banks.

While each of these monetary interventions was largely successful in preventing the economy from falling into a lasting recession by conventional GDP measures, each intervention required more and more effort on the Federal Reserve's part. Whereas a brief series of cuts to 5.69 percent had been sufficient to help the equity markets get back on their feet even after the cataclysmic crash of 1987, it took more than two years of keeping rates down the nation had enjoyed no less than three simultaneous investment booms. The first was in the non-technology stocks, which nearly doubled in value from 2002 to 2007.[21] The second was in derivatives, a leveraged investment whose value is derived from the value of other financial assets, including equities, commodities, and loans, which had become increasingly popular after the tech implosion. Due to their leveraged nature, derivatives are capable of creating huge profits and giant losses alike; in a 2002 letter to his shareholders, Berkshire Hathaway Chairman Warren Buffet described them as "financial weapons of mass destruction." Despite the legendary investor's warning, by June 2008 the notional value of the derivatives market had grown to $683.7 trillion,[22] seven times more than the total value of all the world's stock and bond markets at the time.

Among the assets underlying that vast quantity of derivatives happened to be home mortgages. The housing market, too, had undergone an investment boom; after remaining completely flat in inflation-adjusted terms for nearly twenty years, the median price of an American house rose from 114,294 in 1998 to 245,842 in 2006.[23] Below is a table comparing the annual percentage changes in U.S. interest rates to the annual growth rate of the economy as well as the three investment booms in the stock, derivative, and housing markets. It illustrates the effects of the Federal Reserve's successful attempt to drive interest rates down from 6.5 percent in 2000 to below 1 percent in December 2003. The tremendous effect this had on American markets should not be surprising, as it should be remembered that Japanese interest rates never went below 2.5 percent during the Heisei Boom.

---

21. The Dow rose from 7,181.47 to 14,279.96, a 99 percent gain. The S&P 500 rose 103 percent, from 775.80 to 1,576.09.
22. Bank of International Settlements, "Semiannual OTC derivatives statistics at end-June 2008," Table 19.
23. Case-Shiller National Home Price Index.

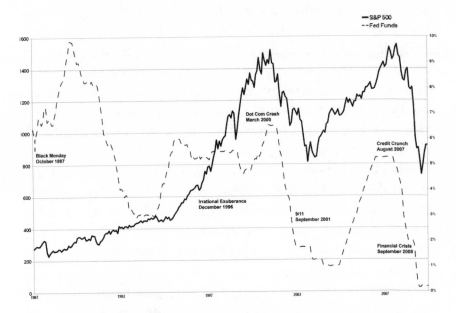

Figure 2.1. Federal Funds Rate & S&P 500, 1987–2009

around the 3 percent mark to get the economy out of its doldrums in the early 1990s. The diminishing returns appeared to apply to the stock markets as well. Both the venerable Dow Jones and S&P 500 indices were able to return to form and reach new peaks in 2007; the technology-focused NASDAQ, which had previously led the bull market charge, barely managed to recover past the half point of its previous heights. Investors were still willing to buy equities, but after being burned by the dot-com debacle, they increasingly preferred to invest in shares of older, more established companies that offered them less obvious risk rather than in recent technology startups with outlandish names. Not even Google's historic 737 percent IPO run was enough to help the NASDAQ return to its former glory.

Google's magnificent run ended in October 2007, not long after the Dow and S&P 500 peaked. Throughout this short but impressive bull market, U.S. economic growth had nevertheless been moderate, slowing gradually from 3.6 percent in 2004 to 2.0 percent in 2007. But despite this relatively sluggish rate of growth,

Table 2.2. U.S. Investment Booms and Busts, 2002–2008

Year	Interest Rate[24]	S&P 500[25]	Derivatives	Housing	GDP
2002	-56.96	-17.89	27.42	7.99	1.8
2003	-32.34	17.52	39.18	10.58	2.5
2004	19.47	5.43	30.80	12.09	3.6
2005	38.52	9.37	15.42	15.68	3.1
2006	54.35	14.20	39.37	11.51	2.7
2007	1.01	14.12	43.51	-2.10	2.1
2008	-61.75	-35.45	14.85	-13.95	0.4[26]

While this aggressive campaign to flood the markets with financial liquidity succeeded in sparking GDP growth and raising stock prices, the bank got a little more than it bargained for as what was supposed to provide a spark wound up setting the global financial system on fire. As can be seen in all three of the markets shown above, the rate of growth in investment asset prices was much faster than the level of underlying economic growth that was theoretically supposed to justify it. The Fed's actions were becoming increasingly clumsy; it alternately stepped on the financial accelerator and slammed on the brakes in response to the markets' reactions to its decisions, creating a vicious circle of continuous overreaction.[27] The housing market was the first to respond to the braking action begun in 2004, but as GDP growth slowed too, Ben Bernanke, the Federal Reserve's new chairman, lost his nerve[28] and began slashing rates again when a sizeable decline in housing sales

---

24. Federal Reserve Statistical Release, "H.15 Selected Interest Rates: Federal funds (effective) annual."

25. Except for GDP, all numbers are percentage changes. S&P 500 performance is calculated October to October in order to capture the full extent of the price movement. All others are annual, January to January, or Q1 to Q1, as normally reported.

26. GDP growth for 2008 had been reported at 1.1 percent, but was revised down to 0.4 percent on July 31, 2009.

27. *"Although this episode appears to have been triggered largely by heightened concerns about sub-prime mortgages, global financial losses have far exceeded even the most pessimistic projections of credit losses on those loans. In part, these wider losses likely reflect concerns that weakness in U.S. housing will restrain overall economic growth."* - "Housing, Housing Finance, and Monetary Policy," Remarks by Chairman Ben S. Bernanke at the Federal Reserve Bank of Kansas City's Economic Symposium, Jackson Hole, Wyoming, August 31, 2007.

28. *"The unusual disruptions in the mortgage market, including a significant rise in jumbo loan rates, resulted in a fairly high number of postponed or cancelled sales...."* Lawrence Yun, Senior Economist, National Association of Realtors. August 2007 report.

confirmed earlier indications of a housing top during the liquidity crunch of August 2007.

Bernanke had taken office in 2006 after being named the four-teenth chairman of the Federal Reserve. An experienced economist who had studied the Great Depression and written an esoteric book about it, he was nicknamed "Helicopter Ben" for a 2002 speech in which he concluded that a government can always generate higher spending under a paper money system through the power of the printing press.

In the Helicopter speech, Bernanke anticipated the obvious objection to his contention that economic growth was merely a matter of printing sufficient quantities of money.[29] He explained that the reason Japan had not been able to inflate its way out of its twelve-year economic difficulties was due to the serious financial problems of its banks and corporations, and the way in which the Japanese government's giant debt-burden impeded its ability to increase government spending, especially when fear of compre-hensive economic reform and the unemployment and bankrupt-cies that would result from it had created political deadlock. While the Bank of Japan had been correct to fire up its printing presses and pursue an aggressive monetary policy, these complications had rendered the bank's efforts ineffectual. It was fortunate, Bernanke concluded, that the U.S. economy did not share Japan's problems, and he was confident that if the United States ever did find itself facing a deflationary situation, the monetary authorities possessed ability and the knowledge to deal with it.

Ironically, it was not long before the Federal Reserve chairman-to-be would discover that United States was facing very similar problems and that the tools at his disposal were not quite as effec-tive as he had previously believed.

---

29. *"[I]t's a disastrous and entirely predictable [nomination]. I called this one back in June, as did vir-tually every other contrarian who saw how Bernanke was being given more face-time in the media. Bernanke is the one who believes that all financial problems can be solved by increasing the money supply ala the magic printing press. However, this doesn't mean that he'll actually be successful in inflating the US economy out of recession, as he'll likely run into the "pushing on a string" problem that so worried Greenspan."* Day, Vox, "Helicopter Money on the Horizon," Vox Popoli, October 24, 2005.

The Mortgage Meltdown

Vox Day: The chief economist for the National Association of Realtors is forecasting that home prices will remain flat in 2008.

Peter Schiff: Well, what do you expect? They denied that there was a problem, there was no bubble. Then they said it is going to be a soft landing....I don't know why anybody even pays any attention to what their economists say because it's really advertising or propaganda, whatever you want to call it. It has nothing to do with some kind of objective economic analysis of the housing market.[30]

In 1977, Congress passed the Community Reinvestment Act. This law required banks to make loans to loan applicants from low-income neighborhoods, and was conceived to surmount the residential security maps that banks used to refuse loans to applicants who lived in high-risk areas. Since the banks were accepting deposits from customers in those areas, it seemed unfair, perhaps even predatory, for them to refuse to loan money into the areas in which they did business. In 1992, the Federal Housing Enterprises Financial Safety and Soundness Act was passed, which required the Federal National Mortgage Association and the Federal Home Loan Mortgage Corporation, usually known as Fannie Mae and Freddie Mac, to ensure that a portion of the home loans they purchased and resold as secured investments had been used to buy properties deemed "affordable housing." While neither the CRA nor the FHEFSSA initially made a noticeable difference in the rate of American homeownership, they did provide the Clinton administration with a means of pursuing its goal to help low-income Americans buy homes as tools to pressure the mortgage banks to be more liberal with their loan policies.

For thirty years, the homeownership rate had remained flat, but in 1995 the Clinton administration's efforts began to show

---

30. Interview with Peter Schiff, March 23, 2008. It may be of interest to learn that while NAR's chief economist predicted median existing home prices to hold essentially even at $218,300 in 2008, I forecast a year-end decline to $175,000 or less prior to the release of the February report. On January 27, 2009, NAR reported: *"The median price crashed 15.3% year over year in December, to just $175,400."*

results. Over the next decade, the percentage of Americans owning their own homes increased 7.8 percent. By 2005, 69 percent of Americans were homeowners, the highest rate in the world. Housing prices increased rapidly as more people bought homes, existing homeowners took advantage of low interest rates to refinance their homes, and wealthy homeowners bought second, third, and in some cases, even fourth homes. As the housing boom was approaching its last days in 2006, Fannie Mae reported that refinancing activity accounted for nearly half of all home loans being made; more than a quarter of these were the risky adjustable-rate variety. Since at that time 30-year mortgages were less than a percentage point away from their then-historic lows, millions of home buyers were making what was assured to be a losing bet in the long term.[31]

While the increase in homeownership meant that more Americans were buying homes, it was only because low interest rates and relaxed lending standards made it possible for them to buy them; it did not mean more people were actually capable of affording them.

Despite the belated efforts of various Republican commentators to place retroactive blame for the housing bubble and its resulting aftermath on the Carter and Clinton administrations, it is important to recognize that the drive to increasing homeownership was an entirely bipartisan effort. While both mortgage-related acts were passed by Democratic majorities in Congress and signed by Democratic presidents, Republican President George W. Bush was not only willing to carry on with what his predecessors had started, his administration actually pursued very liberal homeownership policies that were far more expansive than anything either Carter or Clinton had envisioned. In 2002, President Bush pledged to create 5.5 million new minority homebuyers in the next

---

31. Amazingly, adjustable-rate mortgages have actually turned out to be a profitable gamble to date so long as they are not the two-year exploding variety. Due to the Fed's attempts to stave off financial collapse after the 2007 credit crunch, 30-year mortgage rates declined from 6.14 percent in December 2006 to an all-time low of 4.81 percent in April 2009. Nevertheless, one sincerely hopes that most of those homeowners who still have ARMs will convert to fixed-rate loans before rates rise again, as they eventually will.

eight years[32] and called for a $2.4 billion dollar tax credit to encourage affordable urban single-family housing. Later that year, he hosted a conference on minority homeownership. In 2004, Federal Housing Commissioner John Weicher announced what he described as the most significant federal housing initiative in more than a decade: the Department of Housing and Urban Development's decision to eliminate the legal requirement for a minimum 3 percent down payment for first-time homebuyers.[33] The commissioner declared that the Federal Housing Administration's zero-down payment mortgage would create 150,000 new homebuyers in the first year alone as an important part of meeting the president's pledge.

In the past, would-be homeowners had been presented with a limited range of loan offerings from mortgage lenders, who were primarily commercial banks, savings institutions, and credit unions. These depository institutions loaned out money they were holding on deposit for their clients and derived a modest but reliable profit from the spread between the interest they paid savings accounts and the monthly payments they received from their mortgage customers. The home loans they offered were characterized by four factors: 1) if they were government-backed or not, 2) the amount and term, 3) the type of property that secured the loan, and 4) if the borrower would be residing in the property or not. The creditworthiness of the borrower was not factored into the equation, as the decision to approve or reject a loan depended solely upon whether the borrower met the underwriting criteria for it. So long as the criteria were met, an approved loan recipient could expect to pay essentially the same price as every other borrower.

32. "The problem is we have what we call a homeownership gap in America. Three-quarters of Anglos own their homes, and yet less than 50 percent of African Americans and Hispanics own homes. That ownership gap signals that something might be wrong in the land of plenty. And we need to do something about it. We are here in Washington, D.C. to address problems. So I've set this goal for the country. We want 5.5 million more homeowners by 2010 – million more minority homeowners by 2010." Remarks by the president on homeownership at the Department of Housing and Urban Development, Washington, D.C., June 18, 2002

33. "Bush Administration Announces New Hud 'Zero Down Payment' Mortgage," U.S. Department of Housing and Urban Development, January 19, 2004.

Two financial innovations dramatically altered this conservative business model. The first was securitization, which began in 1970 when the Government National Mortgage Association, known colloquially as Ginnie Mae, began selling investment products known as securities that allowed investors to tap into the cash flow being paid by the homeowners to the banks on their mortgaged homes. Securitization is the process by which a number of loans are combined into a loan pool, then divided into bonds which are sold off to investors. The bonds are secured by the ownership of the underlying property; if the homeowner stops making the payments, thus ending the flow of money, the security holder does not necessarily suffer a loss because his investment is still protected by the value of the house. However, the loan originator, as the original lender is known, does not need to find interested investors himself. He can also sell off the entire set of loans to a financial organization that will create and distribute the securities to various investors. This division of labor allows for heightened efficiency, as it permits the originator to focus on selling loans while the loan buyer's activities revolve around selling securities. However, this introduces an element of potential danger, as the division of labor also has the result of removing the risk of possible default from the loan originator.

For fifteen years, the only asset-backed securities available were based on mortgages. Auto loans were the next asset-backed security product, followed rapidly by credit card, student loan, and equipment leasing securities. The subprime security boom has come and gone, but about 60 percent of American home mortgages are still securitized.[34]

The second important financial innovation to affect the real estate market was risk-based credit pricing. Whereas securitization offered more opportunity and efficiency on the supply side of the mortgage equation, risk-based credit pricing expanded the demand side. Risk-based pricing opened the door to a much wider range of available loan products, wherein less creditworthy bor-

---

34. Z.1 Flow of Funds Accounts of the United States, Federal Reserve Statistical Release, June 11, 2009.

rowers, who would have been automatically rejected in the past, were given the opportunity to take out loans in return for paying a higher rate of interest that would compensate the lender for the increased risk of default.

As is often the case with technological and financial innovation, it was not the established companies that led the way. The depository institutions and government-sponsored enterprises that provided most conventional loans continued to concentrate on servicing their traditional customers; despite the promise of increased interest revenue, traditional lenders were reluctant to accept the accompanying risk while Ginnie, Fannie, and Freddie were prohibited by law from departing from their previous criteria. Mortgage companies, either independents or depository affiliates given greater leeway in their loan operations, quickly filled the void. Independent mortgage companies were particularly inclined to take advantage of the opportunity presented by risk-based pricing, as a disproportionate percentage of the loans they offered were the higher-priced, higher risk variety. Despite providing only 27.8 percent of the total home loans provided in 2004, the independents were responsible for more than half of all higher-priced loans.

Securitization and risk-based credit pricing were an unmentioned, but nevertheless important, corollary of President Bush's plan to increase homeownership. The number of subprime mortgages, the riskiest and most expensive home loans, increased dramatically. These loans were made predominantly to individuals whose credit rating and income did not permit them to obtain a conventional prime rate mortgage from mainstream lenders. The subprime share of all mortgage loans made rose from 5 percent in 2003 to 21 percent in 2006,[35] while near-prime, or Alt-A, loans made up another 13 percent of the market. Both subprime and near-prime loans were known to be substantially riskier than the norm, and compounding the inherent risk was a serious structural flaw, as 89 percent of subprime mortgages came in the form of

---

35. *US Economy Analyst*, Issue No. 07/08, Goldman Sachs Economic Research, February 23, 2007.

exploding adjustable rate loans scheduled to increase significantly when the artificially low two-year teaser rate reset to prevailing market interest rates. But if a low-income home buyer couldn't even afford a 3 percent down payment, then how could he possibly afford the inevitable spike in his monthly payment, up to 40 percent, when his mortgage rate reset? Unsurprisingly, 14.44 percent of the 7.2 million subprime loans were already in default by the end of 2007.[36]

The subprime situation was further complicated due to the unconventional way in which these new lending products were created and the frequency with which they were securitized. In its report on the 2006 Home Mortgage Disclosure Act data, the Federal Reserve authors rather drily refer to institutions that originate subprime and near-prime loans as being "specialists" whose business orientation is "quite different" than that of conventional lenders. Unlike the media and the mortgage industry, the Federal Reserve does not identify subprime as a distinct loan category, referring instead to a single higher-priced market segment which is distinguished from the conventional mortgage market by the greater risk involved and higher price of credit it commands. As the Fed noted, not only were most of these higher-priced specialists not depository institutions, they were functionally more akin to the loan brokers they employed. They were essentially loan sale vehicles as, unlike the banks and other financial institutions, they did not maintain a portfolio of loans. Instead, they borrowed money in order to underwrite the loans they made, then immediately sold them. Despite the increased risk involved, subprime mortgages made attractive candidates for securitization because they offered the potential for a rate of return as much as eight times higher than conventional mortgage backed securities.

According to the Federal Deposit Insurance Corporation, in 2005 almost 68 percent of the home loans being provided were securitized. About a third of these were so-called private label mortgage-backed securities. The original mortgage-backed securi-

---

36. "A Snapshot of the Subprime Market," Center for Responsible Lending, November 28, 2007.

ties offered by Ginnie Mae were guaranteed by the U.S. Treasury, and those sold by Fannie Mae and Freddie Mac were considered to come with a similar implicit guarantee, but despite lacking any such guarantee the number of private-label mortgage-backed securities had doubled in only two years. And two-thirds of these securities were considered non-prime. Having tasted of the high-risk fruit without getting burned, institutional investors had developed an increased appetite for it and were willing to purchase as much as the increasingly aggressive mortgage companies could produce.

The natural result of this confluence of factors was no different than in past investment booms. Fraud and foolishness abounded. Fortunes were made in a few short years and lost in an even shorter period of months. And when thirty-year mortgage rates bottomed at 5.38 percent in May 2005, the two-year time bomb on the adjustable-rate sub-prime mortgages began ticking. Housing prices peaked a year later at $245,842, before beginning their long march downward. The combination of declining home prices and rising interest rates had a speedy and devastating effect on non-prime mortgage holders, the independent mortgage companies, and the mortgage-backed securities market alike. In the ten years prior to 2006, the average national foreclosure rate had been 0.42 percent of home loans. Only two years after the housing peak, the foreclosure rate had risen to 1.37 percent. Presumably due to President Bush's efforts to increase minority homeownership, 87 percent of the defaulted mortgage dollars were located in four states that had been the primary recipients of Hispanic immigration, California, Arizona, Nevada, and Florida. California, where the housing boom had gotten particularly out of control, alone accounted for most of the foreclosures.[37] Whereas the national average for the median price of owner-occupied housing had been 2.4 times the median family income in 2000, the California average in 2007 was 8.3

---

37. While the statistics cited in this section are taken from government sources, they mostly come by way of Steve Sailer's excellent iSteve blog. Sailer, whose iconoclastic but statistically sound approach to the subprime crisis has led to conclusions that some may find uncomfortable, has assembled a sizeable body of evidence showing how the political drive to increase minority homeownership played a significant role in determining the particular form that the housing bubble took from 2004 to 2007. A large collection of informative posts on the subject are online at http://isteve.blogspot.com/search/label/real%20estate.

times income, a hopelessly unsustainable ratio even for homeowners much wealthier than the typical subprime mortgage holder.

As the conventional risk models had always predicted they would be, mortgage defaults were concentrated among the subprime mortgage holders. And if the independent mortgage companies had sprung quickly into existence – AmeriQuest, the nation's largest provider of subprime mortgages, had only converted itself from a small local bank into a pure mortgage lender in 1994 – they disappeared even faster. The rise in home loan defaults caused more than 169 high-priced specialists to go bankrupt in 2007,[38] including the nation's second-biggest subprime lender, New Century Financial Corporation. Just the year before, these defunct mortgage companies had accounted for 7 percent of the national loan activity reported in the Federal Reserve's HDMA report.

In only a few years, risk-based credit had proven to be fatal. But thanks to securitization, the damage was not limited to the real estate market, although few realized it at the time. In March 2007, the *Wall Street Journal*'s MarketWatch ran a headline that now looks deeply ironic with the clarity of hindsight:

In financial sector, subprime's loss may be brokers' gain.

Shares of brokerage stocks rose Monday while most subprime mortgage lenders slipped as financing worries continued to trouble investors but some were betting that major investment banks would be able to pick up assets on the cheap. In the brokerage sector, the Amex Securities Broker/Dealer Index rose 0.8%. Lehman Bros. (LEH +16.0%), Goldman Sachs (GS: 2.97%) and Bear Stearns (BSC:+2.38%), who all reported earnings last week, gained.

It did not take long for the markets to learn that they had seriously misinterpreted the situation. While the investment banks were able to pick up the assets of the failing mortgage lenders at what appeared to be a bargain price, they soon learned that the assets were rapidly declining in value. In February 2007, Citigroup

---

38. Ibid. The 2007 HDMA Data, A109.

acquired an option for buying Argent Mortgage and AMC Mortgage Services, two of AmeriQuest sister companies, from ACC Capital Holdings. Seven months later, Citigroup bought Argent and renamed it Citi Residential Lending. The following March, Citigroup announced that it was strengthening its U.S. residential mortgage business by consolidating its operations, policies, and procedures in order to achieve greater operational efficiency; in other words, the bank shut down the subprime mortgage operation they'd acquired only six months before.

Even worse, the markets also discovered that the billions of dollars in mortgage securities that the banks and other institutional investors had been purchasing over the last few years weren't worth anywhere near what they'd paid for them. The investment bank Bear Stearns was the first to crack, as in June 2007 it informed investors in two of its hedge funds, the High-Grade Structured Credit Strategies Enhanced Leverage Fund and the High-Grade Structured Credit Fund, that they would no longer be permitted to withdraw their money from them. Two weeks later, one of Bear Stearns's creditors, Merrill Lynch, seized $800 million worth of assets it had been holding as collateral and sold them off to cover its exposure; other creditors such as JPMorganChase, Bank of America, and Goldman Sachs elected to hold off on making any similarly drastic moves in order to avoid upsetting the financial markets.

In July, the Dow Jones Industrial Average peaked at its all-time high. A month later, as banks around the world discovered the size of their massive exposure to the subprime mortgage market, the credit crunch began. Some of the largest banks in the world, including Union Bank of Switzerland, Citigroup, HSBC, and the Royal Bank of Scotland, were forced to begin writing off what would eventually add up to $295 billion in subprime mortgage security-related losses. The panic and uncertainty surrounding the real value of assets that had previously served as loan collateral caused banks to stop lending and start hoarding cash; in response, the central banks of the United States, the European Union, and Japan united to inject $266 billion into the global banking system in order to help the banks cover their losses and calm the credit markets.

But even these extraordinary measures were not enough. As mortgage lenders went bankrupt, more and more financial institutions began to announce unexpected losses in increasingly incredible amounts, until finally, in October, the chairman of the Federal Reserve and the secretary of the Treasury were both forced to publicly admit that the bursting of the housing bubble could have serious ramifications for the global economy.[39] A $100 billion superfund was created as a public-private partnership between the U.S. government and the large American banks to buy mortgage-backed securities from endangered institutions, but the plan fell apart when the three biggest banks, Citibank, Bank of America, and JPMorgan Chase, withdrew. Complicating the situation, stocks finally began to follow the collapsing housing market and the Dow began to retreat from its all-time high.

In keeping with its role as an innovative leader in the asset-backed securities market which had been among the first to adopt the securitization model, Bear Stearns was the first major banking institution to succumb to the spreading financial virus. Bear Stearns was acquired by JPMorgan Chase at a valuation of $1.1 billion on March 28, 2008[40] at the behest of the Federal Reserve, which promised to take responsibility for up to $30 billion in potential losses from the merger. Just a year before, Bear Stearns had been the seventh-largest American securities firm, with its stock trading at a market cap of 20.3 billion.

Bear Stearns was the first large casualty of the crisis that was not a mortgage lender. But it was not the last. In July, *Bloomberg* reported that banks and brokers had lost $495 billion in the market value of collateralized debt obligations during the previous eighteen months.[41] Also in July, the seventh-largest mortgage lender in the country, IndyMacBank, collapsed in the fourth-largest bank

---

39. In January 2008, Paulson had confidently declared: "The long-term fundamentals of the economy are strong, and I believe our economy will continue to grow." Nine months before that, Bernanke reassured the Senate that "the impact on the broader economy and financial markets of the problems in the subprime market seems likely to be contained."

40. The original deal was only for $236 million at $2 per share, but the threat of a class action lawsuit by Bear Stearns's shareholders caused JPMorgan Chase to retroactively increase its offer to $10 per share.

41. "Merrill Lynch Posts Fourth Straight Quarterly Loss," Bloomberg.com, July 17, 2008.

failure in U.S. history. The crisis arrived in earnest two months later, in September, when the Federal Housing Finance Agency announced that it was nationalizing Fannie Mae and Freddie Mac, before the pressure that rising loan defaults were placing on their balance sheets wiped them out. Between them, the two mortgage giants owned or guaranteed the mortgages upon which $5.2 trillion in debt securities was based. A week later, Lehman Brothers went bankrupt and Merrill Lynch was acquired by Bank of America in order to prevent it from doing the same.

Regardless of what one thinks of the Bush administration, it cannot be said that it was slow to intervene when the American financial system was briefly believed to be on the verge of a complete collapse. In the span of barely three weeks, it announced the takeover of the two mortgage giants, it changed the tax laws to permit one bank buying another bank to write off all of the losses accumulated by the acquired bank against its own profits, and it proposed the Emergency Economic Stabilization Act of 2008. Thus began the cycle of bankruptcy crisis and subsequent federal bailout that has persisted since that September. While both the financial crisis of 2008 and the government response to it merit a much more detailed examination, for the purposes of contemplating their likely consequences it is enough to know that the instability in the financial markets was potentially calamitous and the conventional explanation for these events is that they were caused by the significant loosening in the standards for American subprime mortgages from 2004 to 2007.

> *"What went wrong with global economic policies that had worked so effectively for nearly four decades? The breakdown has been most apparent in the securitization of home mortgages. The evidence strongly suggests that without the excess demand from securitizers, subprime mortgage originations (undeniably the original source of crisis) would have been far smaller and defaults accordingly far fewer. But subprime mortgages pooled and sold as securities became subject to explosive demand from investors around the world. These mortgage backed securities being "subprime" were originally offered at what appeared to be*

exceptionally high risk-adjusted market interest rates. But with U.S. home prices still rising, delinquency and foreclosure rates were deceptively modest. Losses were minimal. To the most sophisticated investors in the world, they were wrongly viewed as a "steal." The consequent surge in global demand for U.S. subprime securities by banks, hedge, and pension funds supported by unrealistically positive rating designations by credit agencies was, in my judgment, the core of the problem."[42]

If one looks at a graph of the amount of higher-priced mortgages securitized from 2001 to 2008, Greenspan's explanation certainly appears to be convincing. The value of subprime and Alt-A mortgage-based securities increased eight times in only six years, then dwindled away to virtually nothing within two years. One can even see how institutional investors began to lose their appetite for risk as housing prices soared; starting in 2005, less-risky Alt-A mortgages began to claim an increasing percentage of the securities market that had been previously dominated by the subprime-backed investments.

However, the key word in Greenspan's testimony is when he describes the excess demand from securitizers as it related to the subprime mortgage originations as being "the core of the problem." He did not say, the reader will note, that they represented the problem in its entirety. In another speech, given a year before during the joint IMF-World Bank meetings in Washington, DC, the former Federal Reserve chairman was rather more informative when he described the crisis as an accident waiting to happen that was "triggered" by the mispricing of subprime securities and ominously noted that if it had not been subprimes setting it off, it would eventually have erupted in some other sector or market.[43]

The reason Greenspan's choice of words demands close inspection is because of the widespread assumption on the part of the American public as well as the financial media that the 2008 crisis

---

42. Testimony of Dr. Alan Greenspan, U.S. Senate Committee of Government Oversight and Reform, October 23, 2008.
43. "Sub-prime crisis was 'accident waiting to happen': Greenspan," *The Financial Express*, Oct 22, 2007.

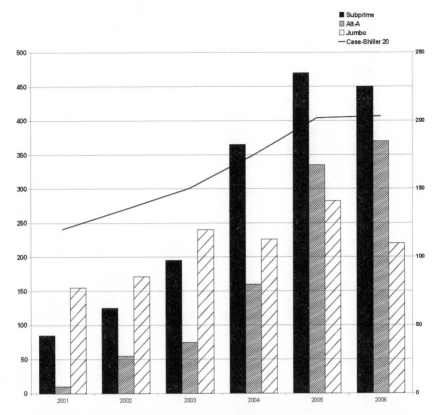

Figure 2.3. Mortgage-Backed Securities and Home Prices, 2001–2006

consisted primarily, if not entirely, of the problem with subprime mortgage-backed securities. The crisis is, in fact, usually known as either "the subprime crisis" or "the subprime mortgage crisis." But it is worth noting that the trigger is neither the whole of the gun nor is it the part that actually causes damage to the target. This is not a pedantic observation; remember that Greenspan spent nearly two decades having his every word and intonation scrutinized by the world's wealthiest investors and largest financial institutions more closely than the haruspices of ancient Rome ever examined a sheep's entrails. Federal Reserve officials often speak with all the clarity of the Delphic oracle, but even their most nebulous statements are usually made with great care.

The reason for Greenspan's verbal precision is very simple. It is that subprime mortgage securities did not represent the entirety of the subprime mortgage crisis since they were never more than a very small fraction of the ongoing *global debt* crisis.

BUBBLE, BUBBLE,
DEBT AND TROUBLE

The current financial and economic crisis is a classic bust of a credit boom, the boom having been fueled by policies whose combined effects were to increase the demand for debt to unsustainable levels.
—BENN STEIL, *Lessons of the Financial Crisis,*
The Council on Foreign Relations, 2009

C REDIT, MORE commonly known to the economically unso-phisticated as debt, is presently considered by mainstream economists to be the lifeblood of the modern industrialized econ-omy. Most of the herculean efforts made by the financial and monetary authorities since 2008 have revolved around their con-cerns that insufficient credit is available to borrowers; esoteric terms such as *LIBOR*, *EFF*, and *the Ted Spread* are often cited as metrics that economists use to determine the probability of eco-nomic recovery. But what these various measures are actually used to estimate is simply the amount of lending activity that is taking place, or rather, how much debt is being created on a daily basis. The assumption, therefore, is that increased lending activity is syn-onymous with economic growth.

The reason the amount of debt being created is tracked so closely is that the current financial system is similar to a white shark that must keep swimming in order to stay alive. While some sharks can pump water over their gills simply by opening and closing their mouths, white sharks are among those that have to keep moving in order to avoid death by oxygen deprivation. Just as reducing the amount of oxygenated water flowing over the shark's gills will weaken a shark by reducing the amount of oxygen its body is receiving, reducing the amount of debt being created weakens a modern debt-based economy. If a white shark stops swimming, its body will receive none of the oxygen it needs and it will therefore die. In like manner, if the financial institutions stop creating new debt by making loans, they will receive no interest income and they will eventually go bankrupt as they pay out interest on the deposits they are holding. Since the financial institutions hold the majority of American savings, a sufficient number of them going bankrupt will therefore cause the financial system to collapse.

The observant reader will likely note one problem with this analogy. Sharks, like most living beings, require a near-constant supply of oxygen to survive. Without it, they will die in a matter of minutes. But most interest payments are made on a monthly basis, not a minute-by-minute one; even the very short term overnight loans made by the Federal Reserve to the investment banks don't require repayment until the next day. So, it would seem that this process of bankruptcy would take a very long time, because at any given moment, the percentage of new loans being made is a small percentage of the total outstanding loans from which the banks are receiving interest income.

While this observation is true, it does not account for modern fractional reserve banking. Under the fractional reserve model, banks are technically insolvent all the time. In the terms of the analogy, imagine the shark has been motionless for some time and is only moments away from death. This is the natural state of the modern banking system, which, like Peter Pan, requires happy thoughts in order to fly. It's no secret that the vast majority of the money deposited in a U.S. bank doesn't sit there safely in the bank vault until the bank's customer wants it back, but is loaned out instead. What is less well understood by most Americans with bank accounts is that for every dollar deposited into their savings, less than one penny actually stays in the bank. The 10.3 percent cash reserve ratio that most people believe applies to bank deposits is only required of depository institutions with more than

$43.9 million in net transaction accounts and does not apply to corporate, foreign, or government deposits. This means that if even 1 percent of the average U.S. bank's customers closed their accounts and demanded their cash, the bank would be wiped out.

Defenders of the fractional reserve concept often like to compare it to a bridge, which also is not designed to tolerate being simultaneously used by everyone it is expected to serve. However, the analogy is flawed for four reasons. First, it is appropriate for the bridge owner to restrict access to the bridge by the bridge-crossers because it is his property, whereas the money deposited in a bank account does not belong to the bank, but remains the private property of the depositor. Second, it is not only unlikely, but impossible, for the maximum number of potential bridge-crossers to be physically present on top of the bridge at the same time. This is not true of banks in this age of electronic banking; a virtual bank run could theoretically empty a bank of its deposits and eliminate its assets in a very short matter of time without anyone ever removing a single dollar of cash from the bank vault. Third, a bridge can be closed for an extended period of time without causing panic or creating doubts about its safety. A bank, on the other hand, has to permit its customers to access their accounts via ATM machines even outside its official hours of business, and could not possibly shut down for weeks without losing a significant percentage of its customers.

Fourth, and most important, the sort of crisis that might require an unusually high traffic load capable of stressing a bridge to the point of collapse doesn't happen very often,[44] as even the large-scale evacuations inspired by incoming hurricanes usually proceed in a relatively orderly manner. Bank failures, on the other hand, occur on a regular basis even in the absence of a major systemwide crisis; the Federal Deposit Insurance Corporation lists ninety-one failed American banks since 2002. Of course, crises tend to increase the rate of failure and many of these banks have failed since the

---

44. I am quite aware that bridges collapse from time to time, although it's usually a structural failure that's responsible rather than a traffic overload. The 35W bridge across the Mississippi River that collapsed in 2007 was one I used to drive across on a regular basis.

credit crisis began. Calculated Risk, which keeps a running total of U.S. bank failures, reported the fifty-second bank failure of 2009, the $963 million Westsound Bank in Worth, Illinois, on July 2. Now, the Reason Foundation reports there are 596,980 highway bridges in the United States, rather more than the 8,195 commercial banks and savings institutions presently insured by the FDIC. Based on the national statistics, banks have been failing six thousand times more often than bridges collapse,[45] so it is clear that the bridge analogy is not a viable defense of the theoretical safety of fractional reserve banking. Describing the concept as being "as safe as houses" would be a more relevant comparison.

When the banking system is described as fractional-reserve banking, the reserves involved really are fractional, a very small fraction indeed. These reserves are public information, as the Federal Reserve publishes a report every month detailing exactly how much cash the banks are keeping in reserve throughout the banking system.

Required Reserve Ratio as of December 2008

Total Bank Deposits:	$7,189 billion
Required Reserves:	$53.7 billion
Reserve Ratio:	0.75 percent
Loan Multiplier:	133.33x

The reserve ratio means that for every dollar deposited in a bank, about three-fourths of a penny must be retained as a cash reserve in order to meet potential withdrawal demands. The rest is available to be loaned out, allowing the bank to create as much as $133.33 in new loan money. This is very profitable for the bank, because even if mortgage rates are as low as 5 percent, each new dollar deposited and converted into loans will produce $0.56 in interest income every month, or $6.67 every year. The bank must

---

45. According to ABC News, there have been 12 U.S. bridge collapses in the last 40 years, so the annual chance of an American bridge collapsing is approximately one in 2 million. The annual chance of a commercial bank failing, on the other hand, has been one in 333. Since 2008, one in 163.

pay interest on the dollar, of course, but since interest rates are low, it has to pay the depositor only around 1 percent on that new dollar at the end of the year. Therefore, the bank can expect to make $6.66 in profit for every dollar deposited if it is running at peak efficiency and loaning out the maximum amount possible. Of course, this optimal performance assumes three things. First, that the bank is able to find enough borrowers to loan out the $133.33 created. Second, that the depositor doesn't want his dollar back. Third and most important, that the borrower will faithfully make his mortgage payments and avoid defaulting on the property. Defaulting is a serious problem for the fractional-reserve bank, because it not only stops the flow of interest revenue, but means the bank will not be repaid the money that it loaned out and could actually lose money on the deal when the original dollar, plus its penny interest, is withdrawn.

It is not difficult to see how the banks have gotten extremely nervous about loaning out the money they are holding ever since the subprime crisis began and the number of loan defaults began to increase. In April 2008, total bank reserves exceeded required reserves by only $1.85 billion, or 4.4 percent. A year later, these so-called excess reserves had ballooned to $881.6 billion, 15.4 times more than the 57.2 billion required!

U.S. Actual Reserves in millions[46]

Apr 08	43,562	41,718	1,845
Aug 08	44,565	42,571	1,993
Dec 08	821,055	53,655	767,400
Apr 09	881,555	57,173	824,381

This tremendous increase in bank reserves explains the strange lack of interest that economists and politicians have shown in preventing additional foreclosures or finding ways to help homeowners make their mortgage payments in the middle of what is commonly

---

46. Federal Reserve statistical release, H.3 (502), Table 1, "Aggregate Reserves Of Depository Institutions And The Monetary Base," May 7, 2009.

supposed to be a housing-related crisis. Indeed, more than a few commentators have noticed that the $700 billion that is being funneled to the banks under the TARP plan is more than enough to have paid off, in full, every single home loan that has defaulted in the United States since the beginning of the subprime crisis in 2008. The total loan value of the 437,955 Notices of Default filed in California during 2008 is estimated to be about $190 billion.[47] It also explains why the White House and the Treasury Department rejected FDIC Chairman Sheila Blair's proposal to use TARP money to prevent foreclosures even though the estimated cost of the agency's plan was only $24 billion, barely thrice the $7.5 billion that the U.S. government metaphorically burned in the failed bailout and subsequent bankruptcy of the Chrysler Corporation.[48]

It is worth noting that even before the end of the housing boom had transformed into what was recognized as the subprime crisis, the primary concern of the monetary authorities with regard to the possibility of mortgage defaults was always their potential effects on the banking system. In a speech entitled "Reducing Preventable Mortgage Foreclosures," in which he expressly drew attention to the rise in mortgage delinquencies since mid-2005, Federal Reserve Chairman Ben Bernanke claimed that various parties were already working on ways to help distressed borrowers:

> "Policymakers and stakeholders have been working to find effective responses to the increases in delinquencies and foreclosures. Steps that have been taken include initiating programs designed to expand refinancing opportunities and efforts to facilitate and increase the pace of loan workouts....

---

47. "Notices Of Default Nearly Double," January 13, 2009 ForeclosureRadar, California Foreclosure Report for December 2008 and year-end summary.

48. The reason that the White House was willing to bail out Chrysler and General Motors had nothing to do with preserving car industry jobs, but because the American automotive companies have essentially been large financial institutions with car companies attached for many years. For example, as of December 31, 2008, GMAC Financial Services reported $189 billion in automotive finance, real estate finance, insurance, and commercial finance assets. The Federal Reserve accepted GMAC's application to formally become a bank holding company on December 24, 2008, thus making it eligible to receive TARP money as the 11th largest bank in the United States. Chrysler Financial reports a global portfolio of around $50 billion.

Of course, care must be taken in designing solutions. Measures that lead to a sustainable outcome are to be preferred to temporary palliatives, which may only put off foreclosure and perhaps increase its ultimate costs. Solutions should also be prudent and consistent with the safety and soundness of the lender."[49]

Notice how the help, which is nominally supposed to be for the borrower, takes the form of salvaging the home loans and their related interest payments rather than what would clearly be the most effective solution, which is to eliminate the loan altogether. Repayment plans are the favored loss-mitigation approach, followed by interest rate reductions, loan extensions, and in the worst-case scenarios, capital balance reductions. Ironically, in light of subsequent events, Bernanke even theorized that perhaps the reluctance of lenders to write down loan principal could be addressed by convincing mortgage-backed security holders to accept a devaluation of those securities by investors. This could be done, he proposed, through modernizing the Federal Housing Administration by permitting it more flexibility in setting the acceptable standards for mortgage underwriting and the interest rate prices for high-risk loans. The chairman even suggested that despite the banking industry's historical distaste for loan writedowns, the unusual combination of low equity rates and falling house prices could mean that reducing the amount of principle owed by the borrower would increase the expected value of the loan by reducing the risk of default and foreclosure. However, neither the Fed nor the banks elected to pursue this strategy of sacrificing reward to reduce risk, as was seen in the subsequent foreclosure and default statistics.

Due to the Fed's tendency to place the interests of the financial institutions first, the lender-centric approach by policymakers and stakeholders to the problem of financially distressed homebuyers failed in a manner that can only be described as complete, if not epic. Their range of carefully designed solutions did not reduce in

---

49. Chairman Ben S. Bernanke, speech at the Independent Community Bankers of America Annual Convention, Orlando, Florida, March 4, 2008.

the slightest foreclosure starts from the pace that Bernanke reported in his speech as being 1.5 million foreclosure starts per year. Despite their efforts, foreclosure filings proceeded to rise to an annual rate of 4.1 million, 342,038 in the month of April 2009 alone.[50]

Although the Obama administration's Homeowner Affordability and Stability Plan offers $1,000 to mortgage holders for each loan modification they make, the number of loan modifications in April actually declined from the previous month. A recent study of subprime and Alt-A loans by Wells Fargo showed that banks continue to prefer foreclosures and liquidations to loan modifications involving writedowns despite the fact that: a) the average writedown amounts to only 6 percent of the loan value, and b) the average loss per writedown is only $13,077 compared to $141,953 per liquidated foreclosure. This $141,953 loss was equal to 64.7 percent of the original loan balance on average.[51]

There were three reasons for the reluctance of policymakers and stakeholders to address the problem directly. The first reason was the political problem, to which the Federal Reserve chairman referred obliquely in his mention of moral hazard. Bernanke correctly anticipated that the millions of Americans who had conservatively managed their household spending, bought houses they could reasonably afford, and made their mortgage payments on time, would not be amenable to seeing their irresponsible neighbors bailed out. Indeed, exactly this sort of resentment was explicitly voiced in Rick Santelli's famous Tea Party speech from the trading floor of the Chicago Board of Trade, when the CNBC reporter lashed out against the Homeowner Affordability and Stability Plan,[52] an outburst that provided inspiration for more than

---

50. "April 2009 U.S. Foreclosure Market Report," *RealtyTrac*, May 13, 2009.

51. Alan M. White and Jonas Herrell, "Columbia Collateral File Summary," Wells Fargo. May 26, 2009.

52. This $275 billion plan to permit the federal government to subsidize interest rate reductions for up to 9 million homeowners had been announced the day before, on February 18, 2009. Notice how despite the plan's title, the primary beneficiaries of these subsidies were the lenders, not the homeowners, because most of the rate reductions would be covered at the government's expense.

750 tax protests across America on April 15, the day that U.S. income tax statements must be filed.[53]

> How about this, President and new administration? Why don't you put up a web site to have people vote on the Internet as a referendum to see if we really want to subsidize the losers' mortgages.... This is America! How many of you people want to pay for your neighbor's mortgage that has an extra bathroom and can't pay their bills? Raise their hand![54]

Given the furious and overwhelmingly negative public reaction to the Obama administration's relatively modest proposal, the Fed chairman was right to assume that providing direct government subsidies to homeowners would be politically unpopular. However, it must also be remembered that the administration's plan was presented after the American public had already witnessed the various Wall Street bailouts and the GSE nationalizations passed against their will, so they almost certainly would have accepted federal assistance for distressed homeowners had it been presented as an alternative to the far more expensive handouts being given to the large financial institutions. The polls tend to support this conjecture. While Americans rejected subsidizing mortgage payments 45 percent to 38 percent in a Rasmussen Reports poll taken the week after Santelli's call to arms, 56 percent were against the banking bailouts and 64 percent opposed the GM and Chrysler bailouts.

The second reason that direct assistance for homeowners wasn't seriously considered by the monetary authorities is that, although the ultimate cost to the banks would have certainly been less than not providing it turned out to be, there was good reason to believe that capital and interest reduction might prove insufficient, while paying off home loans in their entirety would have harmed both the lending institutions and the mortgage-backed security holders enough that it might have triggered the credit crisis even sooner.

---

53. "Tax Day Is Met With Tea Parties," *The New York Times*, April 15, 2009.
54. Rick Santelli, CNBC, April 19, 2009.

In his speech, Bernanke cited lender fears that writing down loan principal was seen as a no-win situation. If house prices continued to fall, they would come under pressure to reduce the amount owed again in order to prevent the homeowner's equity from becoming negative, while if prices rose, they would see no benefit from the homeowner's increased equity. More importantly, every form of loan modification, from extensions to payment and principal writedowns, would reduce the value of the mortgages as well as the size of the income streams that provided the value for the securities they backed. Since the financial institutions were already under considerable pressure at the time for reasons not related to the real estate securities market, the forced devaluation of their mortgage-backed securities could have proved fatal.

Consider, for example, the typical subprime mortgage loan of 2006, which originated at an average value of $199,750. The *Wall Street Journal* reported that in 2006, the average high-priced loan was 5.6 percentage points higher than a Treasury security of similar maturity; since the average rate for thirty-year treasuries was 4.9 percent that year, this gives us an average interest rate of 10.5 percent. This is a reasonable estimate, perhaps even a conservative one, as the same *Wall Street Journal* report describes an adjustable-rate loan of 8.2 percent that rises to 14 percent after two years. The expected income from this average subprime loan stood in contrast with the expected income from a prime loan as follows:[55]

Interest rate	10.50	6.41
Monthly payment (360)	1,827.19	1,250.76
Principal repayment	199,750.00	199,750.00
Total interest	458,038.40	250,523.60
Interest % of security	69.63	55.63

When viewed this way, it's not hard to see why the mortgage-backed security sellers were so easily tempted by high-priced home loans, since they offered considerably more room for profit. Nor is it difficult to see why paying off distressed homeowners' mortgages

---

55. Note that this does not take into account the full effects of an adjustable-rate mortgage.

was not considered to be a viable strategy by the Federal Reserve. A loan payoff was almost as threatening to the holders of mortgage-backed securities as the risk of default, since a complete interest write-down would cause the security holder to take a 70 percent loss on its original value!! Of course, this is precisely why so many subprime loans came with provisions penalizing or even barring early payoff. And not every troubled loan would go into default, while loan payoffs would guarantee massive losses on every security backed by a mortgage that qualified for one.

Third, in a debt-based economy, even the risk of probable future defaults are merely a potential problem, while the issue of banks hoarding their reserves and refusing to make loans is an emergency demanding immediate attention. The political and monetary authorities are practicing a form of financial triage; they simply don't have the time or the resources to worry about a badly bleeding leg wound while they are trying to staunch what is the equivalent of a slashed jugular vein under their economic model. This is why the subprime crisis is considered to have reached its crescendo when the banks began increasing their excess reserves in October 2008, and why financial commentators are so often heard declaring that the most pressing need facing the country to get the banks lending again. For example, Christina Romer, chairwoman of the Obama administration's White House Council of Economic Advisers, was quoted on CNN as saying that America needed to get Fannie Mae and Freddie Mac "lending like crazy," which no doubt struck many Americans as rather peculiar considering that Fannie and Freddie had required a government takeover a few months previous because they were doing precisely that. She was far from the only government figure to underline the extreme importance of bank lending to the fate of the economy.

> "At a time when events naturally make even the most daring investors more risk-averse, the needs of our economy require that our financial institutions not take this new capital to hoard it, but to deploy it."
> —Henry Paulson, Treasury Secretary, October 14, 2008

"The French state will not let any banking establishment go bankrupt."
—Nicolas Sarkozy, President of France, October 14, 2008

"Gordon Brown and Alistair Darling last night began piling the pressure on British banks to start lending again, telling them to honour the commitments they made as part of the £37 billion bailout."
—*The Times*, October 31, 2008

"Governments on Both Sides of the Atlantic Push to Get Banks to Lend"
—*The New York Times*, November 6, 2008

"The public in many countries is understandably concerned by the commitment of substantial government resources to aid the financial industry when other industries receive little or no assistance. This disparate treatment, unappealing as it is, appears unavoidable. Our economic system is critically dependent on the free flow of credit, and the consequences for the broader economy of financial instability are thus powerful and quickly felt."
—Ben Bernanke, Chairman of the Federal Reserve, January 13, 2009

"I am in no doubt that the single most pressing challenge to domestic economic policy is to get the banking system to get lending in any normal sense. That is more important than anything else at present."
—Mervyn King, Bank of England, February 23, 2009

"The concern is that if we do not re-start lending in this country, our recovery will be choked off before it even begins. You see, the flow of credit is the lifeblood of our economy. The ability to get a loan is how you finance the purchase of everything from a home to a car to a college education; how stores stock their shelves, farms buy equipment, and businesses make payroll."

> —Barack Obama, President of the United States,
> February 24, 2009

"We're not going to get out of this financial crisis and we're not going to stabilize our financial system without healthy banks."

> —Larry Summers, Chief Economic Advisor, March 27, 2009

"This is just the beginning and we are going to keep working to try and make sure this financial system is in...a strong enough position so it can provide the credit necessary for recovery."

> —Tim Geithner, Treasury Secretary, May 7, 2009

While people often talk about the Federal Reserve creating paper money out of nothing with Ben Bernanke's famous printing press, this only refers to the physical cash currency that usually makes up about 10 percent of the total money supply. Money in its broadest form is known as *M3* and includes a variety of monetary instruments, including savings deposits, institutional money funds, and repurchase agreements. A significant portion of this expanded form of noncash money is created by the member banks rather than the central bank. As was shown above, as recently as last year, banks were able to loan out as much as $133 for each dollar on deposit; this would result in an expected $6.66 returning to the bank in interest payments in the first year. But where do the various homeowners come up with the $6.66 they make in interest payments? And where will the $133 in loan capital come from when it is repaid? It has to come from the profits produced by economic activity, which most of the time isn't growing anywhere nearly fast enough to make such repayments possible. Therefore, it is obvious that in order for there to be enough money to repay these loans, the pool of money from which repayments will be made must be continuously expanding.

At this point, I should warn the reader that most mainstream economists would criticize this description of the way in which a bank creates money as being excessively simplified. However, their textbook model of bank-created money isn't actually that different, for as Paul Samuelson describes it in his landmark *Economics: An Introductory Analysis*, it is the banking system that is creating the money rather than the individual bank itself. The only substantive difference is that Samuelson's model attempts to account for the way in which the money that is loaned out by the bank is eventually deposited in a dispersed collection of second-generation banks, whose subsequent loans are then deposited in third-generation banks, thus creating a chain of deposit creation that comes to an end only when no bank anywhere in the system possesses cash reserves exceeding the reserve ratio. And if one troubles to enter an actual reserve ratio into the algebraic formula that Samuelson helpfully provides to estimate the amount of money created through this systemic deposit creation, one will discover that it comes to precisely the same 133.33 multiplier that was derived above from the Federal Reserve's historical report on required reserve ratios.

But regardless of whether one blames the individual bank or the banking system as a whole, this suggests that a debt-based economy is little more than an economy-sized Ponzi scheme. Yesterday's loans are paid off with the money created by loans taken out today, which will then be paid off by the creation of even more loans tomorrow. Unlike other monetary systems of the past, a debt-money system must grow or die, hence the panic exhibited by former Treasury Secretary Henry Paulson when the House of Representatives initially rejected his hastily concocted plan. Recall that Paulson warned of everything from martial law and the saddling of the Four Horsemen of the Apocalypse, to cats and dogs living together, if he was not immediately given a blank check for $700 billion with which to bail out the banks. And this fear-mongering blackmail of the American people began only weeks after it became apparent that U.S. banks were increasing their reserves in response to the subprime crisis instead of continuing to lend out 99 percent of their depository holdings.

The danger with debt is that it acts as what the military calls a force multiplier. As the aforementioned example of the fractional-reserve system shows, it permits a much more rapid expansion of economic growth as measured in GDP terms than would otherwise be possible. Even if one assumes that an entrepreneur will be successful, it will take a long time for one investing in a new restaurant or manufacturing facility to turn into one dollar into $6.79 in profit. Most new businesses don't break even and only a small fraction can reasonably expect to earn an eventual return of more than 500 percent on their original investment, let alone the first year. As one Swiss banker once told me, there is no faster way to make money than to sell money. This is why the financial sector's share of total U.S. corporate profits was 22.9 percent in 2006, even higher than its previous peak in 1999. And yet, even if nonfinancial corporations can't expect to take advantage of the full multiplication effect that financial firms do, debt still gives them the means of increasing their profits much more rapidly than they might otherwise hope to accomplish.

But if leveraged profits make bigger gains possible, they also increase the risk of larger losses. This combination of higher reward with higher risk means that large, heavily indebted corporations tend to be more inherently fragile than their smaller, more solvent competitors.

I learned this lesson from one of my friends after he was hired by a $15 million technology services company to be their corporate attorney. Four months later, that company was bought by a larger company in a cash-based acquisition. Having made a good impression during the acquisition process, my friend was asked to stay on as one of the corporate attorneys at the acquiring company, a consulting services conglomerate with revenues of around $575 million. A little more than a year later, that company was bought by an even larger company as the largest of seventy-six acquisitions it made over the course of three years. However, the $1.9 billion acquisition proved impossible to digest, and the acquiring company incurred massive losses as a result. Its stock dropped from $60 to $0.20 in the span of a year, until it filed for Chapter 11 bankruptcy with almost $4 billion in debt. Less than three years after being hired as the sole corporate lawyer for a relatively small Midwestern company, my friend was rather shocked to find himself appointed a corporate director by creditors of the bankrupt multinational, charged with the responsibility of flying around the world in order to shut down dozens of corporations everywhere from France to Australia. He ended up spending more than two years liquidating or selling off eighty of the bankrupt company's ninety corporate entities.

The business catchphrase "grow or die" is often a misnomer. "Grow and die" is usually the more accurate summation. Nor is this fatal philosophy necessarily tied to debt, even if debt almost always winds up being the instrument that eventually kills the organization, thanks to a concept that economists call the *acceleration principle*. This principle, developed by John Maurice Clark and incorporated into mainstream orthodoxy by Paul Samuelson, states that economic growth can come to an end, not because consumption has declined, but because consumption has merely grown at a slower rate than before.[56] This problem is due to a decline in gross investment triggered by insufficient income. It's not necessary to go into the theory here, which has largely been replaced by the Keynesian demand-gap model anyhow, to point out that there is an obvious solution to the problem. Even if a company's income is insufficient to produce any net investment, this does not mean that it cannot obtain funds with which to pay for an increase in its productive capacities, for, as we have seen previously, the banks are more than willing to provide the necessary funds in the form of a loan. Of course, once on the debt treadmill, the company needs to keep growing fast enough to make the interest payments on the loans that permit it to stay in business.

The acceleration principle is not the only pressure on corporations to embark upon the grow-and-die process. In 2009, the

---

56. The formula for the Acceleration Principle is $I = Á \Delta t$. I represents net investment in year t, A represents the accelerator coefficient, and Δt represents the annual change in income. I'm more than a bit skeptical of this "law," as Samuelson calls it, but it's useful in understanding that there are often intellectual roots lying beneath some of the seemingly illogical business practices and concepts that exist today.

Council on Foreign Relations director of international economics calculated that U.S. corporations were penalized 42 percent for making investments financed by equity rather than debt due to their ability to deduct interest from their taxes and to depreciate debt-financed investments at a faster rate.[57] This penalty had the expected result of encouraging them to pay for capital expenditures and acquisitions by borrowing the money rather than selling their stock and left them operating in a highly leveraged manner that rendered them more vulnerable to everything from a general economic downturn to rising interest rates. These two factors may explain, in part, why outstanding nonfinancial corporate debt increased from 2.5 trillion in 1990 to 7.1 trillion in 2008, a rate much faster than either inflation or GDP growth.

While the acceleration principle is a somewhat obscure and largely forgotten economic principle, the same is not true of the persistent idea that credit is a fundamentally beneficial, even necessary, aspect of a modern economy. For example, in his still-influential *General Theory*, John Maynard Keynes confidently asserted that as long as the rate of interest is positive, it is always better to buy a debt than to hold cash. One imagines, however, that Bear Stearns, Lehman Brothers, and the many other institutional investors brought to the edge of bankruptcy by their purchase of mortgage debts sliced up into various risk tranches could offer some compelling arguments in favor of cash. An interesting aspect of economics is the way in which crisis often plays a role in refining economic theory, mostly by conclusively demonstrating the inability of the current orthodoxy to explain what is happening. Just as the pressures of wartime lead to an increased pace of weapons development and the rapid obsolescence of existing technologies and tactics, economics crises tend to illustrate the deficiencies of existing theoretical models while spurring the development of new ones.

With the exception of the 1970s stagflation episode, the long period of post-World War II peace and prosperity has left many economic assumptions relatively unquestioned, but the sheer mag-

---

57. Benn Steil, "Lessons of the Financial Crisis," Council on Foreign Relations, Council Special Report No. 45, March 2009.

nitude of the potential problems today suggest that this may not be the case for long. Consider this defense of the federal debt by Paul Samuelson, written in 1948:

> There are also burdens involved in an internally held public debt like our present one, but the burdens of an internal debt are qualitatively and quantitatively different from those of an external debt. This is the first and most important lesson to be grasped, without which nobody can go far in understanding the economics of the public debt. The interest on an internal debt is paid by Americans to Americans; there is no direct loss of goods and services. When interest on the debt is paid out of taxation, there is no direct loss of disposable income; Paul receives what Peter loses, and sometimes – but only sometimes – Paul and Peter are one and the same person .... In the future, some of our grandchildren will be giving up goods and services to other grandchildren. That is the nub of the matter. The only way we can impose a direct burden on the future nation as a whole is by incurring an external debt or by passing along less capital equipment to posterity.[58]

This perspective probably sounded entirely reasonable back in 1948, when the federal debt of $250 billion was roughly equal to the U.S. GDP of $269.2 billion and had been amassed in order to defeat National Socialist Germany and Imperial Japan in a globe-spanning war. Samuelson mentions his own belief in the possibility that in the postwar period, the public debt might be reduced more than half by 1973, although he feared the potentially depressing effect of high taxes used to gradually reduce the debt. At that time, the debt was owed almost entirely to Americans, with the largest creditors being commercial banks and individuals. Regarding Peter and Paul, in 1948 the Federal Reserve had assets of $44 billion, equal to 16.3 percent of national income, half of which was the Treasury debt used to fund the war.

---

58. Paul Samuelson, *Economics: An Introductory Analysis* (New York: McGraw-Hill, 1948, 426-427).

The situation looks somewhat different six decades on. At an estimated $11.2 billion in 2009, the total U.S. federal debt is about 80 percent of the $14.2 billion U.S. economy. Of course, the country doesn't have the excuse of just having finished winning a major war fought across Europe and Asia; today's debt is more the result of domestic spending and entitlement programs. But the creditors have changed significantly, as 28 percent of the interest on the debt now goes to foreign creditors, who hold $2.8 trillion worth of Treasury securities, while the Federal Reserve's assets have increased to one-third the national income, twice what it was before. This represents both a major transfer of internal wealth, since Americans are increasingly paying interest to the very small percentage of Americans who own the central bank and other depository institutions, as well as an imposition of a direct burden on the future nation since more than a quarter of the debt is external. It also represents a form of tax, since 7.26 percent of the debt is held by either state and local governments or their pension funds.

Despite Samuelson's blithe assurances, the national debt is not essentially free but comes at an increasingly heavy cost to the vast majority of both present and future Americans, even though the relative weight of it has been reduced by 13 percentage points. And Samuelson's insistence that there is no loss of disposable income when interest on the debt is paid out of taxation is not correct because taxes are derived from private income. If the interest payments on the debt were not required, the taxes to pay for them would never have been taken out of private paychecks. Therefore, the percentage of income that would have otherwise been taxed would be available to be spent or saved at the discretion of the taxpayer.

While we now know why the fiscal and monetary authorities are so frightened of a liquidity crisis, we recognize what the potential rewards motivating banks to provide loans are, we understand some of the perverse incentives that encouraged corporations and individuals to take out those loans, and we have seen that credit is not without real cost, none of this necessarily explains the underlying assumption of how debt is supposed to be beneficial to the economy at large. As is so often the case when searching for the rationale behind what appears to be modern economic madness, the answer can be found in Keynes, whose economic theories about credit often had the benefit of telling influential people in positions of power exactly what they wanted to hear.

Keynes explained that the granting of a loan created three consequences he described as tendencies. The first was the tendency of output to increase. This is not difficult to understand; a car manufacturer that is already running at full capacity which borrows the money to build a second manufacturing facility can obviously produce more cars than if it hadn't taken out the loan. The second was that this additional productive capacity will tend to increase in value in terms of wage-units, and the third was the wage-unit will tend to rise in terms of money. Keynes pointed out that these three tendencies could affect the way that income was distributed among the population, and more importantly, he claimed that these tendencies were to be expected even if the increase in output had taken place without any loan being provided, and in fact, would have the same effects regardless of whether the increase in output had come about as the result of a loan or not. Keynes was asserting that there was no real difference between investment that came from savings and investment that came from borrowing, except that in the case of the latter, income would rise at a faster rate than the rate at which investment increased. Even better, so long as the economy was not in a state of full employment, this increase in income would not be inflationary! Keynes also anticipated Samuelson's chain of deposit creation, as he pointed out that any savings which resulted from this increase in real income would be no different than any other savings. The one potential problem, he admitted, was that unexpected investment in one area or another could have the effect of causing an irregularity in cumulative savings and investment rate that would not have taken place had it been anticipated. But this was hardly something to worry about when compared with all the potential benefits to be gained from increases in output, real income, and employment!

When one reads Keynes and Samuelson, the virtues of credit appear to border on the limitless. The banks profit, output increases, the economy grows, real wages rise, corporate profits increase, and everyone is better off. Not only that, but governments can also spend money pursuing a whole range of desirable policies without inflicting a burden upon any of its citizens, present or future. With such a bevy of benefits assured to result from the wonders of bank-credit, it would appear be downright irresponsible for governments and central banks to fail to encourage as much loan creation as possible. Once one understands that Keynes and Samuelson still represent the core of mainstream economic thinking and have had an extraordinary impact on the fundamental thinking of the most influential economists today, it is not hard to understand how the present situation was not only permitted to come about, but was downright encouraged by the fiscal and monetary authorities.

But one is forced to ask, what is likely to happen if this core assumption of the inherently beneficial nature of debt on an economy-wide scale happens to be wrong?

NO ONE KNOWS
ANYTHING

*This is an art of various forms, the object of which is
to give to ordinary observations the appearance and
character of those of the highest degree of accuracy.*
—CHARLES BABBAGE, *Reflections on the
Decline of Science in England*, 1830

O UTSIDE OF the scientific fields of astrology, hepatoscopy, and
evolutionary biology, there are few intellectual arenas where
estimates, calculations, and expectations fail as reliably as economics. Ever since Thomas Malthus predicted mass starvation on the
basis of his belief in the geometric ratio of population growth out-
pacing the arithmetical ratio of growth in food production, economists have been constructing economic models that do not describe reality with any degree of accuracy. Yet not even abject and
repeated failure is capable of inhibiting economists from resolutely
plugging new numbers into old formulas and reporting the results
to the eagerly awaiting financial markets. Is there anything more
absurd than seeing Wall Street embark upon a buying frenzy due
to a report that is less dismal than was expected, only to read the
revised report a month later which shows that the numbers actually
turned out worse than had been originally predicted?

Lamentably, the financial media is extraordinarily forgetful of
these failures and sweeps them into the electronic dustbin of history even as it cheerfully supplies new and equally unreliable projections to replace them. Due to this unfortunate disinterest in the
past as well as the increasing predilection of the various statistical

agencies to engage in historical revision, I have made a habit of collecting various predictions and economic statistics in order to better understand recent history even as it is being rewritten. For example, it may interest those who still remember the 2001 recession to learn that according to the Bureau of Economic Analysis, which tracks Gross Domestic Product, that recession no longer took place.[59] Less spectacular historical revisions take place almost every time a report on the economy is released, this is why I keep track of the four different figures that are provided for each quarterly GDP report, which are the Advance, Preliminary, Final, and Revised numbers.[60]

Table 4.1. Quarterly GDP Revisions, 2007–2009

	Advance	Preliminary	Final	Revised[61]	Max Variance
Q1 2009	-6.1	-5.7	-5.5	-6.4	$127.6 billion
Q4 2008	-3.8	-6.2	-6.2	-6.3 (-5.4)	$358.7 billion
Q3 2008	-0.3	-0.5	-0.3	-0.5 (-2.7)	$349.1 billion
Q2 2008	1.9	3.3	2.8	2.8 (1.5)	$260.9 billion
Q1 2008	0.6	0.9	1.0	0.9 (-.7)	$244.4 billion
Q4 2007	0.6	0.6	0.6	-0.2 (2.1)	$329.8 billion
Q3 2007	3.9	4.9	3.9	4.8 (3.6)	$184.3 billion
Q2 2007	3.4	4.0	3.8	4.8 (3.2)	$223.9 billion
Q1 2007	1.2	0.5	0.6	0.1 (1.2)	$147.1 billion

The differences from report to report may appear to be relatively small, but because the sums involved are so large, the average variance is more than $245 billion within the same quarter. This average variance is 1.7 percent of the $14.2 trillion economy, which until the most recent revisions represented a margin of error

---

59. The popular definition of a recession is two consecutive quarters of real GDP contraction. According to the BEA's revised numbers, the economy only contracted in 2001 Q1 and Q3 and the economy grew 1.1 percent that year, therefore what is recalled as a historical recession never happened. So, who are you going to believe, the BEA or your lying mind?

60. Do a search for "GDP Watch" at Vox Popoli. http://voxday.blogspot.com. However, note that the BEA announced that they are switching from the four-release "Advance, Preliminary, Final, Revised" system to a three-release "Advance, Second, Third" one in the latter half of 2009.

61. The BEA released post-revised revised quarterly figures dating back to Q3 2005 on July 31, 2009. The lastest numbers are in parentheses.

large enough to make the difference between economic growth and economic contraction in fully half of the quarterly figures reported in 2007 and 2008. This means that even with the most updated statistical figures for reference, government policymakers cannot possibly be certain of something as basic and fundamental to their decisions as if the economy is presently growing or contracting.

Nor are these revisions limited to recent periods. John Williams of Shadowstats[62] has analyzed various government statistical figures since 1971 and has concluded that three of the major ones, the Gross Domestic Product (GDP), the Consumer Price Index (CPI), and the unemployment rate (U-3), are essentially unreliable. CPI and U-3 were structurally modified during the Clinton administration, ostensibly for the purposes of increased accuracy but actually to increase the amount of subjective interpretation involved in the process. GDP is revised every five years, during which time data dating back as far as 1929 are revised. These modifications and revisions exhibit a distinct tendency to fudge the statistics in the government's favor, showing lower inflation, higher employment, and faster economic growth than would previously have been the case, an upward bias that Williams describes as "Pollyanna Creep."

The importance of GDP to the field of macroeconomic analysis can hardly be overstated. The statistic was declared to be the Department of Commerce's greatest achievement of the twentieth century and it is considered to be one of the three most influential measures affecting the financial markets in the United States. That being said, I have already shown that current GDP data are given to variation of as much as 2.5 percent over the course of a few months. What is striking about the historical scorekeeping at Shadowstats is the way it shows how the figures given for the past years are subject to even greater variance!

Williams shows that what was reported as a $2.708 trillion 1980 GDP in 1992 somehow managed to grow to $2.786 trillion in

---

62. See www.shadowstats.com.

the 2004 reports, an increase of 2.9 percent. The historical 1990 GDP managed to grow even more in the twelve years from 1992 to 2004, adding $589 billion, or 5.3 percent, to the previously reported figure. These increases weren't just random additions made for no rational purpose, but reflected modifications in the method of calculation that tend to exaggerate current data as well. These modifications are known as the comprehensive National Income and Product Accounts (NIPA) revisions, which were recently revised by the BEA on July 31, 2009. "For 1929-2008, the average annual growth rate of real GDP is 3.4 percent, 0.1 percentage point higher than in the previously published estimates."[63] As the table showing the modifications to past GNP figures[64] also demonstrates, the amount of exaggeration appears to be on the increase.

Table 4.2. Historical GNP Revisions, 1950–2004

	1950	1984	2004	Increase
1929	103.8	103.4	104.4	0.57 percent
1933	55.8	55.8	56.7	1.61 percent
1940	101.4	100	101.7	0.29 percent
1950	284.2	286.5	295.2	3.87 percent
1960	—	506.2	529.5	4.54 percent
1970	—	992.7	1044.9	5.26 percent
1980	—	2631.7	2823.7	7.30 percent

Needless to say, if the current models are exaggerating average GDP figures in a manner similar to the way they have inflated the average GNP revision by 3.35 percent, then the U.S. economy has not been in recession since the third quarter of 2008, but for the greater part of the last decade! Williams himself estimates that the United States has seen only positive GDP growth for one quarter since the turn of the century, and that was in late 2003.

Another indication that GDP growth may be exaggerated stems

---

63. *National Income and Product Accounts, Comprehensive Revision: 1929 Through First Quarter 2009*, Bureau of Economic Analysis, July 31, 2009.

64. Gross National Product, or GNP, was the measure of economic activity more commonly used by economists until about 20 years ago.

from comparing the data for the GDP deflator, which purports to correct GDP for inflation, with the Consumer Price Index, which is more commonly used as the primary measure of inflation. If one chooses 1983, the base year of index to which all of the historical CPI data are chained, one will find that the GDP deflator reports inflation of 79.1 percent over the last 26 years, while the CPI figure shows 114.1 percent inflation over the same period. While the two statistical measures are based on different criteria, their comparison shows the inverse of what one would tend to expect since CPI reflects the price of imported goods while the GDP deflator does not. And, as anyone who has been paying attention to the balance of trade over the last two decades will recognize, foreign imports tend to cost less than domestically manufactured products. Another oddity is the way in which an increase in the price of imported oil *reduces* the GDP deflator, thereby exaggerating GDP growth when the price of oil rises and reducing it when it drops. It's interesting to note that when GDP is corrected for inflation using the CPI rather than the deflator, the real U.S. economy appears to be significantly smaller than it is presently believed to be. For example, whereas the GDP deflator shows growth from $3.1 trillion to $8.0 trillion over the last 26 years in 1983 dollars, using GDP-CPI would indicate a real 2009 GDP of only $6.6 trillion.

The effect of these statistical variances should not be underestimated. David Runkle of the Minneapolis Federal Reserve Bank notes that "The fact of data revision is generally well known, but few academic studies have considered the effects that it can have on the conduct and understanding of economic policy. This is an unfortunate omission. Revisions in estimates of real output growth and inflation have historically been large, and these revisions can cause at least two types of significant distortions." The implications of these distortions are significant. First, they indicate that the information upon which policy decisions are made is often inaccurate. Second, they mislead economic researchers who attempt to analyze historical policies on the basis of information that differs from that which was available to the historical policy makers. The Fed researcher cites an example of how the initial estimates of the decline in real GDP during the 1974-1975 recession were nearly triple that of the 1998 estimates,[65] then provides a series of charts graphically demonstrating the extent of the historical GDP revisions that show his example to be far from an anomaly.[66]

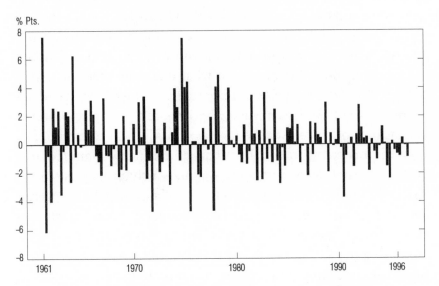

Figure 4.3. Revisions in One-Quarter Growth Rates, 1961–1996[67]

Inflation

> *JIM ROGERS: I know that the figures about productivity and inflation are doctored, butchered. They are a sham! A total sham …I have had BLS guys write me and say, "Look, we were told that we have to smooth out the numbers." I know they are faking the numbers. And so does the rest of the world.*
>
> *DANIEL YERGIN: So, do you think the GDP numbers are faked too?*

---

65. Runkle cites a revision from a 5.8 percent decline between the second quarter of 1974 and the second quarter of 1975 to 2.0 percent. That was in 1998; the present data shows a 1.9 percent decline. Since the BEA's most recent comprehensive revisions only go back to 1995 at this point, by the time you read this it may have been even further reduced.
66. David E. Runkle, "Revisionist History: How Data Revisions Distort Economic Policy Research," *Federal Reserve Bank of Minneapolis Quarterly Review*, Vol. 22, No. 4, Fall 1998, pp. 3–12.
67. This is "Chart 1 Real Output" from David E. Runkle's 1998 paper.

JIM ROGERS: I know they are faked! The whole thing is faked.
—*Financial Sense Newshour*, February 3, 2003

Despite the obvious variance between the two statistics, substituting the Consumer Price Index for the GDP deflator is not likely to be an effective means of correcting for suspected exaggerations of economic growth. Although the intrinsic unreliability of the GDP statistics is obvious, it is the CPI that appears to be more actively manipulated for several reasons. The CPI, or more specifically, the CPI-U, is considered by mainstream economists to be a reasonable metric for the general level of inflation across the economy. Most inflation calculations, including those used in this book, are based on this figure, which is released monthly by the U.S. Department of Labor's Bureau of Labor Statistics and covers the period from January 1913 to the present. The index figures are chained to a 1982-1984 base year dollar, by which the BLS means that a value of 100 means $100 during that time; according to the historical table,[68] the moment at which the price index base is pegged is at the end of July 1983. With only a few exceptions, CPI has steadily increased throughout its existence, rising from 9.8 at its inception to 213.24. This indicates that over the last ninety-six years, the U.S. dollar has lost 95.4 percent of its value.

Because CPI is used as the determinant for both public and private cost-of-living adjustments, it is a highly political statistic. A relatively small percentage increase in CPI can result in very large expenditures for government agencies and corporations alike, which is why there is a great amount of pressure on the BLS to avoid reporting CPI increases regardless of the actual rate of monetary inflation or changes in the prices of goods that consumers actually buy. The BLS has used a variety of means to keep the rate artificially low, ranging from hedonic adjustments that allow subjective modification of actual price data to attempting to exclude whole categories of prices from the price index. Hedonic adjustments range from discounting the price of a computer because it runs faster than a computer that cost the same amount of money in the

---

68. The US Inflation Calculator helpfully makes all the historical statistics available in a big table on their Web site. http://www.usinflationcalculator.com.

past to the presumed benefits of cleaner air provided by gasoline additives. Regardless of the merits of these value arguments, the fact remains that they have nothing to do with either the price of a consumer good, or in many cases, the purpose for which the consumer good is used. To give one example, it is theoretically possible that a faster CPU might allow for productivity improvements if one happens to be a 3D artist doing complex and time-consuming renders. And yet, that faster CPU is not going to do anything for the average computer user who does nothing more than send e-mail and write text using a word processor. The fact that someone else might be able to use the computer in a more effective manner doesn't actually reduce the cost of the new e-mail-and-text machine, and as anyone who has ever suffered through the technology hell of a new Microsoft Windows release knows very well, newer technology is not always indicative of improved value.

The BLS report that makes use of the exclusion technique is known as the "core inflation" figure, which is usually described by the media as "excluding volatile food and energy" prices. I've always found this to be rather amusing because, after all, so few consumers buy groceries, heat their homes, or fill their cars with gasoline. Since home prices and indirect taxes are also excluded from the CPI figure, this means that the core inflation concept is designed to eliminate more than 50 percent of household spending from the price index. If, at this point, you are wondering what could possibly be the purpose of a price index that excludes most common expenses, be comforted in knowing that you are not alone. Mark Wynne, a senior economist at the Federal Reserve Bank, concluded a paper on the concept of core inflation in the following manner: "[B]efore choosing a measure of core inflation we need to specify what it is we want the measure for....if the measure of inflation we are interested in is the cost of living, then it is not clear why we would ever want to exclude the effects of oil price increases or indirect taxes. Thus it must be the case that when measuring core inflation we have some other inflation concept in mind."[69]

---

69. Mark A. Wynne, "Core Inflation: A Review of Some Conceptual Issues." Federal Reserve Bank of St. Louis Review, May/June, Part 2, 2008, 205.

That other inflation concept, one tends to suspect, is whatever will serve to keep Social Security payments and any other cost-of-living adjustment down. The 2009 COLA increased the estimated average monthly Social Security benefit payment for all eligible recipients from $1,090 to $1,153, a 5.8 percent increase that cost the federal government an additional $3.14 billion per month. That increase came courtesy of the CPI-W, which tends to increase at a slightly slower rate than the CPI-U. The massive number of Social Security recipients, 51 million in 2009, means that for every 1 percent increase in the CPI, the Social Security Administration is forced to pay $6.5 billion more annually. Since the autoworkers' and other union contracts also have cost of living adjustments written into them, there is powerful political pressure on the BLS to keep the CPI as low as possible in order to reduce the burden it imposes on all levels of government as well as many large corporations.

This pressure may account for the decision of the BLS to modify the way in which the CPI was calculated during the 1990s, as important policymakers, including Speaker of the House Newt Gingrich and Federal Reserve Chairman Alan Greenspan, waged a public media campaign for the financial benefits of what they rather disingenuously described as a more accurate price index. The weighting of the basket of goods was changed from arithmetic to geometric weighting, which tended to reduce the weight of goods with rising prices and increase the weight of goods with declining prices. The cumulative effect of these changes are estimated by Williams in one of his two CPI adjustments, called 1980-base SGS, to amount to approximately a 7 percent reduction in the rate of reported inflation; 3 percent of the lowballed reporting is attributed to the geometric weighting, and 4 percent to the various methodological changes including hedonic adjustments. If correct, this means that instead of flirting with deflation and remaining essentially flat, the prices of goods and services will continue to rise despite the continuing collapse of investment and other asset prices. In fact, they will continue to rise even if the CPI figures show deflation, as they do at present.

Williams's criticism was taken so seriously by the Bureau of Labor Statistics that, in August 2008, it published a seventeen-page paper entitled "Addressing Misconceptions About the Consumer Price Index," which was very clearly aimed at the iconoclastic critic despite refusing to identify him by name.[70] Instead, the report made reference to the Shadowstats site as "a widely cited alternative index." However, the agency's attempted defense of the price index for which it is responsible turned out to be remarkably incompetent, as in addition to incorrectly reporting the cumulative ten-year effect of the aforementioned 7 percent annual correction as 155 percent instead of 147 percent, the BLS economists actually managed to demonstrate that the CPI-U was, in fact, significantly underreporting the actual changes in the prices of consumer goods.

Table 4.4. Price Comparisons, April 1998 and April 2008 [71]

Price and Income	April 1998	April 2008	CPI-U (32%)	Actual Increase
White bread, per lb.	$0.86	$1.37	$1.14	59.3 percent
Fresh whole milk, per gal	2.67	3.8	3.52	42.3 percent
Tomatoes, per lb.	1.4	1.77	1.85	26.4 percent
Peanut butter, creamy, per lb.	1.81	1.98	2.39	9.4 percent
Cola, non-diet, per 2 liters	1.07	1.33	1.41	24.3 percent
Beefsteak, per lb.	3.67	5.28	4.84	43.9 percent
Gasoline, all types, per gal.	1.11	3.49	1.47	214.1 percent
Fuel oil #2, per gal.	0.92	3.88	1.21	321.7 percent
Utility piped gas, 100 therms	65.87	142.73	86.95	116.7 percent
Electricity per 500 kwh	45.74	62.15	60.38	35.9 percent
Median single family house	132300	200700	174636	51.7 percent
Mortgage payments	719	966	949	34.5 percent
Income	22753	27530	30034	20.9 percent
BLS avg weekly wages	441	454	582.12	2.9 percent

70. As of May 26, 2009, this report was still being advertised on the front page of the BLS's Web site, complete with a helpful FAQ entitled "Common Misconceptions about the Consumer Price Index: Questions and Answers." I suspect that if any BLS economist happens to read this book, it's not going to be up there for long. http://www.bls.gov.

71. "Misconceptions about the CPI," *Monthly Labor Review*, August 2008, Table 1.16.

Whereas the BLS officially reported CPI-U as rising 32 percent over the ten-year period, the prices they specifically selected to show the inaccuracy of the Shadowstats figures indicate inflation of more than twice that amount at 71.7 percent! Moreover, if one omits the two income-related figures, which one really must since they are: a) not consumer goods or services, b) not included in any price index, and c) heavily influenced by changes in labor force factors such as the estimated 1.8 million legal and illegal immigrants[72] who arrived annually during the ten years between 1998 and 2008, the increase in the BLS basket of consumer prices averaged 81.7 percent. In light of this, it is intriguing to note that the second of Williams's two CPI adjustments, 1990-base SGS, reported inflation over this period as being 77 percent. This suggests that of all the various inflationary measures, including CPI-W, CPI-U, CPI-U for All Items Less Food and Energy, (also known as "core CPI"), 1980-base SGS, and 1990-base SGS, the 1990-base SGS is the most reliable. The BLS economists argue in the report that if it weren't for that pesky increase in energy prices, the performance of the CPI-U would have been pretty good, but that defense would be far more meaningful if we still lived in a society that depended upon horse-drawn carriages for transportation and firewood for heating. Moreover, even if the three energy-related prices are excluded, it's not hard to see that the CPI-U comes in on the low side of the actual prices reported two-thirds of the time, 4.5 percent on average. That would still indicate an additional 0.5 percent of unreported inflation per year.

The implications of this underreporting of inflation are profound for the economy. If inflation is rising at the 1990-base SGS corrected rate of 2.5 percent rather than falling 0.7 percent over the last 12 months as the BLS's CPI-U presently reports, then the real economy has grown even less in recent years than substituting CPI-U for the GDP Deflator would indicate, and it is now shrinking even faster in the current recession. Fortunately, so long as the official CPI remains negative, it should be easy for even the non-

---

72. "Annual Immigration to the United States: The Real Numbers," The Migration Policy Institute. May 2007, No. 16.

statistically inclined to note its inherent inaccuracy should prices at the supermarket and the mall continue to rise.

The unemployment rate is the third major statistic that is considered to be fundamentally unreliable, and like the previous two it is closely watched by politicians, economists, and Wall Street. Like GDP and CPI, it is an estimate, though it is theoretically a little less difficult to estimate due to the obvious fact that there are far more economic actions and goods being sold than there are people in a national economy, so the challenge of figuring out how many of those people are working is somewhat reduced. This does not mean that it is difficult, though, since the definition of employment can vary greatly from one individual to the next. It's pretty easy to decide if a factory worker is employed or not; he either has a job where he gets paid to manufacture things or he doesn't. It's a little harder to determine if someone who lives on a farm is employed or not, because while it's obvious that the farmer out plowing the fields is, it's a little harder to say the same of his wife who feeds the chickens or a child who milks the cows. It gets downright difficult once one starts to consider the writer who has been working on the same unpublished masterpiece for years, the musician who plays in a garage band, or the game designer who spends weeks on end leading the Alliance to victory over the wretched Horde in Alterac Valley.[73] And is it really fair to say that the stoner who hasn't worked a day in his life since graduating from college eight years ago is an unemployed member of the labor force when the only way he's ever going to put down the bong and get a job is if he gets hired by Marlboro as a product tester when marijuana is legalized?

Unemployment, then, is somewhat of a subjective concept, which makes it a very nebulous one from which to produce an objective measure of the extent to which the labor supply remains unused. This doesn't stop the heroic analysts at the Bureau of Labor Statistics from producing six alternative measures of labor underutilization, the more important of which are usually considered to

---

73. I spent the greater part of a month doing that a few summers ago – 55 victories in 60 battlegrounds. It was absolutely work! I just had to, you know, be certain I grokked the fullness of the design mechanics.

be U-3 and U-6. U-3 is the official unemployment rate and is defined as the total number of unemployed, as a percentage of the civilian labor force. The BLS defines the civilian labor force somewhat unhelpfully: "all persons classified as employed or unemployed in accordance with the definitions contained in this glossary." I shall save you the trouble of consulting the BLS glossary, as combining the two definitions indicates that the civilian labor force is defined as follows:

> Persons 16 years and over in the civilian noninstitutional population who, during the reference week, a) did any work at all (at least 1 hour) as paid employees; worked in their own business, profession, or on their own farm, or worked 15 hours or more as unpaid workers in an enterprise operated by a member of the family; and b) all those who were not working but who had jobs or businesses from which they were temporarily absent because of vacation, illness, bad weather, childcare problems, maternity or paternity leave, labor-management dispute, job training, or other family or personal reasons, whether or not they were paid for the time off or were seeking other jobs, excluding persons whose only activity consisted of work around their own house (painting, repairing, or own home housework) or volunteer work for religious, charitable, and other organizations, plus persons aged 16 years and older who had no employment during the reference week, were available for work, except for temporary illness, and had made specific efforts to find employment sometime during the four-week period ending with the reference week or were waiting to be recalled to a job from which they had been laid off.

Since there's very little chance that your eyes didn't glaze over while reading that, the pertinent fact is that the BLS doesn't count people who aren't working and haven't actively looked for work in the last four weeks as unemployed. So, while the conventional understanding of the term "unemployed" would mean "not employed," the U-3 official unemployment rate represents only 14 percent of the American civilian noninstitutional population 16 years and older who are not working. The raw data are obtained from two surveys, the Household Survey and the Payroll Survey. The Household is a monthly sample survey of 60,000 households while the Payroll is a monthly sample of 150,000 businesses and government agencies. The BLS itself admits that periodic discrepancies between the two surveys take place and it is reported that neither survey has ever been reconciled to within 1 million jobs of the other.[74] The payroll survey also shows the same tendency towards inaccuracy that was seen in the GDP measure, as in the first five months of 2009 the Payroll Survey has had to revise its previously reported job losses by an average of 86,200 per month. At 431,000, these cumulative revisions actually exceed the average 335 thousand job losses that the BLS has reported monthly since it declared the recession to have begun in December 2007.[75] Compounding this confusion is the dynamic nature of the labor force; men have been continuously exiting the labor force since 1950 while the percentage of women in it has nearly doubled over the same period. In sixty years, the U.S. labor force has grown 147 percent, from 62.2 million to 153.7 million, nearly 50 percent faster than the rate of population growth.

U-6 is a broader measure which attempts to account somewhat for the more obvious flaws in the official statistic, as it includes nonworkers who are outside the labor force but are "marginally attached" to it. These marginally attached individuals include discouraged workers who are not looking for jobs for one of five specific reasons,[76] those who have not looked for a job in the previous four weeks due to a variety of reasons including family responsibilities and a lack of transportation, and involuntary part-time workers. Because it includes more of the non-employed and underemployed workers that are excluded from the arbitrarily restricted definition of the unemployed, U-6 provides a more realistic perspective on

---

74. John Williams, "Employment and Unemployment Reporting," August 24, 2004.
75. "Since the recession began in December 2007, payroll employment has fallen by 5.7 million." Bureau of Labor Statistics, "The Employment Situation: April 2009," May 8, 2009, 3. The perceptive reader will note that according to the BEA's GDP figures, the economy grew 0.9 percent and 2.8 percent in the two quarters immediately following what the BLS declares to have been the start of the recession.
76. "The five specific reasons for discouragement are 1) thinks no work available, 2) could not find work, 3) lacks schooling or training, 4) employer thinks too young or old, and 5) other types of discrimination." U.S. Bureau of Labor Statistics, "Issues in Labor Statisics," April 2009.

how many people are not working and it usually runs approximately 75 percent higher than U-3. According to a BLS report entitled *Ranks of Discouraged Workers and Others Marginally Attached to the Labor Force Rise During Recession*, the unemployed exit the official labor force at about half the rate that the employed lose their jobs. At the time of this writing, the seasonally adjusted U-3 unemployment rate is reported to be 9.5 percent and U-6 is 16.5 percent.

The fundamental problems with both U-3 and U-6 are readily apparent. The logical flaws of basing an objective measure in part upon the subjective opinions of discouraged individuals should be obvious to even the most superficial observer. Nor does it make sense to take into account either the motivations or the inclinations of the non-employed since the purpose of the unemployment measure is to determine the rate of labor underutilization. The fact that a housewife prefers to stay home and care for her children or that a philosophy major prefers to spend seven years in a university pursuing a doctoral degree does not render them incapable of performing paid labor, it merely means that the amount they are likely to command based on current wages is insufficient to tempt them into the labor force. In fact, the arbitrary division of the civilian population into those who are in the labor force and those who are not in the labor force is a violation of the most fundamental law of economics, the Law of Supply and Demand.

Adam Smith's famous law, about which more will be said later, dictates that the supply of a commodity will always rise with an increase in price if other factors remain constant. This is just as true of labor as it is of any other commodity. If her prospective salary is too low, a mother cannot afford day-care for her children and so will not even contemplate joining the labor force. Even if her prospective salary is enough to afford the cost of caring for her children, she may decide it is not enough to compensate her for the sacrifice of her maternal instincts. But, in most cases, there will be a prospective salary, however unlikely it might be that she would command it, that would be sufficient to cause her to join the labor force. The same is true of the hypothetical philosopher; it is much easier to disdain a salary of $27,530 in favor of higher learning than it is to turn one's back on a salary of $1 million. The unemployment rates therefore say much less about the rate of labor underutilization than they do about the momentary preferences of millions of individuals regarding their place on the aggregate supply-demand curve for labor. And because these preferences are both individual and subject to change at any given moment, the unemployment rates don't say very much about them either.

These are not the only problems with the unemployment rate data. It makes little sense for the labor force to exclude military personnel, especially since other government employees are counted and military salaries are included in GDP as part of the government spending (G) component. Although at present military personnel would comprise only 0.5 percent of the employed, in the past, the military has accounted for as much as 8.14 percent of total employment. It might initially seem quite reasonable to argue that, because military jobs are implicitly unproductive if not downright destructive, they should not be included as part of the labor force. However, this argument simply doesn't hold water once you take into account what the tens of millions of drug enforcement agents, driver's license bureau clerks, tax collectors, civil rights compliance officers, and other government bureaucrats are contributing to the economy. If you consider that the United States enjoyed noticeable increases in its balance of trade as a result of both world wars[77] as well as the way in which the U.S. military's destruction of vast swathes of European and Asian manufacturing capability during World War II contributed to American postwar economic growth, then compare this with the annual regulatory burden that is reported by the OECD to have been estimated as high as $17,000 per private sector employee, you will see there is a reasonable case to be made that if any government employees are to be counted as

---

77. According to the statistics provided by Robert E. Lipsey in *Price and Quantity Trends in the Foreign Trade of the United States* (Princeton, NJ: Princeton University Press, 1963), American exports averaged $511 million annually during the decade from 1914 to 1923, significantly exceeding the average annual imports of $368 million. 1923 was the only year that the United States ran a negative balance of trade.

part of the labor force, military personnel should be among the first to be included.

And as if the unemployment figures were not unreliable enough already, the Obama administration has recently introduced a new employment metric it describes as "jobs created or saved." This takes unemployment from the subjective into the realm of pure political fantasy, as it is impossible to measure alternative futures. Thus, when President Obama declares that his stimulus program had saved or created at least 150,000 jobs, as he did on June 9, four days after the BLS reported an increase in U-6 unemployment to 15.9 percent,[78] he can do so with impunity, knowing that no one has any statistical measure capable of determining if a job that exists today would not have existed were it not for federal intervention.[79] The White House might as reasonably have declared that 1.5 million or even 15 million jobs were "saved or created" by its actions in the month of May.

The more you consider the various weaknesses, inconsistencies, and logical flaws of the methodology behind these three major economic statistics from an empirical perspective, the more readily it becomes apparent that attempting to measure a national economy through objective measures is a hopeless task, implausible in practice even if one assumes that it might be possible in theory. To illustrate just how hopeless this task is, it may be helpful to consider the testimony of one of the very monetary authorities, whose job it is to not only measure but manage the economy, the inspector general of the Federal Reserve Board of Governors, when she appeared before the House Subcommittee on Oversight and Investigations Committee on Financial Services.

The inspector general, Elizabeth A. Coleman, was nominally appearing before Congress to present a statement entitled "The Role of Inspectors General: Minimizing and Mitigating Waste, Fraud, and Abuse." The real purpose of her appearance was to lobby the

---

78. Since U-6 rose to 16.8 percent in the month of June, one shudders to think of what might have happened if so many jobs had not been created or saved.

79. William McGurn, "The Media Fall for Phony 'Jobs' Claims," *The Wall Street Journal*, June 10, 2009.

members of the subcommittee in favor of legislation that had been proposed by the chairman, presumably at the behest of the Federal Reserve, to significantly reduce the workload of the central bank's Inspectors General. The proposed law was intended to revise the legal requirements for material loss reviews for troubled banks, which currently are triggered when a bank loses $25 million or 2 percent of its assets. The inspector general, wanting to avoid the current legal requirement to investigate and produce a report every time such a petty and insignificant sum is lost, was lobbying for an increase in the statutory threshold to $400 million and promised that the new law would ensure that the most substantial banking failures would still be reviewed.

What the inspector general was not expecting, however, was that Democratic Congressman Alan Grayson, a member of the subcommittee, would take the opportunity to ask her about a February *Bloomberg* article in which it was reported that the Federal Reserve, the Treasury Department, and Federal Deposit Insurance Corporation had committed to spending $9.7 trillion in response to the various challenges posed by the financial crisis and the contracting economy.[80] The congressman was concerned that a large part of the loans, $7.8 trillion of which were under the direct control of the Federal Reserve, had been provided to unknown parties.

> Representative Alan Grayson (D-FL): Well, I have a copy of the Inspector General Act here in front of me and it says among other things that if you're responsible, you can conduct and supervise audits and investigations relating to the programs and operations of your agency.
>
> Inspector General Elizabeth A. Coleman: That's correct.
>
> Grayson: So I'm asking you if your agency has in fact, according to *Bloomberg*, extended $9 trillion in credit, which by the way works out to $30,000 for every single man, woman, and child in this country. I'd like to know if you're not responsible for investigating that, who is?

---

80. This amount was updated to $12.8 trillion a month later. Pittman, Mark and Ivry, Bob, "Financial Rescue Nears GDP as Pledges Top $12.8 Trillion," *Bloomberg*, March 31, 2009.

Coleman: We, actually... we have responsibility for the Federal Reserve's programs and operations, to conduct audits and investigations in that area. In terms of who is responsible for investigating... would you mind repeating the question one more time?

Grayson: What have you done to investigate the off-balance sheet transactions conducted by the Federal Reserve, which according to Bloomberg now?

Coleman: I'll have to look specifically at that Bloomberg article. I'm not... I don't know if I have actually seen that particular one.

Grayson: That's not the point. The question is have you done any investigation or auditing of off-balance sheet transactions conducted by the Federal Reserve?

Coleman: At this point, we're conducting our lending facility project at a fairly high level and have not gotten to a specific level of detail to really be in a position to respond to your question.

Grayson: Have you conducted any investigation or auditing of the losses that the Federal Reserve has experienced on its lending since last September?

Coleman: We are still in the process of conducting that review. Until we actually, you know, go out and gather the information, I'm not in a position to really respond to this specific question.

Grayson: So are you telling me that nobody at the Federal Reserve is keeping track on a regular basis of the losses that it incurs on what is now a $2 trillion portfolio?

Coleman: I don't know if... you're telling me that there's... you're... missing... that there are losses. I'm just saying that we're not... until we actually look at the program and have the information, we are not in a position to say whether there are losses or to respond in any other way to that question.

Grayson: Mr. Chairman, my time is up, but I have to tell you honestly, I am shocked to find out that nobody at the Federal Reserve including the Inspector General is keeping track of this.[81]

So, nobody at the Federal Reserve is keeping track. And nobody outside the Federal Reserve can even try to keep track either since the Fed has arrogantly refused to release its records despite repeated requests from members of Congress, the passage of Ron Paul's House bill to audit them, and lawsuits filed by media organizations in order to gain access to them. This means that $12.8 trillion, an amount equivalent to more than three-quarters of the national economy, was spent or loaned out in less than a year, and virtually no one knows where much of it has gone, much less what happened to it. And yet, none of that money appears to have had any effect on any of the major economic statistics yet, which is remarkable considering that it is nearly equivalent to the amount produced in a year's worth of national economic activity. Had they simply given all that money to the public, U.S. GDP would have nearly doubled, although presumably a sudden 91 percent growth in a statistic that has averaged 3.4 percent since 1929 might call the validity of the measure into question.

It is the socionomist Robert Prechter who has beautifully demonstrated that no one, least of all the financial media, actually has much of a clue regarding what is taking place at any given moment within the extraordinarily complex and all-encompassing abstraction that is "the economy." He did so by analyzing two speeches given by Alan Greenspan in 2004 and examining not only the reaction of the stock market to those speeches, but the subsequent coverage of the speeches and the reaction of the market. "The stock market rallied for half an hour on the morning of April 20, peaked at 10:00 a.m., and sold off for the rest of the day. Almost every newspaper and wire service claims that the market sold off because Greenspan told Congress that the nation's bank-

---

81. Dotsub.com. http://dotsub.com/view/60d05559-ed86-47b2-a2bf-4bb565ea10ed/view Transcript/eng.

ing system is well prepared to deal with rising rates, which the market interpreted as a new signal the Fed will tighten its policy sooner rather than later. Is this explanation plausible?"[82]

Prechter lists no less than ten reasons why this explanation is not only implausible, but impossible. They include: 1) Greenspan began speaking around 2:30 PM, but the market had already peaked and was heading south four and one-half hours earlier. 2) The same stories also reported that most economists don't expect the Fed to raise rates at its next meeting, which directly contradicts the explanation for why investors sold stocks. 3) There is no reliable evidence indicating that an increase in the Federal Funds target rate makes the stock market go down. 4) The very next day, Greenspan repeated his comments and the stock market went up. As Prechter correctly points out, the "explanations" are simply ex post facto rationalizations sans any evidence that a single trader bought or sold a single stock for the reasons provided.

The truth is that nobody really knows anything, and the mass of numbers, and figures, and reports, and statistics are all very crude approximations that do little more than create the illusion of accuracy. The stock market is not physics. Nor is economics. And to paraphrase the physicist Richard Feynman, reality must take precedence over public relations and the pretense of precision if one is to have a successful economy, because the Invisible Hand cannot be fooled forever.

---

82. Robert Prechter, Jr. "The Stock Market is not Physics," *The Elliott Wave Theorist*. May/June 2004, pp. 9-12.

Chapter 5

N-BODY ECONOMICS
AND THE RICARDIAN VICE

Any extension of the sphere of monetary calculation causes misunderstanding. It cannot be regarded as constituting a kind of yardstick for the valuation of goods, and cannot be so treated in historical investigations into the development of social relationships; it cannot be used as a criterion of national wealth and income, nor as a means of gauging the value of goods which stand outside the sphere of exchange, as who should seek to estimate the extent of human losses through emigration or wars in terms of money? This is mere sciolistic tomfoolery, however much it may be indulged in by otherwise perspicacious economists.

—LUDWIG VON MISES, "Economic Calculation in the Socialist Commonwealth," 1920

I N HIS *Principia*, Sir Isaac Newton provided a solution to the two-body problem by demonstrating how it was possible to determine the exact way in which two bodies with gravitational attraction for each other would move with respect to one another. Armed with Newton's equations and the accurate observational data, this would allow an observer to calculate the relative positions of those two bodies in the future. Newton attempted to extend his approach to allow for similarly precise calculations of three bodies in his attempt to show that the motion of the Moon could be computed from the gravitational influences upon it, which required taking both the Earth and the Sun into account. However, the adding a third body to the equation significantly increased the complexity of the problem and not even the surpass-ingly brilliant mind of Newton was able to find an answer for it despite his development of the Theory of Perturbations. The three-body problem, as this problem came to be known, is so complicated that although certain specific cases have been solved, mathematicians have yet to discover a universal equation that will permit them to solve the general problem.

The n-body problem, which involves a variable and infinite number of bodies, is even more difficult. It is widely believed to be almost impossible to solve, since the addition of one or more bodies to a two-body system introduces small gravitational influences, or perturbations, from each body to each of the other bodies, which disrupts the path and exponentially multiplies the range of potential paths each body may follow. Every additional body added to the situation introduces new perturbations and new complications, thus making it harder to predict the location of any one body in the system. Since we are informed that the three-body problem already exhibits chaotic tendencies,[83] the n-body problem seems likely to remain outside the realm of rational order.

Like many sciences, economics borrows heavily from the language and style of the hard sciences on which Newton left such an indelible mark. Economists are nearly as enamoured of complicated equations littered with Greek letters as physicists and mathematicians, and there is a whole branch of economics, called "econometrics," which is dedicated to applying rigorous statistical methods to economic theory in an attempt to transform it from a science primarily based on observational logic to one that is solidly grounded upon empirical evidence. The various statistical measures cited throughout the previous chapter are an important part of that process. But economists face a tremendous challenge in collecting empirical evidence, for several reasons. First, it's not practical to recreate a national economy in a lab. This doesn't necessarily preclude precision, though, as astrophysicists and other scientists have successfully surmounted the same handicap. Sec-

---

83. Patricia T. Boyd and Steven L.W. McMillan, "Chaotic scattering in the gravitational three-body problem." Chaos 3, 507 (1993). Abstract.

ond, it's difficult to obtain economic information, although the move towards trackable electronic credit and currency will make obtaining price data easier in the future. Third is an issue analogous to the n-body problem in classical mechanics, as n economic actors interact with each other and exert varying degrees of influence over one another through those interactions. And the fourth is something that could be described as the economic uncertainty principle or the n-mind problem, which is the additional complication that every single one of these multitudinous economic bodies is a dynamic actor capable of modifying its value judgments and altering its economic orbital trajectories at will.

For hundreds of years, economists have attempted to address these chaotic and complex challenges facing them by simplifying them. They have usually done so by manufacturing logical justifications to eliminate as many factors as possible, which, to give one well-known example, allows them to reduce something as large and as massively complicated as a national economy to just five variables, Consumer spending, Investment, Government spending, eXports, and iMports.[84] In effect, they attempt to take an insoluble n-body problem and turn it into a two-body approximation. This naturally renders all economic calculations inherently imprecise; you can no more expect an economic equation to provide a reliably accurate result than you could reasonably hope to correctly calculate the Earth's orbit relative to the Sun and Moon without taking the gravitational influences of the rest of the solar system into account. As absurd as it might sound to suggest that astronomers would ignore Venus, Jupiter, and Mars, the analogy is actually too favorable to economists because the combined gravitational influence of all the other objects in the solar system is about 25,000 times weaker than the cumulative influence of the two largest factors. And yet, even less significant factors can be meaningful, as it was the perturbations that caused Uranus to deviate from its predicted path which led to the discovery of the planet Neptune.

---

84. This is the formula for Gross Domestic Product (GDP), in case you have forgotten.

These attempts to simplify a complicated problem has often led economists into constructing economic models that are not only hopelessly inaccurate, but sometimes downright absurd. One of the more influential of the classical economists, David Ricardo, whose theory of comparative advantage is still the primary justification for free trade and provides the intellectual basis that underlies political entities such as the European Union and treaties such as the North American Free Trade Agreement, concocted a theory of profit in which he purported to prove that all profits depend upon the price of food, more specifically, wheat. In his grand survey of the history of economic thought, Joseph Schumpeter wryly praises Ricardo's profit theory as an excellent one that could never be refuted, given its lack of nothing but sense, then proceeds to give this process of conceptual oversimplification a name.

> "His interest was in the clear-cut result of direct, practical significance. In order to get this he cut that general system to pieces, bundled up as large parts of it as possible, and put them in cold storage – so that as many things as possible should be frozen and 'given'. He then piled one simplifying assumption upon another until, having really settled everything by these assumptions, he was left with only a few aggregative variables between which, given these assumptions, he set up simple one-way relations so that, in the end, the desired results emerged almost as tautologies....The habit of applying results of this character to the solution of practical problems we shall call the Ricardian Vice."[85]

The reason that so much of modern economics is guilty of this Ricardian Vice is not due to the influence of Ricardo, however, but due to that of John Maynard Keynes. Keynes's conclusions differed greatly from Ricardo's, but his aims and methods were similar, so similar, in fact, that Schumpeter describes them as brothers in methodological spirit and goes so far as to note that every word in a lengthy paragraph explaining the success of Ricardo and his

---

85. Joseph Schumpeter, *History of Economic Analysis* (London: Oxford University Press, 1963), 472-473.

school could just as easily be written in reference to Keynes, whose theories are the foundation of most modern macroeconomic models and policy prescriptions. Indelible signs of the Ricardian Vice can be seen in the calculation of nearly every macroeconomic statistic. The definition of the labor force eliminates nearly half the population of the United States from consideration, while the CPI core index excludes the three most vital consumer goods: food, housing, and energy. The very monetary prices used to measure most of these statistics are themselves an oversimplification, for as Mises declared in the quote at the beginning of the chapter, monetary calculation cannot be rationally used as a criterion of national wealth and income as it is in computing GDP, for the obvious reason that the price of a good can only reflect the market value of a specific good or service assigned by two specific parties in a specific transaction on a specific date. To assume that this very specific and subjective value can be applied objectively across the entire economy – or the entire world – for a whole year, then compiled en masse with millions of other similarly specific and subjective values to achieve a meaningful result, defies both logic and empirical data.

This may sound overly pedantic as well as willfully iconoclastic, but if you think the matter through, you'll soon understand how it is absolutely true. The mark-to-market aspect of the credit bubble, in which the huge difference between the prices paid for various assets by financial institutions and the dynamically adjusted values of those assets recorded on the institutions' balance sheets according to their present market value, not only had a large impact on the solvency of those institutions but demonstrates the way in which past prices paid cannot be considered a reliable measure of value at a later date. The importance financial risk managers assigned to Value-at-Risk, a calculation of the risk of mark-to-market loss to an asset portfolio over a given time frame that must be regularly disclosed by all regulated financial intermediaries, is sufficient to prove that one cannot use dynamic prices in relatively static models and expect to achieve any meaningful degree of precision.

Moreover, the use of money as a base measure for the economy is inherently questionable due to the inability of anyone to define precisely what it is or how much of it is out there. Until three years ago, the Federal Reserve published data for three monetary aggregates, M1, M2, and M3, all of which included but were not limited to the actual supply of currency, which in combination with bank reserves held on account at the central bank is known as M0. So, in addition to requiring a significant amount of simplification in its calculation, the terms in which the criterion of national economic activity is reported are both dynamic and uncertain.

Ricardo's theory of profit was abandoned long ago. It is doubtful there is a single economist on the planet who believes that profits are reliant upon the price of agricultural products for anyone but farmers and corporate agricultural concerns. But while the conventional economic statistical models based on classical and Keynesian concepts have been modified, tweaked, and massaged in a thousand different ways since government economists began using them, they are still fundamentally the same exhibitions of the Ricardian Vice put into practice that they were when they were adopted in the first half of the twentieth century.

A few of the various problems with the data being entered into the economic statistics were chronicled in the previous chapter. One might reasonably conclude, on the basis of the GIGO principle, that this means that these statistics are therefore inaccurate and useless, and there is an entire school of economic thought to which I am sympathetic that concludes precisely that. But, in the interest of engaging in a scientific inquiry rather than a purely philosophical one, it behooves us to examine the predictive capacity of the models used to produce these statistics and discover if our logical conclusions regarding their inaccuracy are justified or not.

At this point, it seems appropriate to point out that, although you might have reached the conclusion that I am contemptuous of mainstream economists' efforts to calculate economic activity, this is not actually the case. The task to which they have set themselves is a staggering one, very probably an impossible one, and for the most part they make the best of an incredibly difficult job. Unlike scientists in other disciplines where complexity renders precision impractical, economists are usually quite willing to admit the imperfect nature of their models. Of course, this is probably less the result of the superior character of economists and more the consequence of the greater media coverage to which their predictions are inevitably subjected. A paleontologist can announce a new discovery that shows his previous projections were off by 200,000 years without fearing for his future credibility, but an economist who predicts the Dow rising to 36,000 just prior to the start of one of the biggest bear markets in history will become both a laughingstock and a punch line – and rightly so.[86]

Still, economists are generally more willing than most scientists to entertain the possibility that they are wrong. Merely expressing even the smallest degree of skepticism about the theory of evolution by natural selection is enough to cause most biologists to start frothing at the mouth, despite the fact that Darwin's original theory has been so heavily modified over the years that it's usually known as the *modern synthesis* in order to accommodate both Darwinist natural selection and Mendelian genetics. And physicists, for all their past successes, seldom take kindly to the implication that their inability to find the greater part of the universe that their theories indicate should be there means that they need a better gravitational model.[87] It is to the great credit of economists that the reports published by the world's most important economic organizations often include a record of exactly how wrong they had it previously. For example, in addition to publishing data from the previous two years and projections for the current and coming year, the IMF's twice-annual *World Economic Outlook* also reports on the difference between those projections and projections for the same time period made in the previous report. For example,

---

86. I have to confess a certain appreciation for James Glassman's sense of humor about the title of the 1999 bestseller he wrote with Kevin Hassett when he admitted that he wished they'd called it *A Treatise on the Declining Equity Risk Premium* rather than *Dow 36,000*. Of course, if I'm completely wrong and 2010 marks the start of a great global economic recovery, I may require a similar sense of humor.

87. *"Dark Matter and Dark Energy…Dark Matter and Dark Energy….Our two explanations are Dark Matter and Dark Energy…and Dark Vapor….Our three explanations are Dark Matter, and Dark Energy, and Dark Vapor…and an almost fanatical devotion to Karl Popper….Our four…no…Amongst our explanations are such elements as Dark Matter, Dark Energy….I'll come in again."* With apologies to Monty Python.

the April 2009 report, "Crisis and Recovery," provides the following overview in the very first table.

Table 5.1. World Economic Outlook Projections, 2007–2010

Year	2007	2008	Projections 2009	2010	Difference from Jan. 2009 Projections 2009	2010
World Output	5.2	3.2	-1.3	1.9	-1.8	-1.1

Naturally, the fact that the admitted difference from their projections four months prior has averaged 0.6 percent for the current year and 0.7 percent for the following one raises some real questions about how accurate the models upon which the IMF economists base their predictions happen to be, especially in light of what we know about the shifting nature of past economic data. And just how accurate were those models? In looking at the nine most recent *World Economic Outlooks*, the predictions for the U.S. economy in 2006 proved to be the most accurate. Economic growth for that year was projected to be 3.6 percent in the 2005 *Outlook* and 3.4 percent in the 2006 edition. Those predictions turned out to be relatively accurate, as the 2007 outlook reported that the actual growth rate came in at 3.3 percent. However, the post-facto revision decreased the precision of the predictions somewhat when the 2008 *World Economic Outlook* reported final 2006 GDP growth at 2.9 percent.

The variances for the Euro area economies and the Japanese economy were of similar magnitude during those four years, as the initial 2005 predictions of 2.3 percent growth for Europe and 1.9 percent for Japan were both impressively close to the final revised numbers of 2.9 percent and 2.4 percent, respectively. However, 2006 was the best year for the IMF's economic prognosticators, and even though the first two predictions are the only ones available for 2009, the Japanese calculations already look as if they have gone completely awry, as the 1.5 percent growth in Japan's GDP predicted in the 2008 *World Economic Outlook* was slashed to -6.2 percent in the most recent publication. Since the Japanese economy was reported to be $4.92 trillion in 2008, this 7.7 percent swing represents a $379 billion modification of the growth prediction and is almost precisely equal to the total amount of economic growth reported for Japan in the four years from 2005 through 2008.

In addition to keeping track of its past predictions and making them publicly available, the IMF is admirably straightforward about the limitations of its current ones. In each *World Economic Outlook*, it prominently features a page entitled "Assumptions and Conventions" immediately following the table of contents. In the 2008 report, it provided the following caveat:

> A number of assumptions have been adopted for the projections presented in the World Economic Outlook. It has been assumed a) that real effective exchange rates will remain constant at their average levels during January 30–February 27, 2008, except for the currencies participating in the European exchange rate mechanism II (ERM II), which are assumed to remain constant in nominal terms relative to the euro; b) that established policies of national authorities will be maintained (for specific assumptions about fiscal and monetary policies in industrial countries, see Box A1); c) that the average price of oil will be $95.50 a barrel in 2008 and $94.50 a barrel in 2009, and remain unchanged in real terms over the medium term; d) that the six-month London interbank offered rate (LIBOR) on U.S. dollar deposits will average 3.1 percent in 2008 and 3.4 percent in 2009; e) that the three-month euro deposits rate will average 4.0 percent in 2008 and 3.6 percent in 2009; and f) that the six-month Japanese yen deposit rate will yield an average of 1.0 percent in 2008 and of 0.8 percent in 2009. These are, of course, working hypotheses rather than forecasts, and the uncertainties surrounding them add to the margin of error that would in any event be involved in the projections.[88]

While more than half of the IMF's working hypotheses proved to be excellent near-term forecasts, the tendency of actual prices to

---

88. International Monetary Fund, *World Economic Outlook 2009: Crisis and Recovery*, April 2009. v.

diverge from these assumptions over time demonstrates some of the difficulty inherent to economic modeling. The table below compares the IMF's 2008 assumptions with the actual price averages for 2008 and the first half of 2009.

Table 5.2. *World Economic Outlook* Performance, 2008–2009

	Avg Oil Price 2008	Avg Oil Price 2009	LIBOR (USD) 2008	LIBOR (USD) 2009	LIBOR (EUR) 2008	LIBOR (EUR) 2009	LIBOR (YEN) 2008	LIBOR (YEN) 2009
IMF 2008 est.	95.5	94.5	3.1	3.4	4.0	3.6	1	0.8
2008-09 actual	91.5	48.8	3.1	1.7	4.6	1.9	1	0.8
Accuracy	96%	52%	100%	50%	85%	53%	100%	100%

While the performance of the IMF economists responsible for interest rate forecasts is quite impressive, the real question is not how well various components of the economic model corresponded with reality, but how well the model as a whole performed. If we stay focused on the year 2008, since it is the latest year for which actual data are available, we can look at forecasts from the 2007 and 2008 outlooks and compare them with the actual data provided in the 2009 outlook. As per its usual schedule, the IMF provided initial projections for 2008 GDP growth for the United States, the Euro area, and Japan, the average price of oil, and the average rate of inflation across the advanced economies based on consumer prices in its April 2007 outlook.

	U.S. GDP Growth	Euro Area GDP Growth	Japan GDP Growth	Avg Oil Price	Consumer Prices
IMF 2007	2.8 percent	2.3 percent	1.9 percent	$64.75	2.1 percent

One of the interesting things about the *World Economic Outlooks* is the way in which one can trace the development of the current crisis through the titles given to its reports throughout the years. While both the "Financial Systems and Economic Cycles" of September 2006 and "Spillovers and Cycles in the Global Economy" of April 2007 mention potential concerns about the expected cooling of the U.S. housing market spilling over into the U.S.

economy, housing did not take center stage until the April 2008 report, "Housing and the Business Cycle." While they made it clear that they believed the balance of risks to the global economy were weighted to the downside in those earlier reports, the IMF economists still estimated that the chance of world economic growth falling below 3.25 percent or less was only one in six. Of more immediate concern at the time was the potential that the intensification of inflationary pressures causing central banks to raise interest rates and that geopolitical uncertainties could cause the price of oil to continue rising.

Even as housing prices turned down in 2007, there was still no realization of the way in which the mortgage-backed securities market had created a connection between the stability of the financial institutions and the housing market. The only housing-related concerns were related to the possibility that the continued deterioration of the U.S. housing market might cause the U.S. economy to slow more sharply than expected; the key question for the rest of the world was its ability to decouple from any potential U.S. slowdown. There was no mention whatsoever of the risks caused by the European housing bubbles that by that time had already burst in Ireland, Spain, and the United Kingdom, while potential inflationary pressures and the likelihood that financial market volatility would increase from its historically low levels were presented as more immediate risks. In particular, the IMF drew attention to concerns about the possibility that rising protectionism might inhibit free trade and foreign investment and thereby reduce global economic growth.

The projections and statistics from this recent three-year time span reflect the failure of economists utilizing the mainstream models to recognize the threat that the credit and investment booms posed to the U.S. and European economies. And despite the excellent performance of the IMF statisticians in forecasting important variables, they also show the flaws in the statistical models used to calculate the amount of economic activity projected to take place in the global economy.

Table 5.3. *World Economic Outlook Projections, 2006–2009*

	2006 GDP USA	2006 GDP Japan	2006 Inflation	2007 GDP USA	2007 GDP Japan	2007 Inflation	2008 GDP USA	2008 GDP Japan	2008 Inflation	2009 GDP USA	2009 GDP Japan	2009 Inflation
2005 Apr	3.6	1.9	1.8	—	—	—	—	—	—	—	—	—
2005 Sep	3.3	2.0	2.0	—	—	—	—	—	—	—	—	—
2006 Apr	3.4	2.8	2.3	3.3	2.1	2.1	—	—	—	—	—	—
2006 Sep	3.4	2.7	2.6	2.9	2.1	2.3	—	—	—	—	—	—
2007 Apr	3.3	2.2	2.3	2.2	2.3	1.8	2.8	-0.6	2.1	—	—	—
2007 Sep	2.9	2.2	2.3	1.9	2.0	2.1	1.9	0.7	2.0	—	—	—
2008 Apr	2.9	2.2	2.4	2.2	2.1	2.2	0.5	0.5	2.6	0.6	1.5	2.0
2008 Sep	2.8	2.4	2.4	2.0	2.1	2.2	1.6	1.7	3.6	0.1	0.5	2.0
2009 Apr	—	—	—	2.0	2.4	2.2	1.1	1.9	3.4	-2.8	-6.2	-0.2
Variance	0.8	0.9	0.8	1.4	0.3	0.4	2.3	2.5	1.3	3.4	7.7	2.2

Again, the percentage variances appear small, but they represent a substantial amount of money. In the case of the U.S. economy, the average variance has been 1.6 percent, or $210 billion per year. This would appear to be remarkably precise, actually, as the IMF's ability to project annual economic results two years in advance is very nearly as accurate as the U.S. Bureau of Economic Analysis's ability to determine the results of the recently completed quarter, as demonstrated in the previous chapter. It is also somewhat mystifying, since it exhibited no similar precision in projecting oil prices over the same time frame. An examination of the IMF's oil price projections for the last seven years shows that predicted prices diverged from actual prices by $25.29 on average; twice, in 2005 and 2009, the statisticians' working hypotheses were off by nearly 100 percent.

So, given what we know about the cataclysmic effect of even minor perturbations on the overall system due to the n-body problem, how is it even remotely possible that the IMF models can input such wildly inaccurate data and still somehow produce a figure that is relatively close to the eventual result? The answer is simple. The IMF models don't correctly predict the actual level of economic activity in a given economy; they don't have to. Instead, they are designed to project a result that promises to correspond reasonably well with the results that will eventually be produced by the economic agencies responsible for tracking the economic data for the various national and supranational economies with which they are concerned. And if the numbers don't happen to match, such as was the case when the April 2007 *World Economic Outlook* reported 3.3 percent growth of 2006 U.S. GDP versus 2.8 percent growth published by the BLS, they can always be adjusted after the fact. The previous table shows how the rate published in the last *World Economic Outlook* in which the 2006 statistics appeared, September 2008, matched the BLS figure perfectly.

Does it actually matter? After all, even if the IMF happens to be off by $210 billion or so every year, that's only about the size of Wal-Mart's market cap; and what difference does it make to you if GDP, CPI, or the six-month London interbank offered rate on U.S.

dollar deposits are reported at 7.7 or 1.2 percent? The reason it matters is that these numbers are not calculated for fun, or even to provide a statistical basis for the fantasy sport that is Wall Street gambling, but to provide the world's fiscal and monetary authorities with metrics to guide their actions and measure the consequences of those actions. The effects aren't always as directly obvious as the link between CPI-W and cost-of-living adjustments to monthly Social Security payments, but they are seldom trivial. Since the central banks of the world have been trying to manage the business cycle for the last sixty years, they have intervened forcefully and lobbied for legislative intervention whenever these macroeconomic statistics have indicated an economy that is "heating up too fast," or looking likely to produce inflation above the usual central bank target of 2 percent, or threatening to slow down enough to drive unemployment up. Significant political matters, such as the income tax cuts that occurred during the Reagan and Bush '43 administrations and the Obama administration's $787 billion stimulus plan, are largely, if not entirely, driven by these statistics and the economic models that consider them to be important.

As if the challenge of forecasting and measuring national economies were not difficult enough, it is complicated by the fact that many of the economists responsible for producing these politically-charged statistics are employed by the very politicians whose careers depend upon what figures the models spit out, and it defies imagination to think that pressure is not exerted upon them. After the Chancellor of the Exchequer, Alistair Darling, presented a doom-laden 2009 budget to the House of Commons, reports in the British media surfaced that he had been under pressure to present a less gloomy portrait to the public. The *Times* reported: "Mr Darling has been less biddable than No 10 would like. In the run-up to the Budget, I am told that the Prime Minister tried to upgrade the growth forecasts to make the economic outlook appear rosier than it was; the Chancellor refused."[89] While Gordon Brown may be one of the most economically incompetent

---

89. Rachel Sylvester, "Bodies are piling up in this Westminster thriller," *The Times*, June 2, 2009.

politicians to ever head a government – in addition to presiding over the U.K.'s credit downgrade, his decision to sell half of Britain's gold reserves at historically low prices in 1999 unnecessarily cost the British people $8.75 billion – it is highly improbable that he is the only politician to attempt putting pressure on those responsible for the economic forecasts and results.

Brown's ham-handed approach is not the only means available to politicians attempting to influence the information that is provided to the public. My first glimpse of the inadequacies of economic forecasting occurred when I was growing up in Minnesota and my family subscribed to the *Minneapolis Tribune*. Around the time I reached high school, I happened to notice that every year, when the paper reported on the state budget, the story would invariably mention that tax revenues from the previous year had either been lower than expected or higher than expected. But the strange thing was that revenues were usually lower than expected after tax increases, and higher than expected after tax cuts. After reading the stories a little more closely, I realized that the paper's forecasts were reliably wrong because the paper was applying a simple static model to the changes in tax rates. They assumed that an increase in taxes from 5 percent to 6 percent could be expected to bring in an additional penny. The model was unreliable because it failed to account for the fact that humans and their economic activities are dynamic, not static.

That was more than twenty years ago, and yet politicians are still applying these crude and overly simplistic static models. The *Wall Street Journal* reported that the Maryland state government found itself out $206 million in expected tax revenue in 2009 one year after adding a special millionaires' tax bracket that raised the combined state and local income tax to 9.45 percent in its major cities. If the result was predictable to everyone but politicians, the extent of the effect is still surprising; one-third of Maryland's three thousand millionaires disappeared from the tax rolls in a single year. Instead of producing an additional $106 million in revenue, the higher tax rates resulted in the state receiving $100 million less than it had the year before.[90] The lesson is harsh, but clear. Economic models matter.

To understand why certain models are favored and others are disdained, it is first necessary to understand that original, and proper, name for economic science is political economy. Despite the pretensions of econometricians, economics is not, and can never be, a wholly objective physical science. It has too many abstract elements to it, and politics and other petty societal complications will always play a perturbating role. Nor is there a natural economy somewhere waiting to be discovered in the way that scientists in other fields have discovered so many places, properties, and objects, because economics is merely a specialized means of examining certain human activities with the objective of understanding them well enough to predict and influence them. The more that economists attempt to construct purely rational and objective models to describe the economy, the further they will find themselves from being able to accurately predict the cumulative behavior of irrational and subjective individuals. And the more they focus on the aggregate aspects of the macroeconomy, the less likely it becomes that they will be able to ascertain those small but significant influences capable of having a profound effect on the movement paths of the myriad of independent bodies active in the economic system.

---

90. "Millionaires Go Missing," *The Wall Street Journal*, May 27, 2009.

Chapter 6

THE WHORE,
THE FALSE PROPHET,
AND THE BEAST FROM THE SEA

*It is astonishing what foolish things one can temporarily believe if
one thinks too long alone, particularly in economics, (along with the
other moral sciences), where it is often impossible to bring one's
ideas to a conclusive test either formal or experimental.*

—JOHN MAYNARD KEYNES, *The General Theory of
Employment, Interest, and Money*, 1935

I N *THE Mind of the Market*, Michael Shermer describes how he
developed a principle he named "Darwin's Dictum" after a letter the famed biologist wrote to political economist Henry Fawcett
in 1861. In that letter, Darwin discussed his own astonishment
that more people did not understand that observations were not
objective, that their only value stems from their utilization in the
service of one theory or another. According to Shermer, Darwin's
Dictum runs thusly: *all observation must be for or against some
view if it is to be of any service.*[91]

If you measure the success of an economic theory on the basis
of the acceptance of its essential principles, however poorly understood, by the widest possible audience, you will soon be forced to
conclude that history's most successful economists have primarily
been those who managed to most effectively apply Darwin's Dictum
in their works. This is true even of those gentlemen who could not

---

91. Michael Shermer, *The Mind of the Market* (New York: Henry Holt/Times Books, 2007) 9.

possibly have encountered it by virtue of having been buried for decades before Charles Darwin penned his letter to Fawcett, and long before Shermer first articulated it in his first column for *Scientific American*. For economics is inherently ideological and dogmatic, so much so that more than a few observers have been led to conclude that an economic system bears no small similarity to a religion, complete with prophets.[92]

Of the many economists that Joseph Schumpeter chronicles throughout his mammoth *History of Economic Analysis*, three in particular stand out as those who attempted to transform political economy from a logical philosophy of limited practical application into a deductive science capable of providing absolute conclusions. They appear to have been driven to do so by an implicit application of Darwin's Dictum, as their approach does not reflect either the Greek philosopher's search for the truth nor the modern scientist's dispassionate pursuit of evidence, but rather the medieval theologian's desire to rationalize the predetermined conclusion. The need to transform the vagaries of philosophy into the certainties of science stemmed from their desire to dictate specific actions and policies. David Ricardo was the first of this breed; a politician for the last four years of his life, many of the works in which his theories were laid out were political tracts advocating specific positions on the issues of the day rather than intellectual inquiries into basic economic concepts. Ricardo's New Political Economy, supported by James and John Stuart Mill, soon came to dominate the English intellectual scene to such an extent that Ricardo came to be seen as the natural heir to Adam Smith. Despite its prosaic origins, the brilliance of Ricardian economics was such that according to Keynes, it provided the foundation for both the liberal Manchester School as well as the decidedly non-liberal theories of Karl Marx.[93]

It was Ricardo's comparative advantage theory of international trade and his attack on nineteenth century Britain's Corn Laws that provided inspiration to the Manchester School and subsequent

---

92. Anatol Murad, *What Keynes Means* (New York: Bookman Associates, 1962), 16.
93. The General Theory, 15.

followers of *laissez-faire* doctrine, whereas his explication of a labor-embodied theory of value provided Marx with the economic basis of his tripartite pseudo-science. Marx applied Darwin's Dictum to a much greater extent than Ricardo did, as the originator of Scientific Socialism not only expanded the labor theory of value into a full-blown economic theory, but tied it into a holistic socio-political program laden with scientific terminology that specified a variety of very practical and detailed political policies. Whereas Ricardo only sought to rationalize the case for convertible curren-cies and the abolition of Corn Laws, Marx's observations were made with the intention of justifying international revolution, the elimi-nation of private property, and the complete restructuring of the world's governments. And while Ricardo was content to artificially weight his arguments by eliminating factors until he had simplified an issue to drive his desired conclusion, Marx argued from histori-cal inevitability, a contention that only time is capable of refuting.

The Whore

> *I am fully aware that I am claiming that perhaps the most im-pressive intellectual figure I have ever encountered and whose general intellectual superiority I have readily acknowledged was wholly wrong in the scientific work for which he is chiefly known.... Indeed, I am convinced that, through his denial of conventional morals and his haughty "in the long run we are all dead" approach, his influence was disastrous.*
>
> —F.A. Hayek, "Personal Recollections of Keynes and the 'Keynesian Revolution'"

While Marxist economics are now as intellectually defunct as the Ricardian theory of wheat-based profit, it is nevertheless interesting to note how Marx's mention of capitalism's tendency towards over-production in *The Communist Manifesto* points us towards the third and most important of these results-oriented economists, John Maynard Keynes. Despite his status as a self-described priest of Eng-lish classical theory, a school at that time led by Alfred Marshall and steeped in the Ricardian tradition, Keynes broke with this English orthodoxy in order to provide a theory capable of addressing the broad spectrum of economic situations rather than the special case assumed as the basis for most classical theory. In his influential magnum opus, *The General Theory of Employment, Interest, and Money*, Keynes placed particular emphasis on the word "general," which he explained in the introduction to the French edition was meant to indicate that his primary interest was in the behavior of the economic system in its entirety, rather than any of its constituent parts.

Classical economics tended to begin with individual cases and attempted to build general principles from them. If you have read *The Wealth of Nations*, you will almost surely recall Adam Smith's explanation of the division of labor using the famous example of the pin maker's trade. Ricardo explained comparative advantage by postulating two countries, England and Portugal, trading two products. Keynes had no interest in these sorts of microeconomic examples. He believed that the classical method of extending correct conclusions, which was derived from the behavior of specific industries, organizations, and individuals to the system as a whole, had caused important mistakes that might be avoided by looking at the aggregate results of that behavior instead. He was not interested in how one individual saved money, but rather in discovering a way to ascertain how the total volume of savings increased or decreased throughout the economy. He did not seek to understand why one man was out of work, but why the level of unemployment throughout society had changed.

As Darwin's Dictum dictates, Keynes held a view that his observations and his theories were intended to serve. That view long predated the formulation of his arguments; Schumpeter declares that Keynes's vision was distinctly set forth in *The Economic Consequences of the Peace*, which was published not only twenty-seven years before *The General Theory* but more than two decades before he wrote his *Treatise on Money*, which he disavowed in *The General Theory* as being too caught up in the preconceived ideas of the orthodox theories he was attempting to supplant. If Schumpeter is correct, then a perusal of the Keynes's earlier work, which he wrote in 1919 as a British representative to the Paris Peace Conference that led to the Treaty of Versailles, suggests that the great macro-economist's vision was no less utopian, and scarcely less revolutionary, than that of Karl Marx himself.[94]

Whereas Marx promised an eventual Worker's Paradise without offering much in the way of specific explanation for how it would operate or what was necessary beyond incorporating the Ten Pillars of Communism into law,[95] Keynes more credibly sought to offer Man a means of taming the dread business cycle that so reliably turned periods of prosperity into periods of hardship, inflation, and unemployment. Ironically, in light of what we have seen regarding the precision and reliability of modern macroeconomic statistics, Keynes declared that the economic equilibrium postulated by the classical theory was impractical because it was an idealized, hypothetical situation that was seldom relevant to the real world.

> "[T]he characteristics of the special case assumed by the classical theory happen not to be those of the economic society in which we actually live, with the result that its teaching is misleading and disastrous if we attempt to apply it to the facts of experience."[96]

This recognition of the implausibility of realizing practical results from a theoretical model that departed too far from actual economic society did not deter Keynes from constructing a framework to analyze the aggregate economy by utilizing only five variables: the psychological propensity to consume, the psychological attitude to liquidity, the psychological expectation of future yield from capital-assets, the wage-unit, and the quantity of money deter-

---

94. *"[I]t is under the influence of Paris, not London, that this book has been written by one who, though an Englishman, feels himself a European also, and, because of too vivid recent experience, cannot disinterest himself from the further unfolding of the great historic drama of these days which will destroy great institutions, but may also create a new world."* Keynes, John Maynard, "The Economic Consequences of the Peace," 1919.

95. Actually, if you compare Marx's Ten Pillars to current law, you might reasonably conclude we are already living in the Worker's Paradise. Perhaps not all private property has been abolished – yet – but free public education, a graduated income tax, and the centralization of credit in the banks of the state by means of a national bank with an exclusive monopoly certainly sound familiar.

96. General Theory.

mined by the central bank's actions. Today, we more commonly refer to these variables as consumption, investment, the rate of interest, employment, and the money supply. It is even more remarkable to read Keynes mocking Ricardo for constructing a hypothetical world devoid of both common sense and experience, then living in it in preference to the real one, even as he himself reduces the microeconomic world of millions of independent economic actors to a handful of variables dependent upon what he describes as "fundamental psychological laws."

It is striking, when reading *The General Theory*, to see how often the word "psychological" appears in the text. Keynes was highly impressed with Sigmund Freud and considered him to have been endowed with genius. Indeed, without what was then the infant science of psychology to draw from, there would have been no Keynesian framework upon which to hang the aggregate analyses it supports. If the Keynesian approach is beginning to strike you as somewhat illogical, perhaps even bordering on the nonsensical, it is probably worth pointing out that Keynes believed intuition preceded logic, moreover, he asserted that intuition was not only rational, but downright scientific! Thus, modern macroeconomics, with all its mathematical pretensions to precision and scientific objectivity, is largely constructed upon a nonrational foundation that reflects the heavy influences of the early twentieth century's fascination with dream interpretation, psychic apparatuses, and deviant sex theory. Since Keynes was a member of the libertine Bloomsbury Group, it should not be surprising to discover that the intellectual foundations of his theory should be somewhat less than strictly rational. Nor was his flawed economics the only reason to question his intellectual judgment; he was also a committed eugenicist.[97]

But regardless of its underlying sources, Keynes's reasoning eventually led him to one important and counter-intuitive conclusion that ensured the success of his theory as well as his recogni-

---

97. "Keynes also served on the board of directors of the British Eugenics Society in 1945, and said eugenics, the 'perfection of the race' through selective breeding, was "the most important, significant and, I would add, genuine branch of sociology which exists." Ben Leach, "The great economist John Maynard Keynes: A biography," *The Daily Telegraph*. October 18, 2008.

tion as the most influential economist of the century. His "paradox of thrift" asserted that savings was not the primary source of societal wealth that the classical economists had believed, but rather the cause of economic contraction whenever the economy was short of full employment, as it almost always is. While no longer as dominant as it once was, his idea that too much aggregate savings reduces economic growth is still held by many economists, as the following excerpt from a column written by the most recent Nobel Prize winner in the field seventy-three years after the publication of *The General Theory* will show.

> If you want to know where the global crisis came from, then, think of it this way: we're looking at the revenge of the glut. And the saving glut is still out there. In fact, it's bigger than ever, now that suddenly impoverished consumers have rediscovered the virtues of thrift and the worldwide property boom, which provided an outlet for all those excess savings, has turned into a worldwide bust. One way to look at the international situation right now is that we're suffering from a global paradox of thrift: around the world, desired saving exceeds the amount businesses are willing to invest. And the result is a global slump that leaves everyone worse off.
> —Paul Krugman, *The New York Times*, March 1, 2009

The genius of Keynes's general theory was not that it provided an economic model that more closely approximated the real world than classical theory, or even that it promised a means of ensuring stable, long-term economic growth, but that it told politicians exactly what they wanted to hear. As Murad notes, because policy rests on theory, an economic theory which cannot be used to set policy is unlikely to receive much attention regardless of how scientifically valid it might happen to be. Keynes admitted that his theory of analyzing economic output as a whole could be more easily utilized by totalitarian governments capable of exerting direct control over the aggregate variables involved than by free and open societies, but it turned out to be even more attractive to the elected leaders of the liberal democracies for reasons that have nothing to do with economics and everything to do with politics. Because the process of getting elected in a representative democracy has usually involved an amount of fund-raising, patronage has long been a political reality as politicians repay those who funded their electoral campaigns with jobs and influence over areas of interest to the donor.

While still legal in many democracies, what was known as the spoils system had been on the decline in the United States since establishment of the Civil Service Commission in 1883 and the resultant professionalization of the federal bureaucracy. This did not end the patronage system so much as it reshaped it, as instead of providing jobs directly to their campaign supporters, they increasingly began to follow the example of Sen. John Calhoun, who had originated the idea of using federal money to pay for pet local projects some sixty years before. Calhoun's attempt had been unsuccessful, but with the advent of Keynes's general theory, politicians were suddenly handed a powerful justification for distributing financial largesse to their contributors for the good of the nation as a whole courtesy of Keynes's revolutionary concept of counter-cyclical fiscal policy.

Nor was its potential as a replacement for patronage the only appeal that Keynesianism offered politicians. Regardless of whether the nation is enjoying a time of peace and tranquility or is caught up in the throes of crisis, most politicians find it almost impossible to avoid passing laws. Creating new legislation is what they are paid to do – it is what they are *elected* to do, which is why every U.S. Congress adds an estimated 200 laws for every two-year election cycle despite the 20,000 statutes already on the books. Keynes's rationale for fiscal intervention offered more than just an excuse for legislative action, it gave every senator, representative, and member of Parliament the chance to pose as a hero in the never-ending battle against depression, poverty, joblessness, and business decline. And despite protests of the neutrality of its policy implications, Keynesianism armed the progressives with a powerful weapon against economic conservatives; whereas before Keynes it had been possible to argue that the nation couldn't afford the cost of ambitious social programs, in the post-Keynes political world, it could quite easily be argued that the nation couldn't afford to not spend government money on such programs.

Politicians weren't the only ones to succumb to the temptation of Keynes's general theory. A 1965 *Time Magazine* article entitled "We Are All Keynesians Now" declared that the success of Keynesianism had given great status to the men once known as dismal scientists and described how they had come down from their ivory towers en masse to take their places of honor at the side of government leaders and corporate titans, for whom they not only cast their economic auguries, but also made plans and decisions.[98]

The spell that Keynes cast was a broad one, since politicians were hardly the only ones interested in the business cycle. Both economists and businessmen had been aware of the way in which business activity tended to flow from expansion into contraction and back into expansion since the latter half of the nineteenth century. One hundred years later, Joseph Schumpeter would delineate four types of business cycles, ranging from three-to-five-year inventory cycles to the great fifty-year technology cycles of the Kondratieff long waves. But Keynes's general theory, which came to be known as the New Economics, offered a means of conquering the business cycle by flattening it through government intervention. He proposed using government spending to make up for the savings-driven shortfall in consumption during periods of contraction which, combined with loose monetary policy that would reduce the attractiveness of saving and encourage debt-based consumption, would have the effect of returning the economy back to full employment and the economic growth that entailed. His academic champion, Paul Samuelson, whose bestselling textbooks introduced Keynesian economics to nearly 2 million students between 1948 and 1968,[99] likened countercyclical fiscal policy to providing the machine of private economy with a steering wheel it had previously lacked.

---

98. "We Are All Keynesians Now," *Time Magazine*, December 31, 1965.
99. Mark Skousen, "The Perseverance of Paul Samuelson," *Journal of Economic Perspectives*, 1997, vol. 11, issue 2, 137-52.

Of course, Samuelson's textbook on Keynesianism dictated that both fiscal and monetary policy would be utilized in a counter-cyclical fashion, tightening during expansionary periods and loosening during recessionary times. But the historical evidence conclusively demonstrates that the success of the Keynesian model stemmed far more from its political appeal than any serious belief in its economic efficacy on the part of politicians. The chart below, which shows the U.S. federal budget deficit/surplus as a percentage of GDP compared to GDP growth over the last forty years, quite clearly indicates that with the very brief exception of the four-year period of 1998 to 2001, U.S. fiscal policy has not been counter-cyclical, but uniformly expansionary.

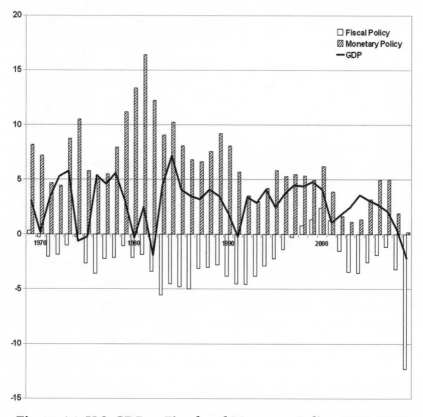

Figure 6.1. U.S. GDP vs Fiscal and Monetary Policy, 1969–2009

If Keynesian policies had been put into practice according to the general theory, you would expect to see that the U.S. government had regularly run surpluses during four decades of economic expansion in which GDP growth averaged a healthy three percent. Instead, throughout that period, the chart shows the white columns indicating regular federal deficits, showing that the U.S. government consistently ran an expansionary fiscal policy with annual deficits averaging 2.5 percent of GDP. And in fact, the fiscal realities are even further removed from the contracyclical policies dictated by Keynesian theory proper when off-budget expenses are taken into account; whereas the official deficit figure for 2008 was $455 billion, the actual increase in federal debt that year was $1,017 billion, or -7.1 percent of GDP rather than the -3.2 percent shown in the chart.

Another problem with the expansionary fiscal policy approach was the matter of timing, which to Keynes's credit he belatedly realized would be a serious problem. He wrote: "Organized public works...are not capable of sufficiently rapid organization, (and above all cannot be reversed or undone at a later date), to be the most serviceable instrument for the prevention of the trade cycle." Unless fiscal stimulus could be implemented immediately, it would exacerbate the expansion rather than limit the contraction. But it already was too late, as the prospect of being able to increase government spending with the justification of saving the economy was far too appealing to the political class to be abandoned on the mere basis of a theoretical revision by the original theoretician. Still, subsequent events proved Keynes's doubts about his own theory to be correct, as Bruce Bartlett demonstrated by comparing the dates of the postwar American recessions to the passage of federal legislation intended to end them.[100]

---

100. Bruce Bartlett, "How not to stimulate the economy," *Public Interest*, Summer 1993, 112; ABI/INFORM Global, 99.

Table 6.2. U.S. Recessions, 1948–1990

Recession Starts	Recession Ends	Anti-Recession Legislation
Nov 1948	Oct 1949	Oct 1949
Aug 1957	Apr 1958	Jul 1958
Apr 1960	Feb 1961	May 1961, Sep 1962
Dec 1969	Nov 1970	Aug 1971
Nov 1973	Mar 1975	Mar 1975, Jul 1976, May 1977
Jul 1981	Nov 1982	Mar 1983
Jul 1990	Nov 1991	Nov 1991, Apr 1993

Monetary policy departed from Keynesian doctrine too, in a manner that was more damaging than it appears from the chart. If the Federal Reserve had taken a dogmatically Keynesian approach, we would expect to see the patterned columns of monetary policy, represented here by the Federal Funds rate,[101] fall below its 40-year average of 6.5 percent when the economy is in recession and rise above it when the GDP is growing at a faster-than-average rate. While there does appear to be a loose correlation between rising GDP and rising interest rates, the correlation is far too weak to be indicative of the close and causal relationship that Samuelson's steering wheel analogy suggests.[102] The monetary policy of the Federal Reserve during the lead-up to the 1980-1982 recession is interesting to note, as the chart clearly shows the decidedly non-Keynesian decision of Fed Chairman Paul Volcker to continue raising interest rates even as economic growth declined and fell into contraction. At a secret meeting of the Federal Open Market Committee on October 6, 1979, Volcker convinced the committee that instead of continuing to try to fine-tune the economy by targeting short-term interest rates as the neo-Keynesian doctrine advised, they should focus on reducing the money supply as per the monetarist model in what his successor later described as "arguably the most important change in economic policy in 50

---

101. The nominal target for the Federal Funds rate is set eight times per year by the Federal Open Market Committee and enforced by the Fed's open market operations. The annual rates in the chart are the average of the twelve monthly historical rates for that year reported by the Federal Reserve, the forty-year average of which is 6.6 percent.

102. A recognition of this weak statistical correlation may explain why Samuelson finally dropped the analogy in the 7th edition of his text in 1967.

years."[103] Volcker's decision to make use of contractionary monetary policy in the midst of what was already considered to be an economic downturn ended the persistent inflation problem of the 1970s and was a severe blow to the credibility of Keynes's core principles as well as that of the dominant neo-Keynesian orthodoxy that had taken Keynes's theories to heart and further expanded them through practical application as well as academic research.

Only fifteen years before, in the laudatory article that served as Keynes's posthumous triumph, *Time* had optimistically asserted that the only economic problems faced by the United States, if any could actually be said to exist, were "the problems of high employment, high growth and high hopes." Such a statement would have been unthinkable in 1980, with high unemployment, no growth, and double-digit inflation, and the pretensions of the neo-Keynesians to have reached the outer limits of economic knowledge were exploded. It was clear that while the General Theory might profitably apply to more cases than classical theory did, it had no answers for the immediate practical case and was therefore neither as general nor as practical as its adherents claimed. Ironically, it was the failure of Keynesian theory to conquer the stagflation of the 1970s that set the stage for the rise of the very man who provided the *Time* writers with their title quote, a University of Chicago economist by the name of Milton Friedman.[104]

The False Prophet

And I beheld another beast coming up out of the earth; and he had two horns like a lamb, and he spake as a dragon. And he

---

103. Alan Greenspan, *The Age of Turbulence* (London: Penguin Books, 2008), 85. It's interesting to see how often financial crises appear to coincide with the appointment of new Federal Reserve chairmen; Volcker had been in office all of two months when the ten-year Treasury spike that goaded him into action occurred. Given Greenspan's own failure to act in a similarly decisive manner even when, by his own account, he was certain that various markets were getting out of hand, one rather gets the feeling that even Greenspan feels his predecessor was made of sterner stuff.

104. Friedman wrote a letter to *Time* the following year to clarify his statement. He explained that to the best of his recollection, he had said: "In one sense, we are all Keynesians now; in another, nobody is any longer a Keynesian." By this, he meant that everyone accepted Keynes's macroeconomic framework and the concept of using government to manage the economy, even if Keyne's specific policy recommendations and theoretical foundations were generally considered to be outdated. Hence the common use of the term "neo-Keynesian."

exerciseth all the power of the first beast before him, and causeth
the earth and them which dwell therein to worship the first beast,
whose deadly wound was healed.
— The Revelation of St. John, 13:11–12

In 1983, international Marxists celebrated the centenary of Karl Marx's death. Always alert for the final economic crisis that would finally bring about the long-awaited collapse of capitalism, they sensed that the predicted moment might have arrived as the intellectual elite outside the ivory towers of academia lost faith in the newly established economic orthodoxy. But while the world moved away from the theoretical revolution wrought by Keynes, the Marxists were bitterly disappointed to discover that, instead of moving further towards the Left and Scientific Socialism, the movement was in the opposite direction. They complained in the customarily grandiose socialist style: "The quack theories of capitalist economists have proved utterly incapable of preventing recessions, which has driven the ruling class to ditch Keynesianism and re-adopt the old measures of "sound finance," of monetarism."[105]

The mass abandonment of Keynesianism came about due to its failure to either anticipate or account for stagflation, which refers to high inflation occurring simultaneously with high unemployment and low rates of growth. This was supposed by neo-Keynesian economists to be impossible; in 1958 an economist from New Zealand named W.A. Phillips published a paper on what he believed to be a statistical discovery of the inherently converse relationship between the rate of inflation and the level of unemployment. The so-called Phillips Curve was popularized two years later in a paper published in *The American Economic Review* by Robert Solow and Paul Samuelson entitled "Analytical Aspects of Anti-Inflation Policy," which explicitly articulated the perceived relationship and calculated the practical applications of it. For example, they suggested that in order to achieve 3 percent unemployment, it would be necessary to have inflation of 4 to 5 percent, whereas maintaining the 2.5 percent inflation that had been con-

---

105. Rob Sewell and Alan Woods, "What is Marxism?," 1983.

sidered the norm during the postwar boom required an unemployment rate somewhere between 5 and 6 percent.

In 1968, however, a Keynesian apostate named Milton Friedman showed that the Phillips Curve described only a temporary tradeoff between inflation and unemployment, not a permanent one, and explained how a simultaneous rise in inflation and unemployment could come about over time. While he did not predict stagflation per se, he had certainly provided a conceptual model capable of anticipating it, which combined with a number of powerful arguments on behalf of monetary policy that made up the theme of his paper,[106] and made economists and policy makers alike take note of his theories when the problem proved to be impervious to conventional neo-Keynesian measures. The fact that his idea of using monetary policy in precisely the opposite manner advised by the Keynesians ultimately allowed the Federal Reserve to tame both inflation and unemployment and only added to the credibility of what had come to be known as Chicago School theory, or monetarism.

It is said that success comes most swiftly and completely to those whose gifts are most completely in harmony with the taste of their times. Few have been so gifted and so perfectly in harmony with the taste of their times as was Milton Friedman in the early 1980s.[107] This had not always been the case; Friedman was an economic advisor to Barry Goldwater's ill-fated presidential campaign and in many ways he was a man well ahead of his time. His book *Capitalism & Freedom*, published in 1962, is a remarkable one that contains the seeds of the greater part of the Reagan Revolution and more. In a slim volume of barely 200 pages, Friedman describes the problems created by government interference in everything from education to affirmative action, and remarkably, even anticipates postmillennial issues such as the international battle now

---

106. Milton Friedman, "The Role of Monetary Policy," *The American Economic Review*, Vol. 53, March 1968.

107. I was practically raised on Friedman. The various books I'm utilizing for this section are the same familiar books that sat on my father's bookshelves throughout my childhood. I can still remember laboriously trying to work my way through *The Optimum Quantity of Money* in junior high. Whatever my differences with his theories might be today, I still have tremendous respect for the man and his accomplishments.

raging over digital piracy and extended copyright protection. After winning the Nobel Memorial Prize in Economics in 1976, Friedman further explicated his case for the connection between economic and political freedom in the 1980 bestseller *Free to Choose*, which was accompanied by a popular ten-part televised series on PBS. Although he had been described as the United States' leading conservative economist as early as 1965, Friedman usually described himself as a liberal in the original sense of the term. If Keynes had followed in the methodological footsteps of David Ricardo, Friedman was an heir to Ricardo's political tradition.

While Friedman's conservative instincts influenced his economic science, his professional background as a statistician[108] and the empirical approach he brought to many of his books indicate that his break with Keynes was less the result of Darwin's Dictum at work and more the case of a brilliant mind following where the facts had led it. Due to his statistical work on consumer surveys, his brief and unfortunately influential experience with the federal income tax system at the Treasury Department, and his research into the role of money in the business cycle for the National Bureau of Economic Research, Friedman was unusually well positioned to see the results that were being gathered by the newly minted tools of macroeconomic measurement. More importantly, he was also in a position to see where those results were departing from the expectations created by the theoretical models used. In his chapter on fiscal policy in *Capitalism and Freedom*, he describes the way in which each failure of Keynes's general theory inspired the creation of new and special cases excusing them. For example, the neo-Keynesian concept of secular stagnation, which concerned the special case of a mature economy in which no substantial new investment opportunities could be expected to arise, was concocted in response to the failure of the New Deal spending programs to

---

108. Although his monetarist school came to be known as the Chicago School of Economics due to his professorship at the University of Chicago, Friedman wasn't a pure academic. Prior to getting his doctorate, he worked as a mathematical statistician for the National Bureau of Economic Research and for the Division of War Research at Columbia University. Remarkably, the great killer of Keynesianism also worked at the U.S. Treasury in 1941-1942, where he helped create paycheck withholding for the federal income tax system. To his credit, he later regretted it.

eliminate unemployment.[109] In addition to comprehending the way in which practical neo-Keynesianism was an implicit confession of the empirical weakness of the original doctrine, Friedman was also aware of the transformation of what had been conceived as practical prescriptions of specific and limited application into a broad license for continuous government expansion. What had been intended for use in flattening out the business cycle had somehow mutated into a security blanket for politicians afraid of seeing an economic downturn occur during their term in office. As Friedman noted, every minor recession spawned a series of new government programs, complete with expenditures that often didn't even take place until after the recession had passed. These delays in implementing the programs meant that, according to the doctrine used to justify them, they would end up having the effect of inflating the economic growth taking place and exaggerating the cyclical effects rather than reducing them. This, of course, was precisely the opposite of what Keynes had intended and also had the long-term effect of exerting a continuous upward bias on federal spending.

But Friedman's break with Keynes was not a complete one. Although he parted from Keynes on fiscal policy, going so far as to cast doubt on the fundamental idea that an increase in the ratio of government spending to tax revenue was intrinsically expansionary and that a decrease was contractionary,[110] he reached the conclusion that monetary policy could be even more effective than Keynes had ever imagined. In 1963, he published *A Monetary History of the United States, 1857-1960* with Anna Jacobson Schwarz, a huge and excruciatingly detailed history of the evolution of the U.S. dollar and the nation's financial institutions. As part of that history, Friedman had naturally paid a great amount of attention to the part of the Great Depression that he labeled The Great Contraction, so much, in fact that the chapter on the period from 1929 to 1933 was later published as a 200-page book in its own right.

Contrary to conventional Keynesian assertions, Friedman knew that the Great Depression had not occurred because of excess Amer-

---

109. Milton Friedman, *Capitalism and Freedom* (Chicago: University of Chicago Press, 1962), 75.
110. Ibid, 79.

ican savings and that it was not the massive government spending of the New Deal that brought the country out of it. In searching for the reason behind the unprecedented extent and length of the contraction, he computed the national money stock, a figure which was not calculated and published by government authorities until 1948, instead of merely looking at the interest rates. He determined the matter of the money stock to be of such importance that the very first table in *A Monetary History*, Table A-1, is a giant chart printed on a special fold-over page that pulls out to show the growth of aggregate currency and bank deposits in the United States for over one hundred years. In the chart, you can see a distinct decline in the three broader definitions of the money supply beginning in 1930 and ending in mid-1933. Friedman decided that it was this untimely decline in the amount of money available in the economy, caused accidentally by the incompetent monetary policy of the Federal Reserve, that aggravated what would otherwise have been an economic downturn of relatively normal duration and magnitude. Therefore, Friedman felt able to assert that, instead of being the result of problems inherent to the private economy as had been previously supposed, the Great Depression was actually caused by the mismanagement of the money supply by the central bank. Since the central bank was a government-established institution, government intervention had been the cause of the Great Depression rather than the solution.

Unlike Keynes, Friedman clearly recognized the dangers implicit in his monetarist theory. While he believed that the power of monetary policy could be used for securing long-term economic growth, he was also aware of the many ways that it could be misused. As a self-described liberal fearful of concentrated power, he considered the most important question about the use of monetary policy to be a structural one. The challenge, as he saw it, was to construct financial institutions in such a manner as to give the government responsibility for the nation's money while at the same time limiting the power that this responsibility would give it by preventing it from using the money power in ways that would reduce societal freedom. Unlike the neo-Keynesians whose knowledge of historical statistics was sparse, Friedman was aware that the post-1913 economy had actually been more unstable, in terms of inflation, money supply, and economic growth, than the less-regulated economy that preceded the establishment of the Federal Reserve. Furthermore, he recognized that the Federal Reserve's behavior during the Great Depression proved that the mere possession of the power required to manage the economy through control of the money supply was no guarantee that it would be managed successfully.

After determining that the primary cause of the depression was mismanagement on the part of the Federal Reserve, he went one step further and sought to find an explanation for why this mismanagement had taken place. His conclusion, which traced the ultimate cause back to the untimely death of the nation's leading central banker in 1928, remains controversial to this day. It cannot be denied, however, that considerable changes in the Federal Reserve structure and policies followed Benjamin Strong's death, or that these changes appear to have played a significant role in the Fed's response to subsequent economic events.

> The explanation for the contrast between Federal Reserve policy before 1929 and after, and hence for the inept policy after 1929, that emerges from the account in the earlier sections of this chapter is the shift of power within the System and the lack of understanding and experience of the individuals to whom the power shifted. Until 1928, the New York Bank was the prime mover in Federal Reserve policy both home and abroad, and Benjamin Strong, its governor from the inception, was the dominant figure in the Federal Reserve System.... If Strong had still been alive and head of the New York Bank in the fall of 1930, he would very likely have recognized the oncoming liquidity crisis for what it was, would have been prepared by experience and conviction to take strenuous and appropriate measures to head it off, and would have had the standing to carry the System with him.[111]

---

111. Milton Friedman and Anna Jacobson Schwarz, *A Monetary History of the United States, 1857-1960* (Princeton: Princeton University Press, 1993), 410.

Of course, this conjecture falls squarely in the realm of alternate history rather than science, but it is not an unreasonable supposition, and, as should be increasingly clear by now, purely philosophical conjectures underlie the greater part of what superficially appears to be mathematically-based macroeconomics. In any case, public acceptance of the monetarist belief in the Federal Reserve's responsibility for the Great Depression reached an amusing apex when on the occasion of Friedman's ninetieth birthday in 2002, the future chairman of the Federal Reserve gave a speech honoring Friedman, his co-writer Anna Schwarz, and their influential *Monetary History*.[112] In his remarks, Ben Bernanke, known to be a student of the Depression in his own right, demonstrated his intimate knowledge of Friedman's work while asserting the supreme importance of a stable monetary background in avoiding economic crises. If Bernanke did not actually declare "we are all monetarists now," he may as well have. And he closed his speech with an apology that is now as well known to economists as the law of supply and demand: "Let me end my talk by abusing slightly my status as an official representative of the Federal Reserve. I would like to say to Milton and Anna: Regarding the Great Depression: You're right, we did it. We're very sorry. But thanks to you, we won't do it again."

By this time, Friedman's monetarist theory had come to be known as the Chicago School of economics, after the Midwestern university where Friedman taught for thirty years. The school produced a formidable group of economists in that time, as its alumni claimed no fewer than nine Nobel Memorial Prizes in Economic Sciences in the last forty years. "In discussions of economic policy," Friedman declared, "Chicago stands for a belief in the efficacy of the free market as a means of organizing resources, for skepticism about government intervention into economic affairs, and for emphasis on the quantity of money as a key factor in producing inflation."[113]

---

112. Ben S. Bernanke, "On Milton Friedman's Ninetieth Birthday," remarks by Governor Ben S. Bernanke at the Conference to Honor Milton Friedman, University of Chicago, Chicago, Illinois, November 8, 2002.

113. Mary Ruth Yoe, "Market Force," *The University of Chicago Magazine*, Jan-Feb 07, Volume 99, Issue 3.

While his devotion to human freedom led some, like Paul Samuelson, to consider his libertarianism as bordering on lunacy, both the untimely death of Benjamin Strong and the unseemly cult of personality that surrounded Alan Greenspan illustrate why Milton Friedman was so convinced about the practical need to eliminate the human element from the management of the money supply. His solution for reducing the prospect for active intervention as well as the margin of human error was to propose the establishment of monetary rules instead of monetary authorities. These rules he summarized as dictating that the central bank would ensure that the money stock, defined as currency plus all commercial bank deposits, would increase on a monthly basis at an annual rate between 3 and 5 percent. Furthermore, he asserted that the precise definition of the money supply, and the exact rate of growth chosen, were less important than the central bank's commitment to what is now known as a fixed inflation target. His longtime *bête noire*, Paul Samuelson, criticized this solution somewhat inaccurately as a machine that would spit out M0 currency at the precise rate that the economic system grew.[114] Friedman's idea was that providing the economy with a reliably growing money supply would permit it to grow steadily without the excess inflation that risked overheating the system.

In short, Friedman's dream remained essentially a Keynesian one of defeating the business cycle and utilizing technical measures to provide a means of permanent economic growth, albeit without the freedom-threatening reliance upon capricious politicians and central bankers that was always such a dubious pillar of the neo-Keynesian program. In the same 1974 speech in which he had laid out the laissez-faire fiscal orientation of the Chicago School, he also made it clear that on the scientific side it was an empirical approach rejecting facts without theory as well as theory without facts. But, as had been the case with Keynes, Friedman's theories were honored more in the breach than by proper application. While some central banks, such as the German Bundesbank, the

---

114. Conor Clarke, "An Interview with Paul Samuelson," *The Atlantic*, June 17, 2009.

Swiss National Bank, Reserve Bank of New Zealand, the Riksbank of Sweden, and the Reserve Bank of Australia, among others, eventually adopted a nonmechanical form of inflation targeting as a strategic approach, more influential central banks such as the Federal Reserve and the Bank of Japan rejected it in favor of a more active approach,[115] as their ongoing attempts to control the economy through manipulating interest rates readily show.

The public profession of monetarism and Keynesianism by many different historical fiscal and monetary authorities that resolutely refused to apply the actual policies dictated by those economic theories tends to suggest that decision makers value economic theory less for its ability to provide them with practical recommendations than for its utility in producing post-facto rationalizations and justifications for their desired actions. Regardless of what we may now think of Friedman's assertion of the power of monetary policy or the validity of a fixed inflation target, time has certainly proved the wisdom of his inherent skepticism about trusting in the discretion of the Federal Reserve and the U.S. Treasury. As far back as 1948, the great preacher of the power of monetary policy was calling for a major reform of the banking system to eliminate fractional-reserve banking and discretionary control of the money supply by the central-banking authorities.[116]

The triumph of the Chicago School was short-lived. Although boosted by the success of the Chicago Boys, young Latin American economists who received their educations at the University of Chicago and went on to become cabinet ministers in Chile and other Latin American countries, the Bank of Japan's inability to lift Japan out of its long slump cast the first real doubts about the omnipotence of monetary policy. In his recent book concerning lessons from Japan's seemingly endless struggle, now approaching its twentieth year, Richard Koo went so far as to conclude that instead of being omnipotent, monetary policy is actually impotent during a bal-

---

115. Ben S. Bernanke, "A Perspective on Inflation Targeting," remarks by Governor Ben S. Bernanke at the Annual Washington Policy Conference of the National Association of Business Economists, Washington, D.C., March 25, 2003.

116. Milton Friedman, *Essays in Positive Economics* (Chicago: University of Chicago Press, 1966), 135.

ance sheet recession and that its effectiveness in such situations is determined by fiscal policy.[117]

But if Japan's economic difficulties cast doubts on monetarism, the devastation in the credit markets that began with the U.S. subprime crisis and subsequently spread throughout Europe and the rest of the financial world has all but confirmed them. For all of the Federal Reserve's vaunted scholarship and expertise, none of its various policy measures appear to be gaining any traction as real estate prices continue to fall and unemployment continues to climb. Only the stock market, always among the least trustworthy of leading indicators, appears to have responded favorably to the Federal Reserve's efforts. The Fed appears to be out of ammunition; popular economics writer Mike Shedlock examined the thirteen specific policy points from Chairman Ben Bernanke's infamous 2002 speech entitled "Deflation: Making Sure 'It' Doesn't Happen Here" and concluded that every single policy mentioned in that speech had been put into practice and failed.[118]

It is the son of a famous neo-Keynesian progressive, John Kenneth Galbraith, who pronounced the intellectual public's verdict regarding the Chicago School even as interventionist policies similar to those advocated by his father come back into political vogue. "The inability of Friedman's successors to say anything useful about what's happening in financial markets today means their influence is finished," James Galbraith, an economist at the University of Texas, told the *Wall Street Journal*.[119] While this observation may be true, it would be unfair to attempt holding either Milton Friedman or monetarism proper accountable for the present crisis since neither the fiscal policies of the Bush administration nor the monetary policies of the Greenspan and Bernanke chairmanships can honestly be said to have put into practice the politi-

---

117. Richard C. Koo, *The Holy Grail of Macroeconomics: Lessons from Japan's Great Recession* (Hoboken: John Wiley & Sons, 2009), 28-33.

118. Mike Shedlock, "Bernanke's Deflation Preventing Scorecard," *Mish's Global Economic Trend Analysis*, April 7, 2009.

119. Stephen Moore, "Missing Milton: Who Will Speak For Free Markets?" *The Wall Street Journal*, May 29, 2009.

cal or economic policies found consistently advocated throughout Friedman's works.

As was the case with Keynes, Friedman's legacy suffers from the conflation of his actual theories and policy recommendations with the policies and pronouncements of those who profess allegiance to them. Despite being known as the great champion of monetary power, Friedman never recommended an activist Federal Reserve, and the aggressively expansionary policies pursued by Alan Greenspan, Ben Bernanke, and other central bankers around the world are precisely the sort of human error that his fixed inflation-rate machine was designed to eliminate. To the extent that Friedman can be shown to have been wrong, it was not his skepticism about the political aspects of political economy that led him into error, but rather the vestiges of Keynesian interventionism that he never quite managed to excise from his economic theories.

The Beast from the Sea

It is of paramount importance to every individual in a modern civilized community that banking credit should have the same solidity as coined money.
—Charles Connant, *Principles of Money and Banking*, 1905

One of the most peculiar things about economics is the way that one of its most significant practical elements is given relatively little attention in the theories presented by the mainstream theoretical schools. It is almost as if Newton had written about the laws of motion and the movement of bodies without ever developing the Theory of Universal Gravitation or even directly considering the question of what gravity actually is. The classical economists, such as Smith and Ricardo, tended to contemplate banking from the perspective of international trade and its effects on the national supply of bullion, while Marx's explicit call for "centralization of credit in the banks of the state, by means of a national bank with state capital and an exclusive monopoly" in *The Communist Manifesto* had no more to do with economic theory than his demand for educating children in free public schools. Keynes mentions central banking a few times in *The General Theory*, but usually in the same sense that he brings up government, as an assumed constant that requires no discussion. Also, his conclusion that private hands cannot safely assume the responsibility of ordering the volume of investment, when viewed in combination with his statement about substituting green cheese for the Moon, tends to suggest that he envisioned a central bank under government control rather than an independent, private institution granted monopoly status.

Unsurprisingly, given his deep and abiding interest in all matters related to the money supply, Milton Friedman's philosophy provides the most theoretical approach to central banking among the major economists. However, his historical accounts of its development, even in the United States, leave something to be desired. In *A Monetary History of the United States*, he and Anna Schwartz describe the creation of the Federal Reserve as a practical solution to technical problems with the monetary system, which is such a superficial and misleading description that it is indicative of historical ignorance, political naïveté or outright deception. Because their history begins in 1857, Friedman and Schwarz omit the long and bitter political battle over central banking that dated back to 1781 and the establishment of the Bank of North America. This omission is astonishing in light of the fact that Friedman's theoretical considerations of central banking tend to be more political than economic. That the political aspect of his thoughts on the money supply take priority over the economic aspect is evidenced by the way in which his fixed-inflation rules are designed for the express purpose of converting monetary policy from a potential threat to societal freedom into a mechanical shield for it.

It is often forgotten that the Federal Reserve System is the fourth central bank in the history of the United States. The Bank of North America voluntarily transformed itself into a private commercial bank less than two years after it was chartered by Robert Morris because of the markets' lack of confidence in its inflated notes. The First Bank of the United States was established ten years later with a twenty-year charter and rapidly launched into an inflationary program that caused 14.4 percent annual inflation in wholesale prices during its first five years.[120] Five years after the bank's charter expired, the Second Bank of the United States was created in 1816 with an identical twenty-year charter. Despite the Daniel Webster-led efforts of Congress to rein in the new central bank's inflationary tendencies with restrictions on its dealing with the state banks, the Second Bank circumvented these efforts by making effective interest-free loans to the state banks and failing to capitalize itself according to its charter by a two-thirds margin. The Second Bank was even more inflationary than its predecessor, as it set the stage for the Panic of 1819 by increasing the money supply 20 percent per annum in its first two years of operation. The result was the foundation of the Jeffersonian free-market, small-government party by Martin van Buren known as the Democratic Party.

Andrew Jackson won the presidency as the Democratic Party's first candidate in 1829, running on a fiscally conservative, anti-central bank platform. In addition to reducing the federal debt from $58.4 million to only $33,700, he vetoed the congressional renewal of the Second Bank's charter in 1931 and his veto was upheld. He then broke the bank's power in 1833 by removing the Treasury's deposits from it and distributing them to ninety-one different banks; the Second Bank of the United States was forced to reinvent itself as the United States Bank of Pennsylvania. The nation survived without a central bank for the next eighty years, but in 1905, one of the chief advocates of economic imperialism and stock market speculation, Charles Conant, published *The Principles of Money and Banking*, in which he advocated the establishment of an advanced form of paper currency managed by a central bank.

Conant's ideas were adopted enthusiastically by Jacob Schiff and Paul Warburg, both of the Kuhn, Loeb & Co. investment bank, who led the charge for the adoption of a fourth United States central bank. Business support for the idea grew after the Panic of 1907, and with assistance of the National Monetary Commission and symposiums held by the American Academy of Political and

---

120. Murray Rothbard, *A History of Money and Banking in the United States: The Colonial Era to World War II* (Auburn: Ludwig von Mises Institute, 2002), 69.

Social Science, the American Association of the Advancement of Science, and Columbia University, public opinion was gradually won over in preparation for the inevitable legislative campaign. The Federal Reserve bill itself was prepared by six men, Senator Nelson Aldrich, Henry Davison, Paul Warburg, Frank Vanderlip, A. Piatt Andrew, and Arthur Shelton, who represented the balanced interests of the Morgan and Rockefeller camps. The secret plan they drew up in 1910 over the course of a week spent on Jekyll Island was presented to the National Monetary Commission in 1911, then, after two years of shepherding the bill through the newly Democratic Congress, was passed as the Federal Reserve Act in 1913.

Unsurprisingly, the new central bank-in-all-but-name lost little time in repeating the inflationary tricks of its predecessors. In its first five years of operation, the Federal Reserve System expanded the money supply at an annual rate of 14.6 percent, almost precisely matching the annual inflation rate of the First Bank of the United States. And yet, despite the consistent history of central bank-induced inflation and the reduction of the value of the dollar note to a nickel in less than a century of the Fed's money management, most Americans still believe that the primary purpose of the Fed is to fight inflation! The reason is that the Federal Reserve's campaign to educate the American people about their need for a central bank to manage their money supply never ended.

In a colorful twenty-two-page, cartoon-laden booklet entitled *In Plain English: Making Sense of the Federal Reserve*, the bank summarizes its purpose and activities thusly:

- The Federal Reserve was created in 1913 in response to the nation's recurring banking panics; its mission has since expanded into fostering a healthy economy.

- The Federal Reserve manages the nation's money supply to keep inflation low and the economy growing at a sustainable rate.

- The Federal Reserve writes regulations and supervises banks to ensure that the banking system is safe, sound and able to respond to a financial crisis.

- The Federal Reserve offers financial services to banks and the U.S. government to foster competition, innovation and efficiency in the marketplace.

In Chapter 3, I demonstrated that the Federal Reserve has failed in its responsibility to maintain monetary stability since the value of the U.S. dollar has been significantly reduced by the 2,060 percent inflation observed over the ninety-six years of the Federal Reserve's financial stewardship. What is less well known, even by economists and financial experts, is its similar failure to ensure the soundness of the American banking system. The common misconception is that there has been a huge reduction in the number of bank failures since the pre-Federal Reserve era. The fact is that the historical period which witnessed the greatest number of bank failures occur was the four years between 1930 and 1933, seventeen years after the passage of the Federal Reserve Act. The large decline in the number of bank failures took place only after the 1933 banking reform that established the Federal Deposit Insurance Corporation. While the Federal Reserve was involved in the various banking reforms, it would be a mistake to give the central bank too much credit for Congressional action that took place due only to the reserve system's initial failure to provide the promised banking stability.

However, it must be noted that even this corrected history is still incomplete and misleading. First, it is not true that 4,000 banks failed in 1933, as is almost invariably mentioned in any discussion of U.S. banking history. The present assertions of the FDIC notwithstanding,[121] the 4,000 failed banks claim is a verifiable historical falsehood. A 1943 report published by the Fed entitled *Banking and Monetary Statistics 1914-1941* stated: "The figures for 1933 are not wholly comparable with those for other years.... The figures for 1933 comprise banks suspended before the banking holiday, licensed banks suspended or placed on a restricted basis following the banking holiday, unlicensed banks placed in liquidation or

---

121. "1933. Approximately 4,000 commercial banks fail. 1,700 S&Ls fail." From fdic.gov: About FDIC > Learning Bank. June 25, 2009.

receivership, and all other unlicensed banks which were not granted licenses to reopen by June 30, 1933." A total of 1,334 of those 4,000 banks were licensed to reopen between June 30, 1933 and December 31, 1936. Another 1,874 were denied federal licenses to operate and were eventually forced to liquidate or merge over the course of the next four years.[122] This indicates that only 792 banks actually failed outright in 1933.

This is not to say that the banking crisis was not a serious matter that demanded attention, since 1,350, 2,293, and 1,453 banks, respectively, had failed in the three previous years. However, the significant reduction in the number of annual bank failures does not mean that the banking system is truly more stable than it was prior to the establishment of the FDIC. While the largest number of post-1934 bank failures to take place in a single year (530 in 1989 is less than half the 1,297 average annual failures of the 1930-1933 period) the problem is that the amount of deposits being held by failing banks has increased greatly over time. The total amount of deposits in the 9,096 banks that failed, were temporarily suspended, or were denied permission to operate by the federal government in the four years between 1930 and 1933, was $5.3 billion. Removing from this total the deposits held by the 1,334 banks that subsequently reopened, and correcting it for 79 years of inflation, that amounts to $68.9 billion in 2009 dollars. By way of comparison, the 530 banks that failed in 1989 alone held $237.7 billion in inflation-corrected deposits; in spite of the deposit insurance provided by the FDIC, the $92.5 billion in losses caused by those failures not only exceeded the $19.9 billion in losses from 1930 to 1933 but was more than the $68.9 billion in deposits held by all of the 9,096 banks that failed, were shut down, or were temporarily suspended during the Great Contraction.

It merits a brief tangent to point out that the relationship between a significant number of bank failures and economic downturn is more complex than is commonly supposed. The decline in the number of Japanese banks during a period of economic growth

---

122. Friedman and Schwarz, A Monetary History of the United States, 1867-1960 (Princeton: Princeton University Press, 1971), Table 14, 426.

from 1926 to 1929 was significantly larger than it was in the following three years of economic contraction due to a major financial
crisis in 1927.[123] A total of 539 banks failed or were taken over in
government-encouraged mergers as the Japanese GDP grew 7.6
percent to the 1929 peak while only 340 did the same as GDP contracted 3 percent through 1932. And the Chairman of the Federal
Reserve himself reached the same conclusion in his studies of the
Great Depression. "The Great Depression was a worldwide phenomenon; banking crises, though occurring in a number of important
countries besides the United States, were not so ubiquitous. A number of large countries had no serious domestic banking problems
yet experienced severe drops in real income in the early 1930s."[124]

Only 106 U.S. banks have failed so far in 2008 and 2009, but
those 106 banks held deposits of $307 billion between them, rep-
resenting 4.2 percent of all American money held by depository
institutions. If the economic contraction continues and the present rate of bank failures holds steady for the next twenty-eight
months, the total deposits held by failed banks will exceed $700
billion, more than ten times worse than before the problem was
supposedly fixed by the 1933 banking reform. This would surpass
the worst previous four-year period in U.S. banking history, the
1988-1991 savings and loan crisis, in which institutions with $407.4
billion on deposit ($666.6 billion in 2009) failed, with $151 billion
in losses to the FDIC.[125]

Defenders of the Federal Reserve and the FDIC can be expected
to point out that bank depositors lost surprisingly little from these
massive banking failures, since the assets and deposits of banks
that failed between 1934 and 2009 were transferred to surviving
banks with net losses of only 15 percent on average. While this is
true, it should also be noted that this is still around half the 29
percent losses during the pre-FDIC era, and net losses during the

---

123. Peter Drysdale and Luke Gower, *The Japanese Economy* (1998), 156.
124. Ben S. Bernanke, *Essays on the Great Depression*. Princeton: Princeton University Press, 2000. 65.
125. Pre-1934 figures are from *Banking and Monetary Statistics 1914-1941*, post-1934 figures are from the Table BF01 Failures and Assistance Transactions reports from the Federal Deposit Insurance Corporation. Inflation corrections utilize CPI-U as of June 2009.

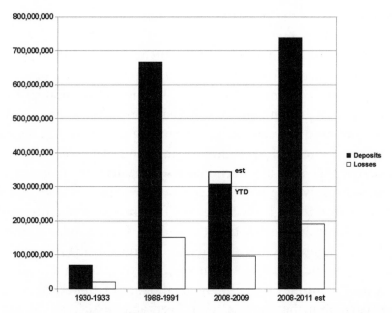

Figure 6.3. Failed Bank Deposits and Losses in 2009 Dollars

savings and loan crisis of 1988 to 1991 were 22.6 percent. I estimate deposit insurance fund losses are running at approximately 26.4 percent of failed deposits since the beginning of 2008, which had the fund around $7 billion in the red as of August 21, 2009. But a focus on losses to the deposit insurance fund misses the more important point, which is that the present system is actually increasing systemic risk over time through growing bank centralization; the FDIC is in effect doubling down each time a bank fails. Whereas there were 30,419 American banks in 1920,[126] there are now only 6,995 commercial banks, plus an additional 1,200 savings institutions. This decline in the number of depository institutions, combined with the huge increase in the amount of failed banking deposits during economic contractions, indicates that neither the Federal Reserve nor the FDIC has been successful in removing risk from the banking system. They have merely been successful at creating an illusion of lowered risk while at the same

---

126. John Thorp and Philip Turnbull, *Banking and Monetary Statistics* (London: Centre for Central Banking Studies, Bank of England in its series *Handbooks* with number 21,2000), 9.

time increasing the real risks and potential costs of catastrophic failure in the future.

The insolvency and eventual closing of the Federal Savings and Loan Insurance Corporation in 1989 despite two recapitalization attempts utilizing more than $25 billion in public money is also evidence that government-guaranteed deposits is not necessarily a successful means of stabilizing the banking system in the long run. While guaranteed deposits do have the effect of reducing the likelihood of bank runs in a fractional-reserve system, the moral hazard created by providing bank executives with a false sense of security appears to outweigh the benefits of increased depositor confidence. Regardless, given that the Federal Reserve has repeatedly failed in its public responsibilities and is arguably the primary factor in systemic risk to the economy, it is truly remarkable that it not only continues to enjoy the confidence of the executive and legislative branches, but has even been able to successfully lobby for increasing the scope of its monetary authority.

The unusual nature of the relationship between private central banks and government[127] is analogous to the nebulous place of central banking in economic theory. Joseph Schumpeter notes that part of the difficulty in tracing a theoretical basis for central banking is due to the fact that central banking was not originally developed by intellectuals or academics, but by practitioners. He traces the basis of the classic theory of monetary policy to two actions on the part of Bank of England Governor J. Horsley Palmer. The first was the 1827 guideline known as Palmer's rule, which tied the bank's liabilities to the gold stock, and the second was Palmer's testimony to the Parliamentary Committee of 1832 when he explained the bank's use of interest rates to control the amount of loans it provided. Of course, the fact that central banking is generally contemplated from a policy perspective rather than a theoretical one should not be surprising since the Bank of England was chartered to act as the English government's banker in 1694, long before the publication of *The Wealth of Nations* established economics as a distinct intellectual discipline.

---

127. The Federal Reserve and the Swiss National Bank are private institutions, just to give two examples, as was the Bank of England until it was nationalized in 1946.

Schumpeter admits that it is not known when central bankers first began to concern themselves with national issues rather than their own profits, assuming that this has ever actually been the case. In light of some of the less explicable actions of the Federal Reserve and other central banks around the world in addressing the present crisis, there would appear to be sufficient reason to wonder if their concerns for the wider economy genuinely rise to the level of their self-interest. But whether they do or not, the inability of the central banks of the world to provide monetary stability, banking security, or steady economic growth indicates that it is long past time for economic theorists to set aside the practical traditions of the past and begin rethinking their assumptions about the proper role of central banking in an advanced global economy.

What the theoretical economists and the practical financiers alike have failed to take into account is that the impossibility of socialist calculation applies to the price of money as well as to the prices of goods and services. A central banker has no more ability to correctly ascertain the intersection of the collective supply and demand curves for money in a modern economy than the historical communist planner was able to calculate the correct number of shoes required in the now-defunct socialist economies. The significant point is not the Federal Reserve's inability to enforce its target price of money or control the size of the money supply, but its inability to know independent valuations of money set on a dynamic basis by its various buyers and sellers according to their momentary needs. Lacking this godlike knowledge, its actions will inevitably be incorrect no matter what it does, which necessarily casts serious doubt on the utility of the concept of central banking.

> [T]o exploit the state for selfish profit is not only immoral; it is criminal, infamous. And so the oracle, which the Pythian Apollo uttered, that "Sparta should not fall from any other cause than avarice," seems to be a prophecy not to the Lacedaemonians alone, but to all wealthy nations as well.
>
> —Marcus Tullius Cicero, De Officiis XXII

AN ANSWER
IN THE ALPS

[T]he moment must eventually come when no further extension of the circulation of fiduciary media is possible. Then the catastrophe occurs, and its consequences are the worse and the reaction against the bull tendency of the market the stronger, the longer the period during which the rate of interest on loans has been below the natural rate of interest and the greater the extent to which roundabout processes of production that are not justified by the state of the capital market have been adopted.
—LUDWIG VON MISES, *The Theory of Money and Credit*, 1912

T HERE HAVE been four major schools of economics since Adam Smith published *The Wealth of Nations*. In the order their ideas became popular, they are usually known as Classical economics, Socialism, Keynesian economics, and the Chicago School of economics. There are many varying strains both within and without these schools, as well as a fair number of relatively minor schools that would merit mention if this were an encyclopedia, but the four major ones are sufficient to cover the broad scope of mainstream economics for the last two centuries.

One of the lesser economic schools began in 1871 with the publishing of *Grundsätze der Volkswirtschaftslehre* by Carl Menger, a professor at the University of Vienna. Among his *Principles of Economics*, as Menger's book is titled in English, was a new and significant theory of value that has become widely accepted in microeconomics although it is still not incorporated into macroeconomics. This new idea was that value was not objective, but rather entirely subjective, and based on the principle of marginal utility. This meant that value of a good was derived from the satisfaction that an individual user of the good obtained from its incremental use rather than an objective measure such as the quantity of labor required to manufacture the good.

Menger's theory had tremendous implications for socialist theory, particularly the dominant Marxian form. The concept of subjective value destroyed the economic basis of Marx's holistic system, since in eliminating labor as the sole source of value, it also eliminated the surplus value that was the primary justification for the class struggle and the socialist redistribution of wealth that were central components of Marxist political policy. Without its foundation of the labor theory of value, the entire structure of Marxian economic theory was rendered irrelevant. However, as was seen later with Keynesian general theory, because the widespread acceptance of an economic theory depends on elements that have very little, if anything, to do with the actual science involved, this abstract undermining of the vast Marxian sociopolitical edifice had very little effect in the material world where politics, power, and personal ambitions tend to count more than mere logic and empirical evidence.

Menger's student, Eugen von Böhm-Bawerk, followed in the creative footsteps of his mentor by expanding the subjective theory of value to incorporate the time-preference principle that further negated the Marxist concept of profit and interest being the result of exploitation of the workers. Böhm-Bawerk's theory of capital and interest did not come to be as widely accepted as subjective value, and therefore the concept of time-preferences remained primarily within what had come to be known as the Austrian School of economics.

What set the Austrian School apart from the onset was not its specific economic theories, but rather its methodological approach. The school derived its identity less from the Austrian nationality of many of its leading lights than from their long-running intellectual conflict with the rival German Historical school. This conflict, known as the *Methodenstreit*, or "Battle over Methods," began when

Gustav von Schmoller criticized Menger's *Untersuchungen*[128] on the grounds of his dislike of Menger's axiomatic-deductive methodology, which is to say that Menger preferred to reason from first principles. Schmoller and the German Historical School, on the other hand, believed in developing social principles from collecting and studying statistics and other historical data.

Plus ça change, plus c'est la même chose. As you may recognize, despite their shared interest in mass quantities of macroeconomic statistical data, the different ways Keynesian general theory and Chicago School monetary theory were developed bear some similarities to the opposing sides represented in the nineteenth century *Methodenstreit.* While Keynesians certainly don't reject empirical data and monetarists readily engage in an amount of axiomatic deduction, the developmental correspondence is an interesting one.

The strong Austrian preference for *a priori* theoretical reasoning[129] in the place of scientific empiricism is due to their belief in the inherent unreliability of utilizing historical and statistical facts to either test or create theory. The Austrian School economist Murray Rothbard, in particular, argues that the complex nature of history and the multitude of inseparable causal factors involved in the formation of any historical fact render any conclusions derived from them inherently false, and even goes so far as to insist that only logic can ultimately serve as an appropriate means of testing an economic theory. The imitation of the physical sciences and their reliable method of controlling and isolating various elements in the laboratory in order to test an economic theory are misguided, as they lead to the Ricardian Vice of reducing theory to the tautological justification of a preconceived idea. Even worse is the approach that involves collecting a mass quantity of statistics in

---

128. Investigations into the Method of the Social Sciences. I am personally convinced that one reason Austrian theory took so long to catch on is because so much Austrian literature involves neologisms constructed by German intellectuals who knew Latin. Mises, in particular, occasionally leads you to conclude that a translation for the English edition is in order. Keynes's forays into mathematics are a breeze by comparison.

129. In illustration of the point made in the previous footnote, this methodological approach is known as "praxeology."

the hope that a theory will magically emerge from the numerical morass. Even if meaningful order can be found somewhere in the historical chaos, that does not mean it necessarily has any application to future events.

The problem is not that economic statistics are inaccurate, although I hope you will be in agreement that this has been sufficiently established in the previous chapters, but that the complexity of causation renders them irrelevant. Ironically, there is no shortage of historical examples to support the idea that even those who nominally subscribe to an empirical approach don't hesitate to abandon their empiricism when the data doesn't support their theories. Consider, for example, how two decades of failing mainstream economic policies in Japan have no more caused mainstream economists to conclude that their theories are incorrect than 70 years of economic failure in the Soviet Union caused socialist economists to abandon Marxism. Some excuse is always found to explain away the theory's failure and rationalize its continued application; if the fiscal stimulus was not too small or too late, then the interest rate hikes were too large or too early. If the federal government's expansionary efforts were unsuccessful during the New Deal, then it must have been due to their being overwhelmed by the contractionary policies of the state and local governments.

Paul Krugman provided a more recent example when, after the Obama administration's $787 billion stimulus plan led to higher unemployment than was projected if the Congress *failed* to pass the stimulus package, he complained Republicans and other skeptics were reaching what would appear to be the perfectly reasonable conclusion that the stimulus had failed.[130] The excuse-making is endless and the only thing of which one can be sure is that the theory will not be abandoned regardless of what the data that is supposed to support it actually is. Not until both the logic and the mass of empirical data are so overwhelming that the consensus of opinion turns against a theory will most adherents finally, re-

---

130. *"At the time, some of us warned about what might happen: if unemployment surpassed the administration's optimistic projections, Republicans wouldn't accept the need for more stimulus. Instead, they'd declare the whole economic policy a failure. And that's exactly how it's playing out."* Paul Krugman, "Not Enough Audacity." *The New York Times,* June 26, 2009. See table 9-4.

luctantly, begin to consider embracing an alternative. Moreover, as Rothbard explains, there is no empirical means of settling the issue between the critics of a theory who claim that an empirically demonstrated failure proves it is incorrect and the adherents who insist such failure only means that it wasn't applied properly. Since any argument between two sides interpreting the empirical results in different ways will necessarily end up being a theoretical one concerning competing premises and logic, a more rational process would be to omit the pointless step of collecting and interpreting the empirical data and begin with the relevant theoretical arguments rather than ending with them.

The inherent unreliability of empirical models can perhaps best be understood by looking at the recent history of the financial world. While complex, the financial markets are a mere microcosm of the economies they purport to represent and they incorporate a much smaller number of more rigidly defined variables. Those attempting to model them and forecast their behavior have a tremendous number of financial and informational resources at their disposal as well as the services of some of Man's most accomplished, best educated minds. And yet their models, which are usually based on historical statistical data, not only fail with regularity, but often fail quickly and completely, and not infrequently in manners which were theoretically supposed to be impossible. But the inevitable appearance of a black swan is nothing more than the consequence of the financial wizards forgetting that most humble investment caveat: past results are no guarantee of future performance. While economists regularly engage in backtesting their theories, and indeed, even attempt to utilize backtests in order to "prove" them, such proofs as they habitually present would only draw a wry smile from any experienced investor since it is well known how this method is known for producing false positives that highlight historical patterns lacking any substantive predictive validity.[131]

---

131. I once produced an investment model that backtested beautifully for more than 20 years and even showed genuine predictive validity, allowing me to identify one major stock market rally down to the hour. Within a few weeks, I had tripled my investment on the options exchange. And then it stopped working....So, I learned the hard way that the Austrian skepticism of historical testing is, at the very least, a reasonable perspective.

It was the German Schmoller who gave the Austrian School its name, as at the time Austria was considered to be an outdated intellectual backwater in comparison with the scientific, academic, and progressive glories of the newly unified Second Reich. The title was originally intended as an insult by the Germans, but is still proudly utilized by its adherents nearly a century after the demise of the largely-forgotten Historical School, whose rejection of universally valid theorems and theories of culture-specific social sciences would border on anathema to most modern scientists regardless of their discipline. Unfortunately, their mania for statistical data survived them and today dominates modern mainstream economics.

The methodological implications of the *Methodenstreit* were largely extraneous to the English-speaking world, though in his preface to the German edition of *The General Theory*, Keynes himself notes that there had always been a large body of German opinion that held to neither Marx nor the Manchester School. And after World War I, the German-speaking world also had to deal with very different economic and political pressures than the victorious Allied Powers due to the Treaty of Versailles, as Keynes had foreseen in his *The Economic Consequences of Peace*. Whereas Marxism was no serious intellectual threat to the Alfred Marshall-dominated economic scene in the West, it harbored much more appeal in the inflation-ravaged lands from which Marx and Engels originally hailed. The Germany Social Democratic Party (SPD) was already the most popular socialist party in the world and was Germany's largest political party from 1919 to 1932; between the SPD and the KPD (Communist Party), Marxists controlled as much as 45 percent of the parliament of the Weimar Republic.[132] Marxism arguably reached the heights of its academic and intellectual appeal at this time, so, it is not hard to understand that with the *Methodenstreit* behind them, a substantial part of the critical attention of the Austrian School economists was directed towards Marxist theory

---

132. Carroll Quigley, *Tragedy and Hope: A History of the World in our Time* (Pasadena: GSG & Associates, 1975), 422.

rather than the Keynesian theory that was rapidly drawing the attention of economists in the West.

The tumultuous period between the two world wars bore witness to the appearance of the Austrian School's two leading lights, Ludwig von Mises and Friedrich von Hayek, who actually worked together in an Austrian government office prior to their respective departures for Geneva and London in the early 1930s. It is a testimony to the keen perceptiveness of these scholars that they recognized the incipient dangers of Hitler and the National Socialists so much earlier than most, although their close proximity to the political situation no doubt allowed them to see the close similarities between the rival left-wing German ideologies[133] that have eluded so many American academics until recently. Their most effective criticisms of socialism were published relatively early in their careers, remarkably early considering that it took the academic world some seventy years to catch up with a brilliant article published by Mises in 1920 entitled "Economic Calculation in the Socialist Commonwealth."

In that article, which he expanded into his prescient 1922 book *Socialism*, Mises laid out the problems that logically resulted from the absence of price information in any centrally planned economy. Known as the Economic Calculation Problem, the problem entails the inability of central planners to know the proper value to place on every product or service available in the planned economy. Since market transactions take place at the price point where supply meets demand, eliminating those transactions, and therefore the price point, leaves the central planner with no means of correctly calculating either the demand or the required supply. The subsequent supply shortages that wracked the Soviet bloc economies for the duration of the Communist era, as well as the famines that still occur regularly in African nations inflicted with socialist govern-

---

133. *"At no point in history has a doctrine found such immediate and complete acceptance as that contained in these three principles of Marxism. The magnitude and persistence of its success is commonly underestimated.... Professed Christians attack the materialism of Marxists, monarchists their republicanism, nationalists their internationalism; yet they themselves, each in turn, wish to be known as Christian Socialists, State Socialists, National Socialists."* von Mises, Ludwig, Socialism (1932), 15.

ments, offered copious empirical support for Mises's philosophical thesis.[134]

The other great Austrian economist, Hayek, became rightly famous for his anti-totalitarian political masterpiece, *The Road to Serfdom*, published in 1944. When Marxists attempted, largely unconvincingly, to respond to the Misean problem of economic calculation by proposing an artificial system of simulated prices, Hayek buried their response by pointing out the many practical problems involved in constructing a theoretical system of market socialism. He later won the Nobel Prize in 1974, two years before Milton Friedman. Prior to that, however, he had a personal relationship with John Maynard Keynes that lasted for 19 years and ranged from initial enmity on Keynes's part[135] to genuine friendship between the two men. While Hayek liked Keynes, admired him, and respected him as an outstanding figure of his age, he also believed Keynes's influence was ultimately disastrous, in part due to Keynes's ill-educated and haphazard approach to economic theory.

> I am afraid this obliges me to say frankly that I still have no doubt that Maynard Keynes was neither a full master of the body of economic theory then available, nor really cared to acquaint himself with any development which lay outside the Marshallian tradition which he had learnt during the second half of his undergraduate years at Cambridge. His main aim was always to influence current policy, and economic theory was for him simply a tool for this purpose.... In these theo-

---

134. Unfortunately, the Western fixation on Keynesian economics has left most academic economists in near-complete ignorance of Austrian School theory. In my Econ 101 class at Bucknell University, my professor was Steve Stamos, one of the authors of the textbook *Economics: A Tool for Critically Understanding Society*. One day, he asked the class: "You plan your day. You plan your week. Why wouldn't you plan something as important as a national economy?" I raised my hand, and when called upon, explained that you wouldn't because you couldn't, as Mises had demonstrated with the economic calculation problem almost seventy years before. He quickly dropped the subject. A few years later, my favorite history professor remarked that he didn't think the economics department's more left-leaning professors ever got over the blow inflicted by the collapse of the Soviet Union.

135. When Hayek published the first part of his critical review of Keynes's *Pure Theory of Money* in the journal *Economica*, Keynes was so infuriated that he published a very querulous and unprofessional response before Hayek had even written the second part of the review. Then, after Hayek published the second part, the mercurial Keynes announced that he no longer believed what he'd written before anyhow.

retical efforts he was guided by one central idea – which in conversation he once described to me as an "axiom which only half-wits could question"– namely, that general employment was always positively correlated with the aggregate demand for consumer goods. This made him feel that there was more truth in that underconsumption theory preached by a long row of radicals and cranks for generations but by relatively few academic economists. It was his revival of this underconsumption approach which made his theories so attractive to the Left.[136]

But the Austrian School is defined by more than that which it opposed. Its best-known aspect, aside from its distaste for empiricism, is its business cycle theory, which Murray Rothbard confidently declared to be the only cycle theory properly integrated into general economics.[137] It was originally developed from the work of the Swedish economist Johan Wicksell, whose theory of interest was expanded upon by Ludwig von Mises, and first appeared in a form that is recognizable today in Mises's *The Theory of Money and Credit*, published in 1912.

Austrian business cycle theory is founded on the logical premise that the economy-wide nature of booms and depressions indicates a causal factor that is both dynamic and capable of reaching all aspects of the economy. This latter requirement separates the business cycle from mere business fluctuations, which are the result of changes that relate only to particular portions of the economy. Since the necessary component of all economic exchanges is the medium of exchange, this points to money as the likely culprit, and more specifically to changes in either the price of money – the interest rate – or the amount of money in the economy. Since the price of money is so heavily influenced by the stabilizing actions of the central bank (or, as in the case of Japan, remains virtually static for years), in a modern economy this indicates that it is the money supply that matters and the interest rate is of significance primarily

---

136. F.A. Hayek, *The Collected Works of F.A. Hayek*, Volume 9 (Contra Keynes and Cambridge), 248.

137. Murray N. Rothbard, *America's Great Depression* (1963), 3, 72-73.

to the extent that it is a correct indicator of changes in the money supply.[138]

When the money supply increases faster than the demand for money, interest rates fall while the price of goods rise. Borrowing becomes less expensive because interest rates are lower and loans can be paid back in future currency that is worth less than present-day currency. Since bank credit costs less, the demand for it increases as more businesses and consumers increase their level of debt. In a credit-based monetary system where fractional reserve banking is practiced, this effect is dramatically pronounced, since an increase in the money supply is, by definition, an increase in the amount of debt.[139] The expansion of bank credit has an inevitable effect on the real economy, because it encourages businesses to invest in producing higher-order capital goods rather than lower-order consumer goods based on their reading of the information provided by the price movements. However, consumers continue to buy in their old patterns since the increase in the money supply is the result of expanded bank credit rather than a genuine shift in consumer time-preferences, which leads to a sudden cluster of business errors. The increased investment in the unneeded capital goods rather than the desired consumer goods turns out to be malinvestment which is wasted and has to be liquidated. This process of liquidation is the cause of the subsequent contraction, which is necessarily proportional to the amount of malinvestment created by the previous expansion. The contractionary process features a reduction of the money supply, a decline in the availability of credit, falling prices, and a decrease in the demand for money, which brings about an increase in the price of money (interest rates). These are all part of a necessary process, and attempting to fight it by increasing government spending, creating more bank credit, or attempting to prevent the liquidation of businesses that are insolvent due to their malinvestments will only prolong and

---

138. The Law of Supply and Demand also suggests that for the purposes of analyzing the business cycle, a distinction between the price of money and the supply of money is not terribly important, especially in a hypothetical free economy without a central bank managing both.

139. See Chapter 3.

exacerbate the contraction. Once the debt burden is removed and the misallocated resources are free, the economy is capable of growing once more, and a new round of credit expansion will usually begin at the earliest opportunity. In summary, the Austrian business cycle features the following pattern:

1. Credit expansion
2. Economic boom
3. Malinvestment
4. Economic bust
5. Liquidation and credit contraction

This is the Austrian business cycle in its traditional form and unlike the orthodox economic theories, it has repeatedly proved reliable in predicting the future course of economic events even if some of its more empirically oriented critics, such as Milton Friedman and Gordon Tullock, assert that it does not backtest particularly well. And yet, despite Austrian disregard for the empirical approach, a number of more recent econometric studies have found results consistent with the Austrian assertion that monetary policy shocks create business cycles.[140] Interestingly enough, the recent work of a heretic Federal Reserve economist whose mainstream credentials are impeccable coexists rather well with Austrian cycle theory. Richard Koo's intriguing concept of balance sheet recessions, which explains the occasional impotence of monetary policy due to heavily indebted corporations paying down debt in lieu of borrowing more money, fits within the general framework of the boom-bust cycle even if it differs in the particulars.

As Hayek pointed out in his 1974 lecture entitled "The Pretence of Knowledge," there are practical limits on the amount of money that can be injected at points of the economic system and these limits may not merely be imposed upon the monetary authority's ability to maintain the rate of the increase of the quantity of money being injected into that particular sector, but by its ability to continue accelerating that rate.

---

140. James Keeler, "Empirical Evidence on Austrian Business Cycle Theory," *Review of Austrian Economics*, Vol. 14, No. 4. (Dec. 2001). pp. 331-351.

In a similar vein, the way in which the Austrian business cycle applies to a post-industrial information and service economy rather than a traditional industrialized manufacturing economy can perhaps be better understood if we broaden our perspective with regards to the malinvestment mechanism and consider how the expansion of bank credit can also lead to malinvestment for reasons that are not dependent upon the shifting dynamic between capital goods and consumer goods.[141] The first important point is to note the obvious causal connection between increased bank credit and price distortions. There can be no doubt that inexpensive credit permits consumers to purchase goods at prices they could not otherwise have afforded; this is precisely why it is offered by the financial institutions. The huge quantity of television advertisements for home mortgages, no-interest furniture loans, zero-down automotive leases, and loan consolidation packages in recent years should suffice to demonstrate the point. The easy availability of cheap credit permits the purchase of everything from houses and cars to college degrees by a much broader range of buyers than would otherwise be the case, so as the law of supply and demand dictates, an increase in the availability of inexpensive debt will lead to an increase in demand that will inevitably drive the price of those goods being purchased by debt higher.

As these debt-financed goods rise in price, more potential suppliers become interested in entering the market while existing suppliers ramp up their manufacturing capacity. This general increase in production capacity requires additional investment in the capital goods that produce them. But it's not necessary to insist that consumers revert to their previous consumption patterns in order to create the malinvestment gap; instead it's enough to note that although consumption patterns are altered in the short term there is a material limit to the extent they are altered, and that the continued increase in capital investment will eventually exceed this

---

141. Rothbard asserts that consumer credit is non-cycle generating, but I don't find his logic to be so much unconvincing as absent. There's no reason that the malinvestment concept cannot be logically applied to various economic sectors instead of limiting it to capital goods versus consumer goods; moreover, consumer credit drives demand, which subsequently causes investment in capital goods to meet that demand.

limit. Once the limit is exceeded, the contraction process will begin, with the negative effects magnified by the fact that productive capacity reaches its peak only after supply has already been driven beyond the furthest limits of demand. This means that prices will tend to decline faster than the shift in consumption patterns would dictate; the post-peak decline will tend to be faster than the preceding rise.

This may sound very similar to the acceleration principle described by Paul Samuelson, but it is actually quite different because it does not rely on any mechanistic assumptions, artificial time scales, or a fixed capital-output ratio. It is actually based on expanding Murray Rothbard's thoughts on the quantity of labor to encompass consumer goods and investment products[142] and requires nothing more than postulating two things. First, that increasing the amount of inexpensive credit will cause demand, price, and supply levels to rise over time, and second, that there are finite price and quantity limits to the maximum quantity of every consumer good or investment good available in the various markets. The chart below shows how the credit-expanded creation of a new demand curve causes upward movement along supply curve S. This upward and outward movement of demand, from D to Dcredit, is the expansionary phase of the cycle, and it will inevitably lead to a collapse in prices to the equilibrium point on the original demand curve due to the inability of suppliers to anticipate precisely when the limits of demand, either Plimit or Dlimit, will be reached. While credit expansion can temporarily push the demand curve past the finite limits of demand in a speculative or consumptive frenzy, this effect can be maintained for only a brief period of time before the collapse takes place. Note that the same contraction will take place regardless of whether the demand limit is based on price or quantity.

Both the recent housing and automotive booms are examples of what for lack of a better term we shall call the Austrian demand limit. Bank credit expansion increased the demand for both houses

---

142. Rothbard, AGD 42-53.

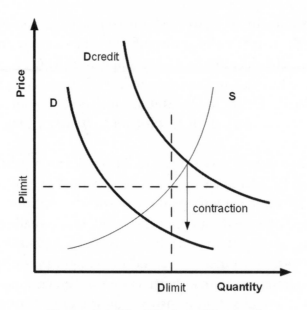

Figure 7.1. The Limits of Demand

and cars, as well as many other consumer products. In the housing market, lower interest rates, then new lending products such as subprime and Alt-A mortgages, expanded the pool of home buyers. At the same time, the plethora of low-interest leasing options vastly increased the number of potential car buyers. Consumption patterns were drastically altered as the demand curve was pushed outward by the increase in the availability of inexpensive credit. The percentage of homes purchased as second and even third residences increased in the United States and in every country where a housing boom took place. Whereas the number of vehicles per household had remained flat, at 1.8, from 1988 to 1994,[143] the average rose to 2.3 per household by 2008 with nearly 35 percent of U.S. households owning three or more vehicles. But the number of houses and cars a consumer believes he can afford to own is finite, even if the precise number is variable and unknown, so the expansion cannot continue indefinitely. Eventually, even the most creative efforts of the financial institutions to expand the demand

---

143. Household Vehicles Energy Consumption 1994, Energy Information Administration.

base will reach the limits of their marginal utility. At that point the contraction begins and the prices begin to fall.

It must be understood that this is very different from the Keynesian concept of underconsumption. There is no shortage of consumption, in fact, the problem is rooted in the credit-based creation of demand in consumers that could not otherwise afford to be buying the consumer goods they are purchasing. It should be obvious that in the real world of economic scarcity and finite resources, there will always be material limits on consumption.[144] Once the artificially enhanced demand limits are reached, or even worse, consumers cannot afford to service their debt on the goods they previously purchased, the boom will come to a hard and fast end. It is important to understand that this is not a fluctuation limited to a single market, it is merely the way in which the general expansion of credit plays out in all of the specific markets to which the credit expansion is directed. The focus on the aggregate economy should not blind us to the fact that the distribution of credit is never uniform throughout the entire economy.

Consider a hypothetical example of an economy in which there are 100 cars being driven every year. Assume that a car lasts for ten years, while every year 10 cars wear out and are replaced. The economy is healthy, people are getting wealthier, and so five households buy second cars. Ten cars wear out, the three car makers each sell five cars, which represents half their maximum productive capacity, and now there are 105 cars in the economy. In the second year, however, there is a brief stock market panic due to the failure of the cashew harvest in Madagascar, so the central bank gets nervous and slashes interest rates. The credit expansion begins, and one sector in which it is focused is the car industry. The auto makers are seeking to expand their market, which they do by taking advantage of the cheap credit to provide inexpensive leases that will allow those who don't have the purchase price of a car to

---

144. Digital media are a theoretical exception to scarcity on the supply side, but remember that on the demand side, there are only so many video games one can play or movies one can watch in a day. Since I have played straight through Heretic in 18 hours and commanded 60 battles in Alterac Valley in three weeks, I believe I can attest that those limits do exist.

buy one. These leases are so affordable that twenty more households decide to buy second cars. Ten cars wear out and are replaced, so there are now 125 cars in the economy. The car manufacturers are now running at their full capacity of 10 cars apiece, so in order to keep up with the growing pace of demand, each year they invest in new capital goods that allow them to produce 5 additional cars apiece. Pleased by the wealth-creating results of its actions and leery of any action that might bring an end to this period of prosperity, the central bank keeps rates low, consumers continue to take advantage of the inexpensive car-financing offers, and three years later there are 275 cars in an economy that five years earlier required only 100. Instead of 1 vehicle per household, there are now 2.75 cars in every garage and driveway, which is getting perilously close to the maximum number that the members of the various households either want or need. For every car enthusiast with 4 sports cars and a sports utility vehicle, there are three families that make do with a sedan and a minivan and an environmentalist couple that owns 1 electric hybrid and a pair of bicycles.

In the seventh year, the car manufacturers continue to increase their productive capacity at the same rate, producing 90 cars. However, since so many people already own cars now, the demand limit is reached when only twenty-five people buy new cars, bringing the total cars owned 300 and increasing the average number of cars per household to the material maximum of 3. After subtracting the 10 annual replacement cars, this leaves a surplus of 55 cars which the car manufacturers have to figure out how to sell somehow.[145] The situation cannot be reasonably described as an underconsumption problem because the consumers are buying three times as many cars as before. It is not an overinvestment problem because the manufacturers didn't invest any more in the seventh year than they had in years four, five, and six; even if they hadn't invested in any additional productive capacity they still would have produced 40 surplus cars. It is, rather, a cluster of business

---

145. This is observably what has been happening in the U.S.A. in 2008 and 2009. Monthly light vehicle sales declined from a seasonally adjusted annual rate of 16 million in 2007 to only nine million in 2009.

errors occurring simultaneously due to artificial demand created by the expansion of credit.

Table 7.2. An Austrian "Acceleration Principle"

Year	Cars Produced	Total Cars	Surplus Cars
1	10	100	0
2	15	105	0
3	30	125	0
4	45	160	0
5	60	210	0
6	75	275	0
7	90	355	55

It should be clear that no conventional macroeconomic solution except allowing the liquidation process to run its course can possibly be effective at this point. Cutting interest rates won't help since there is no demand to be stimulated. Expansionary fiscal policy won't help either, since tax cuts won't create a need for a car in someone who already has one, and even if the government buys all 55 surplus cars, that would merely be a short-term and ineffective measure, because if the automotive manufacturers don't reduce their planned investment, close factories, and lay off workers, thus triggering a contraction, there will be an even bigger surplus the next year. So, as the reasoning exhibited in this example shows, it's not necessary for consumption patterns to return to their previous level of 10 cars per year in order to begin the contractionary process.

Now, it must be admitted that Rothbard asserts that the Keynesian acceleration principle explained fluctuations only in specific industries, not general economic depression, and even declares it to be wholly invalid because it does not take prices into account.[146] But, as I have previously pointed out, prices are an integral part of this Austrian variant on the concept so that aspect of Rothbard's criticism does not apply. There is also no reason that the finite limit

---

146. Rothbard's reasoning is uncharacteristically weak when it comes to the acceleration principle. Speaking as a successful entrepreneur who is the son of a successful entrepreneur, I can testify that his faith in the forecasting abilities of entrepreneurs is almost entirely unfounded.

Rothbard places on the quantity of labor cannot be applied to any other scarce good – indeed, economic scarcity dictates they must be so placed – and reason informs us that price limits clearly exist even though they are neither material nor objective. As for the matter of specific industries versus the general economy, I have already pointed out that bank credit does not expand at the same rate throughout the economy as a whole, but is concentrated in the specific sectors that the financial institutions have targeted as areas of opportunity. This is why the first contractionary signs preceding a general recession will tend to be seen in the price movements of those sectors in which the credit expansion was concentrated.

The addition of a modified acceleration principle to the dynamic ratio of capital goods to consumer goods also has the benefit of applying more directly to the less tangible aspects of the economy such as the service and financial sectors. Services are even more strictly limited than goods in that there is an absolute limit on the amount of services that can be provided by one service worker in a day and the amount of services a customer can receive in a day, as well as a limit on the number of individuals capable of providing any given service. It is not necessary to delve into the question of whether services actually create wealth – it would appear unlikely that an economy dependent upon people exchanging back massages for haircuts is destined to prosper – in order to see how the expansion of bank credit into nonmanufacturing sectors can run into the same material limits as the capital and consumer goods sectors. And while stocks and other investment vehicles are described as financial capital, the way in which they have become increasingly tangential to entrepreneur-driven technological development while becoming ever more closely tied to the process of credit expansion indicates that the modified acceleration principle can be applied to at least some forms of this "capital" as well.

It is difficult to definitively categorize a financial product. Is a certificate of share ownership investment or is it a consumer good more akin to a baseball card? If a share of Toyota is deemed to be capital, why isn't a share in defunct Enron? If solvency is the issue, at precisely what point did shares in General Motors cease to be capital, and what did they become? Is a stock option a capital good or is it more accurately viewed as a lottery ticket? And what is the fundamental difference between trading derivatives and doubling down at the blackjack table?

None of these questions become relevant once we recognize that it is not necessary to place various goods and services into one category or the other in order to understand that they are all affected in the same way by an increase in the availability and affordability of debt. The debate over when gasoline magically transforms from a consumer good into a capital good, or vice-versa, becomes entirely irrelevant once it is understood that the debt-fueled demand for it in either of its forms is going to eventually run into a material limit when no amount of inexpensive credit is going to cause a consumer to drive one additional mile or tempt a producer into ordering one additional delivery of manufacturing supplies. The limits on the demand for financial goods are not material, but they are no less real. Investments can be securitized, divided, repackaged, and leveraged to the point that there are 40 theoretical dollars stacked on top of $1 of actual earnings, and stocks can rocket skyward for longer than any reasonable analyst believes possible, but eventually, the time always arrives when a new buyer cannot be found. The failure of the greater fool to appear and shoulder the risk of the previous fool is the financial equivalent of the first car to roll off the production line for which there is no buyer.

The tech equity bubble that ended in 2000 is an example of the Austrian business cycle at work when the bank credit expansion was focused in the financial sector. The housing bubble that ended in 2007 is an example of the same cycle at work in the housing sector. In the case of the latter, it is interesting to note that even non-Austrian economists began to recognize the connection between the central bank's expansion of the money supply, the creation of an investment bubble, and the economic expansion of the economy. Paul Krugman, who in addition to being the nation's leading neo-Keynesian is an avowed despiser of Austrian business cycle theory, nevertheless wrote the following at a time when it was widely feared that the economy would slump into the recession that followed the dot-com crash.[147]

> Of course capital is wasted in a speculative boom, and much of that capital must be written off. Moreover, the sectors of the economy in which the speculative excess was greatest may not see much new investment for a while; it might be years before the demand for servers or business software resumes rapid growth.... I've always believed that a speculative bubble need not lead to a recession, as long as interest rates are cut quickly enough to stimulate alternative investments. But I had to face the fact that speculative bubbles usually are followed by recessions.[148]
>
> —Paul Krugman, *The New York Times*, May 2, 2001

While most mainstream economists still cling to their technocratic dream of actively managing the economy in order to maintain what Keynes described as a permanent state of quasi-boom, Austrian business cycle theory is rapidly becoming more widely accepted by investment professionals who have less interest in dogmatic allegiances to the theoretical orthodoxy than they do in predictions that enable them to successfully anticipate the direction of future price movements.

The single most important thing to understand about political economy is that the current consensus among professionally credentialed economists is almost always irrelevant. Due to the political aspects involved, there will always be too many tangible benefits to following the consensus to justify granting it any inherent credibility. The rational and scientific approach is to view each theoretical interpretation of the present economic situation as a hypothesis, then consider how well they fare as a predictive model. When viewed from this perspective, it is clear that political economists who utilize Austrian business cycle theory, including Peter Schiff, Marc Faber, Mike Shedlock, Frank Shostak, and Ron Paul, were far more correct about the future of the global economy than

---

147. Or rather, that the economy would slump into the non-recession that the Bureau of Economic Analysis subsequently decided did not take place after the dot-com crash.

148. Paul Krugman, "Dodging the Bullet," *The New York Times*, May 2, 2001.

any of the mainstream economists. The same can be said of several non-Austrians such as Stephen Roach, Robert Prechter, and Nouriel Roubini, whose independent predictions of the downturn that officially began in July 2008 tended to bear more similarity to Austrian School concepts than to conventional neo-Keynesian or monetarist theories. The fact that both neo-Keynesians and monetarists repeatedly vowed that the economy was fundamentally strong and that the Federal Reserve was capable of keeping the United States out of recession should permanently mar their credibility in the eyes of any rational, fair-minded observer.

"There is no real estate price bubble."[149]
—David Learah, Chief Economist of the National
Association of Realtors, February 2006

"Housing boom will not end in a crash, says Harvard."
—*Financial Times*, June 12, 2006

"The evidence is not there. That doesn't mean it can't happen. But the elements of a recession are not yet there."
—Alan Greenspan, September 29, 2006

"[T]he big rally in homebuilder stocks suggests that the economic drag from housing is starting to peter out."
—Larry Kudlow, *National Review*, December 4, 2006

"The impact on the broader economy and financial markets of the problems in the subprime market seems likely to be contained. . . . the weakness in housing and in some parts of manufacturing does not appear to have spilled over to any significant extent to other sectors of the economy."
—Ben Bernanke, March 28, 2007

"The Fed has plenty of room to cut rates further, if it deems such cuts necessary. At the moment, recession is only a possi-

---

149. David Learah, *Why the Real Estate Boom Will Not Bust and How You Can Profit From It* (2006).

bility, and inflation is a bigger worry than deflation.... The truth is that the current Fed governors, together with their crack staff of Ph.D. economists and market analysts, are as close to an economic dream team as we are ever likely to see."
—Greg Mankiw, *The New York Times*, December 23, 2007

"The index indicates a 35.5 percent chance that the U.S. economy is in recession, sharply up from 10 percent last month."
—*Employment Numbers as Recession Indicators*, Joint Economics Committee, United States Congress, January, 2008

"Economists see U.S. avoiding recession"
—MSNBC, March 11, 2008

None of this should be taken to mean that the Austrian School has all the answers to the complexities of man's economic activity at either the micro or macro levels. It does not, nor do any of its advocates pretend that it does. To the contrary, Austrian theory explicitly declares the subjective nature of human action to render many aggregate calculations intrinsically incalculable. But the repeated failure of both neo-Keynesianism and monetarism over the last six decades means that political economy once more finds itself at the same sort of theoretical crossroads it previously faced in the 1930s and 1970s. For the sake of future generations, it is important that this time it is the rational aspects that are given priority over the historical and political elements. George Cooper is entirely correct to declare that the present economic orthodoxy does not accord with the facts, and strictly speaking, does not qualify as a science. He is also correct to assert that only the fittest theories should survive. However, his suggestion that a combination of Hyman Minsky's Financial Instability Hypothesis, James Maxwell's control system theory, and Benoît Mandelbrot's fractal mathematics can serve as the foundation for a more rational economic philosophy is a repetition of the mistakes of the past. It amounts to little more than an attempt to find a new basis for justifying the same structure of centrally controlled economic management that has repeatedly proven to be a failure.[150] Because Austrian theory is more compatible with the intriguing new field of behavioral economics as well as the modern variants of Irving Fisher's debt-deflation theory, and because it has been objectively demonstrated to offer a predictive model superior to the standard macroeconomic and financial models, it is the economic theories of the Austrian School that should provide a conceptual foundation for mainstream economic inquiry going forward.

> Over the past three decades, economists have largely developed and come to rely on models that disregard key factors – including heterogeneity of decision rules, revisions of forecasting strategies, and changes in the social context – that drive outcomes in assets and other markets. It is obvious, even to the casual observer that these models fail to account for the actual evolution of the real-world economy. Moreover, the current academic agenda has largely crowded out research on the inherent causes of financial crises.... In our hour of greatest need, societies around the world are left to grope in the dark without a theory. That, to us, is a *systemic failure of the economics profession.*
>
> —"The Financial Crisis and the Systemic Failure of Academic Economics," Kiel Institute for the World Economy, February 2009

---

150. George Cooper, *The Origin of Financial Crises: Central Banks, Credit Bubbles and the Efficient Market Fallacy.* (New York: Vintage Books, 2008). 158.

A KEYNESIAN CRITIQUE
OF AUSTRIAN THEORY

Whether the views so widely accepted about the effects of fiscal policy be right or wrong, they are contradicted by at least one extensive body of evidence. I know of no other coherent or organized body of evidence justifying them. They are part of economic mythology, not the demonstrated conclusions of economic analysis or quantitative studies. Yet they have wielded immense influence in securing widespread public backing for far-reaching governmental interference in economic life.
—MILTON FRIEDMAN, *Capitalism & Freedom*, 1962

I HAVE OFTEN found that one of the best ways to understand an economic theory is to examine it from the critical perspective. Friedrich von Hayek's explication of the impossibility of socialist calculation is a more useful tool for understanding the actual working mechanisms of Marxian socialism than anything that Karl Marx, with his habitual preference for rhetoric over detailed explanation, ever wrote. And most readers will obtain a more comprehensive knowledge of Keynesian theory from reading Murray Rothbard, Henry Hazlitt, or Hans-Hermann Hoppe than they will from reading the *General Theory* itself.[151] In this vein, it is educational to turn to one of the world's most famous Keynesian economists, Princeton professor and Nobel Prize winner Paul Krugman, who in 1998 wrote an article entitled "The Hangover Theory"

---

151. This is not to say I disdain reading original sources. The critical perspective is most useful in deepening one's understanding of a theory through highlighting its strengths and weaknesses. Reading the original sources is still vital; indeed, doing so often gives one a distinct advantage over many professed adherents who have never actually read them, let alone the critiques.

which is considered by many to be the foremost modern critique of the Austrian theory of economics.[152]

Krugman based his critique around a single question. Are recessions the inevitable payback for good times? While this might seem insufficient to call an entire economic theory into question, an inability to provide a reasonable answer would be as problematic for Austrian theory as subjective value is for Marxian theory or stagflation is for orthodox Keynesianism. One might, of course, take exception to the overly broad language used; it would certainly be helpful to know what Krugman's precise definition of "good times" would be. Is it fifty-seven straight quarters of uninterrupted GDP growth of the sort Japan had during the Izanagi Boom, a ten-fold increase in stock prices the Dow saw from 1982 to 1999, or American house prices doubling from 2000 to 2006? But given the casual context, the question is a reasonable one.

Krugman begins his piece by announcing that he was inspired to write it in response to the charge that he has ignored Austrian theory in his previous examinations of the business cycle. He justifies this failure by declaring his opinion that Austrian theory is "about as worthy of serious study as the phlogiston theory of fire." Although Krugman was still ten years from receiving his Nobel Prize in 1998, it seems that the reader is nevertheless supposed to accept this blatant appeal to his own authority, because Krugman rather strangely elects not to directly address any aspect of the theory, but instead turns his attention to an unidentified worldview that he believes to lie behind it. He characterizes this worldview as "the overinvestment theory of recessions" and "liquidationism" before coining the apt and memorable phrase "hangover theory," which he describes as the concept that economic contractions are the price that an economy pays for the excesses of the preceding expansion. It strikes me as somewhat of a pointless bait-and-switch, but his reason for doing so soon becomes clear.

---

152. Paul Krugman, "The Hangover Theory: Are recessions the inevitable payback for good times?" *Slate*, Dec. 4, 1998. I should also note that I consider Bryan Caplan's essay "Why I Am Not an Austrian Economist" to be a much better critique, but since a response to that critique would require more than one chapter and Paul Krugman is arguably the best-known economist in the world today, I have elected to respond to Krugman's argument here.

Now, even if you set aside the inherent silliness of responding to a charge about your past inadequacies by citing your own opinion, the idea that Austrian theory isn't worthy of serious study was already absurd in 1998. This isn't to say that it is perfect, but it would be virtually insane to say that it is not worth considering since not one, not two, but *three* credit inflation-induced "hangovers" have occurred since 1998 in the United States alone.[153] Moreover, it was primarily Austrian School economists who were repeatedly warning of approaching disaster during the various excesses of the post-1987 expansion while mainstream Keynesians and monetarists were primarily occupied with their concerns about developing economies around the world; the orthodox economists had no fears for the supposedly rock-solid fundamentals of the American economy. Ironically, two years after writing this article, Krugman himself declared that "the risk of an actual depression has receded for now" just as the hangover from the tech equity boom was about to begin.[154] But when one recalls the economic events of the past decade, one could make a much more reasonable case that the only sense in which mainstream economic theory[155] is worthy of serious study is the sense that a flight recorder demands intense examination after an airplane crash. The pejorative manner with which Krugman describes Austrian theory here is simply out of place and amounts to a category error. Imagine a physicist describing gravity in a similar manner, wherein the damage an object suffers in falling to earth is deemed its necessary punishment for having been projected aloft! In his very first paragraph, Krugman provides a telling clue that he has read very little Austrian theory, if indeed he has read any at all, because he mistakenly makes use of a specific term that is precisely how Murray Rothbard predicted Keynesian critics would fail to grasp one of the most basic Austrian concepts twenty-five years *before* Krugman wrote his essay.

---

153. The tech equity boom, the credit boom, and the housing boom, were followed, inexplicably, by the dot-com bomb, the credit crunch, and the housing crash.

154. Paul Krugman, *The Return of Depression Economics* (London: Penguin Books, 2000), viii.

155. Mainstream economics today is largely an incoherent synthesis of Keynsianism with Friedmanite empiricism tarted up with econometrics and flavored with a dash of neo-classicalism. It seldom makes any sense, for the very logical reason that it is not a theoretical system but a collection of concepts taken from various economic theories.

"Overinvestment" or Malinvestment? The second misconception, given currency by Haberler in his famous *Prosperity and Depression*, calls the Misesian picture of the boom an "overinvestment" theory."[156]

While the neo-Keynesians almost invariably continue to confuse malinvestment and overinvestment, Keynes himself got tantalizingly close to grasping the importance of the malinvestment concept for one brief shining moment while explicating his own theory of the trade cycle.[157] Unfortunately, his focus on the marginal efficiency of capital prevented him from looking more closely at the causes and consequences of what he called "misdirected investment" and he concentrated instead on other, less plausible reasons for a declining propensity to consume. Krugman, on the other hand, never considers the matter at all. After a brief tangent into amateur psychoanalysis, wherein he declares Austrian theory to be a perverse form of morality play with seductive appeal to sadists who find pleasure in its failure to offer an easy way out of economic hard times, Krugman answers his own question. No, he declares, recessions are not a necessary consequence of booms and there is no inevitable payback for good times. If, for some unknown reason, a recession should happen to appear, it should be aggressively attacked with policies encouraging people to spend more money, not less. Therefore, "hangover theory" and the austerity it recommends is not only powerfully seductive, but "disastrously wrongheaded" and capable of causing actual harm. He claims that the "liquidationist views" of Friedrich von Hayek and Joseph Schumpeter were not only a major factor in the extent of the Great Depression, but that the same views were also inhibiting recovery in depressed economies around the world in 1998.

The problem is that neither psychology nor morality plays have anything to do with the accuracy or inaccuracy of the Austrian model, they simply aren't relevant to the subject. It is a matter of

---

156. Murray Rothbard, *America's Great Depression*, 30.

157. "*It may, of course, be the case – indeed it is likely to be – that the illusions of the boom cause particular types of capital-assets to be produced in such excessive abundance that some part of the output is, on any criterion, a waste of resources....It leads, that is to say, to misdirected investment.*" p. 336.

the historical record and simple observation, and the reliable frequency with which economic recessions follow expansions can no more be wished away than the consequences of gravity. As Murray Rothbard pointed out, Keynesians like Krugman have no rational explanation for the observable fact that busts do follow booms, which is why their attempts to witch-doctor positive "animal spirits" and "consumer confidence" are so hopelessly ineffective. And again, it is remarkably easy to demonstrate that Krugman is factually wrong, since "liquidationist views" played no role in either bringing about the Great Depression or causing it to spread, because the following statement from the most influential figure from the first quarter of the Depression demonstrates rather conclusively that the liquidationist position was wholly rejected by the pro-intervention financial and monetary authorities in power at the time:

> "[W]e might have done nothing. That would have been utter ruin. Instead we met the situation with proposals to private business and to Congress of the most gigantic program of economic defense and counterattack ever evolved in the history of the Republic. We put it into action. . . . We determined that we would not follow the advice of the bitter-end liquidationists and see the whole body of debtors of the United States brought to bankruptcy and the savings of our people brought to destruction."[158]
>
> —Herbert Hoover, 1932

It is worth noting that Krugman doesn't even appear to know who the chief theorists of the Austrian School were. While Joseph Schumpeter was an Austrian national, an important economist, and an influential critic of Keynes, he is not considered to have been an Austrian theorist because his cycle theory is based on general Walrasian economics rather than Austrian School theory. Krugman's citation of Schumpeter rather than Carl Menger, Ludwig von Mises, or Eugen Ritter von Böhm-Bawerk, the three most influential Austrian School economists prior to the Great Depression, is a strong indication that he knows very little about the theory he is purport-

---

158. Murray Rothbard, *America's Great Depression*, 55. See also Appendix A: 50 Little Hoovers.

ing to criticize. Nor do either of his charges make any sense in a historical context. For how can the views held by economists of the Austrian School, precisely none of whom have ever held any positions of political influence or power of the sort held by various neo-classicalists, Keynesians, and monetarists in the United States in 1929 and 1998, possibly be blamed for the very credit-inflated expansion that they have been uniformly decrying since 1912?

> "It is only in this sense that we can interpret the statement that it is apparently true after all to say that restriction of loans is the cause of economic crises, or at least their immediate impulse; that if the banks would only go on reducing the rate of interest on loans they could continue to postpone the collapse of the market. If the stress is laid upon the word *postpone*, then this line of argument can be assented to without more ado. Certainly, the banks would be able to *postpone* the collapse; but nevertheless, as has been shown, the moment must eventually come when no further extension of the circulation of fiduciary media is possible. Then the catastrophe occurs, and its consequences are the worse and the reaction against the bull tendency of the market the stronger, the longer the period during which the rate of interest on loans has been below the natural rate of interest and the greater the extent to which roundabout processes of production that are not justified by the state of the capital market have been adopted."[159]

So, Krugman's accusation isn't merely incorrect, it is directly contradicted by the easily verified historical facts. Its inherent unfairness is particularly egregious coming as it does from a literal prize member of the economic elite who himself holds precisely the position of national influence that neither Hayek nor Schumpeter ever did. At the time of this article's publication in 1998, Krugman was still seven years away from recognizing the existence of the housing boom as well as the subsequent recession predicted by Austrian theory.

In his next paragraph, Krugman confirms that he has never read Mises, or at least not *The Theory of Money and Credit*, for he postu-

---

159. Ludwig von Mises, *The Theory of Money and Credit* (New Haven: Yale University Press, 1953), 365-366.

lates a variety of Austrian explanations for why an investment boom gets out of hand, ranging from an expansion of the money supply, reckless bank lending, or simply irrational entrepreneurial exuberance. He supposes that Austrians think that excess investment causes the creation of too much productive capacity, which eventually causes investment spending to collapse, thereby creating a recession. However, as the previous quotes from Mises and Rothbard show, Krugman has made three fundamental mistakes in his attempt to summarize the Austrian concept of the credit-inflated business cycle.

First, the investment boom does not get out of hand for some mysterious, unknowable reason. It gets out of hand specifically due to credit inflation, which in the modern era is usually instigated by the central bank. Or, as Mises phrased it ninety-seven years ago, because the banks have forced the rate of interest on loans below the natural rate of interest. Second, it's not a question of excess investment creating too much overall capacity, but rather malinvestment creating too many capital goods devoted to producing output that no one wants, needs, or is willing to go into debt in order to buy. This is simply the repeat of his previous "overinvestment" error anticipated by Rothbard. Third, it's not excess productive capacity that causes investment spending to collapse, but rather the fact that there is insufficient willingness to continue taking out the loans required to sustain demand. This can happen for a variety of reasons, but as Mises points out, it usually occurs because the central bank, belatedly recognizing that asset prices in the credit-inflated market have reached unsustainable heights, decides to stop cutting interest rates and begins raising them instead.[160] Once the money factory shuts down, the goods factories are forced to

---

160. This is how it usually happens. In *The Theory of Money and Credit*, Mises writes: "If our doctrine of crisis is applied to more recent history, then it must be observed that the banks have never gone as far as they might in extending credit and expanding the issue of fiduciary media. They have always left off long before reaching this limit, whether because of growing uneasiness on their part and on the part of those who had not forgotten the earlier crses, or whether they had to defer to legislative restrictions concerning the maximum circulation of fiduciary media. And so the crises broke out before they need hve broken out." On the rare occasions that the central bank doesn't elect to step in and force an end to the expansionary phase, the economy will reach the limits of demand described in the previous chapter. That's my contention; you may recall that the conventional Austrian cycle theory gives the shift from capital goods to consumer goods as the causal factor.

follow suit. It will probably surprise no one to know that the Federal Reserve's actions between 1995 and 2009 show that the U.S. central bank has engaged in three distinct attempts at credit inflation, the first of which produced the tech equity boom, while the second caused the credit boom and housing booms. The third, which is still ongoing, is an attempt to launch a fourth boom that will most likely fail. Ironically, the U.S. housing boom that Krugman still prides himself on detecting was brought to an end in precisely the manner described above,[161] and was subsequently followed by the very sort of economic hangover predicted by the Austrian School that Krugman mocks throughout his article.

Nouriel Roubini, the economist famous for being one of the few non-Austrians to foresee the way in which the subprime crisis would affect the economy as a whole, described the era of the "New Economy" thusly:

> "We've been growing through a period of time of repeated big bubbles. We've had a model of 'growth' based on overconsumption and lack of savings. And now that model has broken down, because we borrowed too much. We've had a model of growth in which over the last 15 or 20 years, too much human capital went into finance rather than more-productive activities. It was a growth model where we overinvested in the most unproductive form of capital, meaning housing. And we have also been in a growth model that has been based on bubbles."[162]

While Krugman is willing to admit that periodic episodes of boom-and-bust do take place, he still wonders why there should be any connection between the cyclical nature of investment demand and ups and downs in the rest of the economy. He informs us that the key to the Keynesian model which he claims made both hangover theory and Austrian theory obsolete[163] was Keynes's real-

---

161. See Table 2.2.

162. James Fallows, "Dr. Doom Has Some Good News," *The Atlantic*, July/August 2009.

163. It seems to have escaped Krugman that despite his attempt to distinguish between what he describes as "the general worldview" that lurks behind Austrian theory and Austrian theory proper, the only other cycle theory integrated into a general economic theory is Joseph Schumpeter's. This is to say, the very same Joseph Schumpeter who *(continued on next page)*

ization that it was the question of why declines in investment demand cause recessions, not why investment demand happens to occasionally decline. It is not enough for an economic theory to observe a correlation, he explains, it must explain the observed correlation. But once more, Krugman is doing little more than demonstrating his complete unfamiliarity with Austrian theory, which articulates a very clear answer as to why the whole economy slumps.

The misallocation of investment resources due to credit inflation means that many of the goods being produced by the economy's increased productive capacity are those that consumers neither want nor need. This, combined with price increases that increasingly put goods out of reach of those who are not the beneficiaries of the credit inflation or are unwilling to go into debt, causes the *consumption* demand gap that so occupies Krugman and his fellow Keynesians. It's a concrete explanation and also happens to be rather more empirically demonstrable than the mysterious disappearance of consumer confidence that the Keynesians blame. It also happens to be directly connected to easily observable factors such as the central bank's management of the interest rate. But, more to the point, there is no reason why Austrian theory should explain a correlation between declining investment demand and recessions for the very simple reason that Austrian theory specifically rejects the correlation! In his criticism of the Keynesian acceleration principle put forth by underconsumptionists like Paul Samuelson, Murray Rothbard declares that the slackening of investment demand would not necessarily be depressive.[164] Krugman then goes on to elucidate what he believes to be the central issue.

> Here's the problem: As a matter of simple arithmetic, total spending in the economy is necessarily equal to total income (every sale is also a purchase, and vice versa). So if people decide to spend less on investment goods, doesn't that mean

---

Krugman erroneously claims to have been an Austrian theorist. By this point, one is forced to the conclusion that Krugman elected to attack a general worldview because he simply doesn't know enough about the actual theory to even begin criticizing it.

164. Murray Rothbard, *America's Great Depression*, 64.

that they must be deciding to spend more on consumption goods—implying that an investment slump should always be accompanied by a corresponding consumption boom? And if so why should there be a rise in unemployment? Most modern hangover theorists probably don't even realize this is a problem for their story. Nor did those supposedly deep Austrian theorists answer the riddle. The best that von Hayek or Schumpeter could come up with was the vague suggestion that unemployment was a frictional problem created as the economy transferred workers from a bloated investment goods sector back to the production of consumer goods.

—Paul Krugman, "The Hangover Theory," 1998

Krugman follows Keynes here in making the error that Joseph Schumpeter dismissed as "the Ricardian vice," as he ignores all but a few variables in order to pose a false dichotomy. If total spending in the economy was necessarily equal to total income, the United States could not be in cumulative debt equivalent to 375 percent of its GDP; like most Keynesians, Krugman is handicapped by the inability of the Keynesian model to account for time-preferences, savings, or the consequences of debt. If someone doesn't buy an equity or an industrial plant, that doesn't mean he must have bought a car instead. Krugman is posing an artificial dilemma that is punctured by the observable facts that (1) not every dollar of income must be spent today, and, (2) not every dollar that is spent today is earned. As to the so-called problem of the rise in unemployment, that is easily explained. When there is a credit-inflated boom that results in your working at a job in which you produce goods that no one wants, needs, or can obtain financing to buy, and which your employer consequently cannot sell, it naturally follows that neither you nor your co-workers are going to be employed in the near future. In their myopic focus on the aggregate picture, Keynesians constantly ignore the reality that inflation, investment, and unemployment all have a *disparate* impact on different areas of the economy at different points in time. While these diverse impacts will eventually have a cumulative effect on the aggregate economy, the Keynesians consistently fail to comprehend that, due to the disparate nature of these effects, analyzing them in the overly simplistic Keynesian manner guarantees that their cumulative net effect will be miscalculated.

If there are any remaining doubts that Krugman is almost completely ignorant of the theory he is affecting to criticize, they vanish in the quoted section. While it is true that Schumpeter did only attempt to explain one form of unemployment, transitory employment, which he explained as a frictional phenomenon in *The Theory of Economic Development*, Krugman is simply wrong about Hayek. And he is clearly unaware of the explanation for unemployment provided by basic Austrian business cycle theory, which is laid out in numerous works by Ludwig von Mises, Murray Rothbard, and others, most notably in the landmark Austrian work *Human Action*. In his magnum opus, Mises not only addresses the issue, but even features a section explaining the important difference between institutional unemployment[165] and catallactic unemployment,[166] as well as why the latter should not be described as frictional. Hayek explains that institutional unemployment is caused by a discrepancy in the distribution of labor between various industries and the distribution of demand for the products of those industries, a discrepancy caused by a distortion of the system of relative prices and wages. That distortion, of course, is the result of credit-inflation on the part of the central bank.[167]

Because he has read so little Austrian School theory, and therefore has no idea what the theory actually is, Krugman winds up attacking a nonsensical straw man of his own creation which, as

---

165. Ludwig von Mises, *Human Action* (Auburn: The Ludwig von Mises Institute, 1998), 595. "Institutional unemployment is not the outcome of the decisions of the individual job-seekers. It is the effect of interference with the market phenomena intent upon enforcing by coercion and compulsion wage rates higher than those the unhampered market would have determined. The treatment of institutional unemployment belongs to the analysis of the problems of interventionism."

166. Also known as market-generated unemployment. It simply means an unemployed state intentionally selected for individual reasons, however noneconomic or irrational those reasons might appear to anyone else. For example, being unemployed because you have decided to attend graduate school is catallactic unemployment, whereas being unemployed because General Motors closed the factory at which you worked is institutional unemployment. Catallaxy: another example of what happens when you permit overly erudite Austrians to create their own lexicon.

167. Friedrich von Hayek, *Full Employment at Any Price* (Institute of Economic Affairs, 1975).

he himself notes, bears little resemblance to what really happens in a recession. Aside from attempting to write a critique of something he has not bothered to learn, his main error is his epic failure to understand that Austrian business cycle theory rests on the inflation of bank credit. A failure to borrow money to expand production capacity does not mean that people must therefore be spending more on consumption goods, so there is absolutely no implication that an investment slump should always be accompanied by a corresponding consumption boom. Krugman is also clearly unaware that the conventional Austrian business cycle rests on the failure of consumer preferences to stay in sync with the shift in investment from consumer goods to capital goods; even his use of the term "investment goods" indicates an unfamiliarity with Austrian theory since Austrians customarily use the term "capital goods" in contrast to "consumption goods."

Of course, if you substitute the limits of demand concept for the shifting goods ratio component, then it does not matter whether the credit-inflated investment boom is directed towards capital goods or consumer goods; if an investment boom can occur in the tulip bulb market, it can obviously happen anywhere that cheap credit is made available to people who believe they can make money buying and selling in a short-term time frame.

Krugman ends his quixotic case against hangover theory by declaring, "A recession happens when, for whatever reason, a large part of the private sector tries to increase its cash reserves at the same time." It's all quite simple, he declares. If the problem is that people want more money than is available, all that needs to be done is to increase the money supply. And, if bad loans and bad investments were made, rather than permitting them to leave perfectly good productive capacity idle, just write off the loans and junk the bad investments. For nobody, he asserts, has ever managed to explain why bad investments made in the past necessitate laying off workers in the present.

I shall understand if you have begun to wonder at this point if I am constructing a cruel parody of Krugman's argument for my own sinister purposes. I can only encourage you to verify the accuracy of my summary by reading the complete text of the *Slate* article, which is available on the Internet.[168] It is very difficult to believe that after Krugman announces the answer to a recession that follows a period of explosive debt, egregious spending, and easy money is more debt, more spending, and easier money,[169] he would accuse the "hangover theory" – which, you will recall, is a general worldview of his own device held by fictional parties and not Austrian theory per se – of being intellectually incoherent.[170] And yet he does! The central problem is not that people want to hold too much cash, the problem is that no one wants, or can afford, or is willing to borrow the means to buy the goods that are being produced. All productive capacity is not created equal; the fact that it exists does not make it "perfectly good." After all, what use is the vast amount of General Motors' perfectly good productive capacity today, when so few people want to buy their cars? It's not as if its factories can immediately be converted to cranking out Victoria's Secret robot girls or anything else that might happen to hold more consumer appeal than oversized, unattractive people movers with poor gas mileage.[171]

I previously noted that numerous Austrian economists have managed to successfully explain why bad investments in the past require the unemployment of good workers in the present. It is because of the many bad past investments in Detroit's auto-making capacity that many Detroit autoworkers have to lose their jobs now. If those investments had instead been made in manufacturing the sort of cars that people want to buy today, or even in manufacturing high-definition flatscreens, then those workers would not have needed to lose their jobs and would still be securely employed. But, because huge auto plants are not easily converted into nail salons, iPod factories, or robot girl production lines, the workers employed there face losing their jobs. It's really not a difficult concept and even a Nobel prize winner should be able to grasp it.

---

168. http://www.slate.com/id/9593.
169. Some call it the "Hair of the Dog" theory.
170. "Nonexistent" would be a more accurate charge.
171. I don't know, that's just the first example that sprang to mind.

The fact that Paul Krugman does not understand even the most basic fundamentals of Austrian theory does not make the theory intellectually incoherent, it merely means the man does not know whereof he speaks. Indeed, when one recalls the shamanistic Keynesian belief in the supreme importance of "animal spirits" to the economy, the idea of a neo-Keynesian criticizing any economic theory as intellectually incoherent becomes downright risible.

Krugman finally brings his article to an end by complaining about how Western commentators have been too prone to blame the problems that various Asian countries were facing in the late 1990s on their previous financial excesses. Contrary to a legion of books and economic papers written by mainstream economists since the collapse of the Nikkei and Japanese real estate, he even questions the propriety of blaming Japan's then-current malaise[172] on the 1980s bubble economy because the Heisei bubble burst almost a decade prior to Krugman's piece. The reason for Japan's difficulties, he explains, is too much austerity. However Japanese interest rates have been below one percent since 1995; presently at 0.1 percent, they are much lower than the 2.5 percent that marked the loose monetary policy of the Heisei Boom![173] This is not monetary austerity, it is extreme monetary liberality. The tripling of Japanese government debt from 65 percent of GDP in 1991 to 182 percent today suffices to show that the Japanese have not been practicing fiscal austerity either.

While the famous Princeton professor did eventually come to terms with the fact that economic contractions really do tend to follow investment booms, he has remained stubbornly ignorant of Austrian School theory. Eleven years after the publication of "The Hangover Theory," Krugman appeared on C-SPAN and was visibly caught off-guard when a caller asked about why neo-Keynesian economists like himself were blindsided by the financial debacle of 2008, especially when Austrians such as the economists of the Mises Institute and Peter Schiff were not. Krugman's response was much more brief, but reflected about the same mastery of Aus-

---

172. This is the malaise that has continued throughout the eleven years since Krugman wrote the article. It's now approaching its second complete decade.

trian theory as he showed in his failed 1998 critique. In another fallacious appeal to authority, he said: "Um, boy, I don't even want to go into the Austrian stuff. It's, ah, it's not major school."[174] Of course, it is the failure of the major economic schools that is precisely the problem occupying many influential minds today, as evidenced by an article published in July by *The Economist*, entitled "What went wrong with economics."

You may well wonder why it matters what one economist, however award-winning and influential, happens to think about a rival school of economic thought. The reason it matters is that if politics is again allowed to trump economic science due to the influence of willfully ignorant men like Paul Krugman, the world may be doomed to lose another four decades to errant economic policies based on intrinsically flawed economic theories. It matters because truth matters. It matters because science, even imperfect science applied to complex matters only dimly understood, matters. And finally, it matters because the president of the United States and other influential men whose decisions are capable of affecting the global economy are listening to certain economists' recommendations regarding the present economic crisis.

> "On the night of April 27, for instance, the president invited to the White House some of his administration's sharpest critics on the economy, including *New York Times* columnist Paul Krugman and Columbia University economist Joseph Stiglitz. Over a roast-beef dinner, Obama listened and questioned while Krugman and Stiglitz, both Nobel Prize winners, pushed for more aggressive government intervention in the banking system."[175]

Two months later, Barack Obama proposed a package of financial reforms that would provide for more aggressive intervention in the U.S. banking system. The *Wall Street Journal* described his proposals as a historic overhaul that would "affect nearly every

---

173. See Figure 1.1.
174. *Washington Journal*, C-SPAN, February 15, 2009.
175. Evan Thomas, "Prisoners of the White House," *Newsweek*, May 18, 2009.

aspect of banking and markets."[176] They included a new federal agency to regulate financial products for consumers as well as an expanded role for the Federal Reserve in regulating systemic risk.

---

176. Damian Paletta, "Historic Overhaul of Finance Rules," *The Wall Street Journal*, June 18, 2009.

Chapter 9

THE RETURN OF THE
GREAT DEPRESSION

The remedy for the boom is not a higher rate of interest but a lower
rate of interest! For that may enable the so-called boom to last. The
right remedy for the trade cycle is not to be found in abolishing
booms and thus keeping us permanently in a semi-slump; but in
abolishing slumps and keeping us permanently in a quasi-boom.
—JOHN MAYNARD KEYNES, *The General Theory of*
Employment, Interest, and Money, 1935

ACCORDING TO Keynesian theory, recessions are caused by excessive savings. In 2005, Ben Bernanke coined the term "global savings glut," a concept which has been embraced as a potential cause of the global recession by a number of economists, including the neo-Keynesian Paul Krugman. The concept is a remarkable one considering that the overall global savings rate was 22.8 percent of world GDP in 2006, which has trended down from 25.5 percent in 1974.[177] The same is true for the United States, only more so, as in 2008 the combined savings rate of American individuals, businesses, and the government sector was only 12.6 percent of GDP, down from 18 percent in 2000. The personal savings rate as a percentage of disposable income had also been falling for more than three decades, from 12 percent in 1974 to -2 percent in 2005.[178]

177. Stephen Roach, "The Shifting Mix of Global Saving," Global Economic Forum, June 04, 2007. Brigitte Desroches and Michael Francis.
178. Massimo Guidolin and Elizabeth A. La Jeunesse, "The Decline in the U.S. Personal Saving Rate: Is It Real and Is It a Puzzle?," *Federal Reserve Bank of St. Louis Review,* November/December 2007, 491-514.

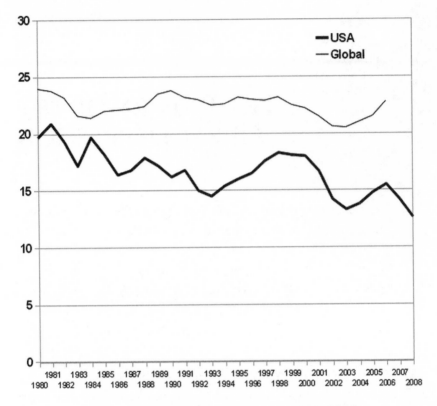

Figure 9.1. Gross Savings Rates, 1980–2008

It's not hard to see why neo-Keynesians like Krugman failed to see the recession that officially began in the third quarter of 2008 coming. Since there was no glut of global savings but merely a shift in global savings patterns from the advanced economies to the developing economies,[179] and because U.S. savings rates have been in decline for 35 years, it is obvious that either there is no economic contraction or the neo-Keynesian theory of recession is incorrect. The Federal Reserve chairman's position, on the other hand, superficially appears to be incoherent. In a 2007 speech to the Bundesbank he returned to his previous theme in discussing the so-called global savings glut from 1996 to 2004. During that

---

179. *"According to IMF statistics, in 1996 the advanced countries of the developed world accounted for 78% of total global saving. By 2006, that share had fallen to 65%. Over the same decade, the developing world's share of global saving has risen from 22% in 1996 to 36% in 2006."* Roach, ibid.

speech, he surprisingly announced that he could find no obvious reason that the U.S. savings rate had *fallen* so precipitously during those same eight years.[180] We can only hope the fact that the interest rate on a six-month CD dropped from 5.71 to 1.02 percent in the period he was referencing slipped his mind, because the idea that the individual most responsible for monetary policy in the present crisis genuinely does not understand that the price of money has a predictable impact on its market supply is too terrifying to contemplate for long.[181] More likely, the Fed chairman understood very well that trouble was looming on the near horizon and was making a futile attempt to shift attention away from the Federal Reserve and its creation of multiple investment booms before the full effect of the subprime crisis was understood.

Monetarist theory asserts that recessions are caused by insufficient growth in the money supply defined as currency plus all commercial bank deposits. Based on Friedman's mechanistic concept of monetary expansion, "insufficient" means below the recommended 3-5 percent rate. Unlike the Keynesian approach to monetary policy, interest rates are not a primary factor, but matter only insofar as they happen to affect the size of the money supply. The Friedmanite monetarist case looks superficially better than the Keynesian one, as the M1 money stock fell from $1,375 billion in January 2006 to $1,368 billion at the start of the current recession in July 2007, which is precisely as according to the theory. The -0.5 percent growth of the money stock fell below the 2.8 percent level of inflation, therefore the economy begins to contract as predicted.

The reason this predictive success fails to prove the reliability of the theory can be seen in the chart comparing growth in the money stock to the inflation rate over the previous three decades. Since 1980, the monetarist model has predicted recession for eleven

---

180. Ben S. Bernanke, "Global Imbalances: Recent Developments and Prospects," The Bundesbank Lecture, Berlin, Germany, September 11, 2007.

181. It may be interesting to consider my previous statements about the calculation problem as it applies to central banking in light of Mr. Bernanke's Bundesbank speech. If he is incapable of understanding that most people are less inclined to save money if they're only going to receive one percent interest instead of nearly six percent, how in the name of the Elder God dreaming beneath the Antarctic ice is he going to correctly anticipate the future demand for money on an economy-wide basis?

of the last twenty-nine years. More usefully, the chart indicates how the contraction of the money supply from 1995 to 1997 made Alan Greenspan, a discretionary monetarist, reluctant to shut off the money spigot and raise interest rates despite his well-known concerns about irrational exuberance in the equity markets.

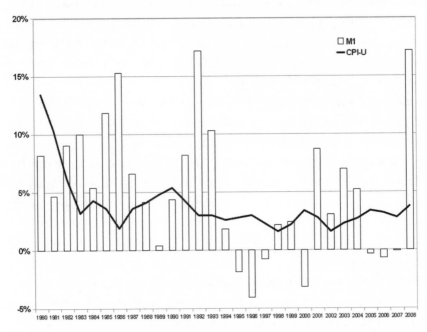

Figure 9.2. U.S. Money Supply and Inflation, 1980–2008

If the Keynesian and monetarist theories fared poorly in predicting the present downturn, is there any evidence that the Austrian School theory fared any better beyond what we have already seen with the various investment booms that took place in the American stocks, credit, and housing? With the caveat that Austrians are skeptical of the utility of aggregate economic statistics, there is nevertheless a large amount of empirical data available because the United States was far from the only country to experience significant bank credit expansion in the last decade. If you recall, Austrian theory asserts that bank credit expansion leads to investment booms, which increasingly creates malinvestment in the form of supply that is mismatched with demand. Liquidation of the malinvestment-created supply causes economic contraction which is marked by a decline in prices, particularly in the market sectors where the credit expansion was focused.

In the United Kingdom, the amount of total personal debt increased a little more than 100 percent from 2001 to 2007. This expansion of bank credit was increasingly focused in the housing sector, as total secured lending on homes increased from 75 percent of total UK personal debt to 83 percent in that time. The six-year period also encompassed an investment boom that saw UK housing prices increase from 77,698 in 2000 to a peak of 184,131 in Q3 2007. The chart below shows how the annual expansion of bank credit coincided with the annual increase in house prices until 2007, when the limits of demand were reached[182] and prices began to crash, falling 14.7 percent in 2008 alone.

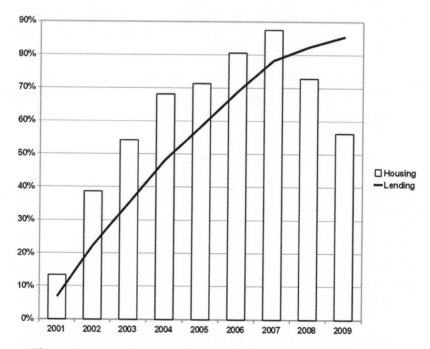

Figure 9.3. UK House Prices & Bank Lending, 2001–2009

---

182. Most likely on the price axis rather than the quantity axis shown in Figure 7.1.

Although the UK's 14.8 percent annual increase in nominal house prices from 2002 to 2006 was nearly double the 7.7 percent U.S. rate, it was not even the most extreme example of the housing boom in Europe. It was fifth, behind Spain at 18.4 percent, Bulgaria at 23.5 percent, Lithuania at 23.8 percent, and Estonia at 36.4 percent. This stood in contrast to countries such as Poland, Austria, Portugal, and Germany, where housing prices increased less than 3 percent per year. According to Austrian theory, the effects of the housing bust on the overall economy should be much greater in countries like Estonia, Spain, and Ireland than in Austria, Germany, and Poland, and to the extent that inexpensive debt was made available to that and other sectors of the economy, we would expect to see that signs of the resulting economic contraction are similarly greater as well. Therefore we should see unemployment rising faster, prices falling further, GDP contracting more, and government deficits growing larger in the three housing boom countries than in the three non-boom ones. Due to the Austrian doubts about the reliability of macroeconomic data, greater credence should be given to historical statistics that are less easily manipulated, such as government deficits and interest rates, rather than GDP, unemployment, and inflation.

Table 9.4. Six European Economies

	Estonia	Spain	Ireland	Germany	Austria	Poland
Unemployment 2007-2009	+10.2 points	+10	+7.5	-1.3	-0.2	0.5
GDP Q1 2009	-15.6 percent	-1.8	-7.4	-6.9	-2.9	0.8
Inflation 2009	0.3% annual	-0.9	-1.7	0	0.1	4.2
Deficit delta 2005-2008	+4.5 percent of GDP	+4.8	+8.8	-3.2	-1.2	-0.4

The results don't match up precisely with what Austrian theory predicts, but they are remarkably in line with them. With the exception of Germany's huge contraction in first quarter GDP and the inexplicable ability of Spain's GDP to resist the negative effects of 18.1 percent unemployment, the figures are entirely consistent with what Austrian theory leads us to expect. Note that Estonia's positive inflation tends to supports the theory rather than contradict it because at 0.3 percent, its inflation is still markedly down from 7.2 percent only eighteen months before.[183] Nor are the data cherry-picked. Some of the other countries that also saw sizable investment booms featured even more horrific figures, such as Lithuania's one-year 12.5 percent increase in unemployment or Latvia's cataclysmic 18.6 percent fall in GDP.

> "People talk about the American subprime problem, but there were housing bubbles in the U.K., in Spain, in Ireland, in Iceland, in a large part of emerging Europe, like the Baltics all the way to Hungary and the Balkans... That's why the transmission and the effects have been so severe. It was not just the U.S., and not just subprime. It was excesses that led to the risk of a tipping point in many different economies."[184]

Although it can be demonstrated to have been applicable to a number of different countries where investment booms took place, the superior performance of the Austrian theoretical model does not prove that it is necessarily reliable as a predictive model of the future. No amount of back-testing, however flawless, can be taken for reliable scientific evidence. It does suggest that Austrian School theory makes for the most reasonable means of analyzing the present situation with an eye towards forecasting the future, though, as the repeated failure of the other models render them of rather dubious utility for such purposes. This leads us to at last contemplate the central question of the book, which concerns whether the global economy in general and the U.S. economy in particular are presently in the throes of what will eventually be recognized as the Great Depression 2.0. Of course, before we can hope to make any such determination, it is necessary to remind ourselves what the Great Depression was in global terms.

---

183. In looking up the Estonian inflation figures, I found myself laughing out loud when reading the past macroeconomic predictions. The Estonian central bank and Ministry of Finance were forecasting that the Estonian economy would have a soft landing "as the property sector cools and credit growth slows." No Austrians there, to be sure.
184. James Fallows, "Dr. Doom Has Some Good News," *The Atlantic*, July/August 2009.

The Global Great Depression

The Great Depression was a global phenomenon, but the economic contraction struck harder and lasted longer in America than it did in Europe or other parts of the world. The United States had seen annual economic growth of 1.7 percent GDP per capita, twice that of the four major European countries in the 16 years leading up to the 1929 peak; from 1922 to 1929 it also experienced significant bank credit expansion that saw a 17.7 percent annual increase in the amount of home loans provided.[185] Europe's subsequent decline was gentler, shorter, and smaller as European governments did not engage in the same heroic attempts to fight the effects of the contraction that the U.S. government did. There was no European Reconstruction Finance Corporation or New Deal to prolong the downturn, so the European economies hit their collective nadir in 1932 and had already grown past their pre-depression levels in 1936. With the exception of Germany, which suffered from the economic complications of a socialist government, crushing war reparations, and the famous Weimar Republic hyperinflation, unemployment in Europe was lower than in the United States. While U.S. unemployment reached an estimated peak of 24.9 percent in 1933, British unemployment peaked at 17 percent in 1932 and French unemployment never even reached double digits. Japan saw neither a big pre-1929 boom nor a massive post-1929 bust, although the results of its successful 1931 invasion of Manchuria and 1937 invasion of China can be seen in the 40 percent growth in the period leading up to 1940.

From 2000 to 2008, the United States saw a 35.4 percent increase in GDP per capita. The combined economies of the European Union have grown 17 percent over the same period by the same measure; the slower European rate of growth is customarily attributed to the economic sclerosis imposed by its more interventionist governments. But if the global economic growth that preceded the Great Depression was faster than in recent years, the same cannot be said for the growth in global debt. The debt-to-

---

185. Colonial to 1970, Series F 10-16 "Growth Rates (Percent) of GNP and Output per Employee for the U.S. and 6 Countries: 1870 to 1969."

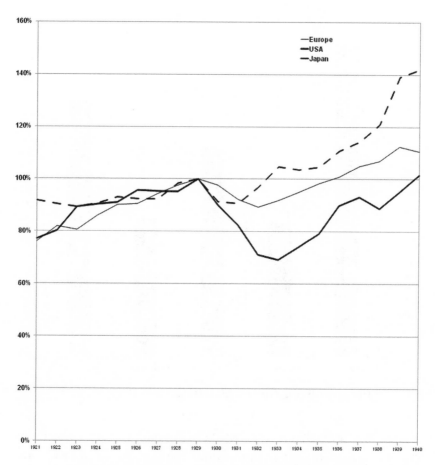

Figure 9.5. GDP per Capita Growth, 1921–1940

GDP ratio is now higher in the three major European countries than it was in 1929, and the ratios are even greater in the United States and Japan. Not since 1933 has the world seen debt-to-GDP ratios this high, and that was after four years of economic contraction combined with price deflation increased debt-to-GDP from 175 percent in 1929 to 299 percent in 1933.

Although the subprime crisis was at first considered to be an American problem, it rapidly spread to infect the financial sectors of other nations due to the scale of European, Japanese, and Chinese investing in the U.S. economy. Swiss giant UBS required a $35 billion bailout from the national bank and was forced to raise $15

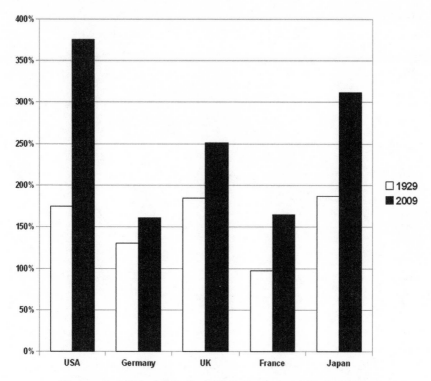

Figure 9.6. World Debt/GDP Ratios, 1929 & 2009

billion by selling shares after losing $37.7 billion from investments in the U.S. housing securities. Halifax Bank of Scotland lost $7 billion and was forced to merge with Lloyds TSB, which itself lost $1.3 billion. The world's largest banking group, London-based HSBC, lost $20 billion, while international banks such as Deutsche Bank, Credit Agricole, Mizuho, Credit Suisse, and the Bank of China all suffered losses counted in the billions.

The smug attitude of many Europeans toward what was initially perceived to be a strictly American problem rapidly disappeared as the effects of the subprime crisis rapidly spread to their countries. In addition to the huge losses to institutions that had invested in mortgage-backed securities, the resulting credit crunch threatened many investment businesses that required large quantities of leverage for their regular operations. Meanwhile, a few European countries were forced to confront the negative consequences of their own investment booms. The UK nationalized one of its largest mortgage lenders, Northern Rock, before it failed. Two of the nations which had enjoyed the biggest booms, Iceland and Estonia, both saw their governments fall as their currencies and real estate markets crashed. But the problems in many European financial sectors were soon complicated by continent-wide problems as well as domestic economic troubles.

The end of the Soviet Union had spawned an investment rush to the east, as Western European investors moved into Eastern Europe to take advantage of the newly opened economies, a wave of overheated economic activity that was further stimulated when the European Union expanded from fifteen nations to twenty-five in 2004. The Treaty of Amsterdam implemented the Schengen Agreement, which provided for the removal of border controls and the free movement of persons throughout most of Europe in 1999 which spurred economic development as labor migrated to the wealthier countries and retirees expatriated to warmer, lower-tax climes. The creation of the unified European currency also had a major effect throughout the continent, mostly due to a 15 percent increase in intra-European trade. The effect of this economic growth was multiplied by the European central bank's decision to follow the Federal Reserve's lead in keeping interest rates low, as did the Bank of England. Fortunately for the sake of European banking stability, the lack of European mortgage securitization meant that the effects remained somewhat localized, but not entirely, as most of the funds for the housing boom in the former Eastern bloc countries were loaned by Western European banks and denominated in Euros or Swiss Francs. This had the result of adding currency risk to the inherent risk of loan defaults. Austrian, German, and Italian banks presently have the most exposure, having made approximately $700 billion in loans to the East.

The sum of these various factors is that the shadow of debt hanging over the global economy is more severe than it was in 1929. The threat is heightened by the fact that this time, eighty years later, it is not only the American authorities that are attempting to fight the contraction with aggressive fiscal and monetary policy, the European and Asian authorities are doing so as well. One of the more ignorant myths of the Great Depression is that Herbert Hoover was a *laissez-faire* president who did nothing in response to the stock market crash or the economic contraction. While it's true that his secretary of the Treasury, Andrew Mellon, did favor a *laissez-faire* policy, Hoover, in his own words, "determined that we would not follow the advice of the bitter-end liquidationists" and embarked upon a revolutionary program of "the most gigantic program of economic defense and counterattack ever evolved in the history of the Republic."[186] FDR may have spent more money in nominal terms and as a percentage of GDP, but what is often forgotten is that the nation's GDP was much larger at the beginning of Hoover's term than at the beginning of Roosevelt's. Ironically, Hoover actually increased federal spending as a percentage of GDP much faster than Roosevelt did, even during the New Deal. The 12 percent increase in federal spending from 1929 to 1932 may look modest, but because the economy contracted to barely more than half its former value in nominal terms during that time, the amount of government intervention saw an increase of nearly 100 percent.

The chart below shows clearly how Hoover aggressively pursued an active depression-fighting strategy once the broader ramifications of the stock market crash became apparent. It must also be remembered that the market did not collapse until October of that year, so 1930 was the first year that countercyclical action showed up in the government's fiscal budgets.

Austrian theory indicates that the heroic, if misguided, efforts of the Hoover and Roosevelt administrations to end the depression by mitigating its effects were the cause of its uncharacteristic length and depth. If events continue to play out in accordance with the theory, this means that Great Depression 2.0 is going to be worse on a global scale than its predecessor, due to the way in which the European nations have imitated the Hooverian interventionist approach which has already been adopted by the Bush and Obama

---

186. Rothbard, *America's Great Depression*, 187.

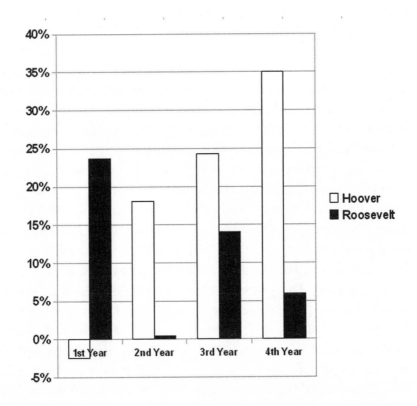

Figure 9.7. Increase in Federal Spending/GDP: USA, 1929–1936

administrations with their various bailout and stimulus plans. The European Economic Recovery Plan, adopted in December 2008 by the European Union and its member states, is nothing more than conventional application of Keynesian fiscal policy. The plan amounts to a commitment to inject countercyclical government spending equivalent to 1.5 percent of GDP, two-thirds to be spent in 2009 and the rest in 2010, and it is intended to be combined with lax monetary policy on the part of the various central banks. The size of the European stimulus is small when compared to FDR's New Deal, which increased federal spending by 4.3 percent of GDP in 1934 and 1935, and the American Recovery and Reinvestment Act of 2009, which amounts to a 5.5 percent increase. But despite its relatively conservative size, the Europeans' collective action will still tend to aggravate the effects of the American and Asian actions. It should also be noted that the $787 billion Obama administration plan was the second American stimulus package to take effect in two years, as the first one, a $168 billion plan equivalent to 1.2 percent of GDP, had been passed almost exactly a year before. Thus, the Bush-Obama stimulus is already one-third larger as a percent of GDP than were the first two years of the New Deal.

The Bush administration plan clearly failed to have the desired results. In like manner, it was very quickly obvious that the Obama administration's stimulus package was not working as advertised either. Prior to Obama's inauguration, his economics team produced a white paper entitled "The Job Impact of the American Recovery and Reinvestment Plan," which assumed a stimulus plan of $775 billion, just barely smaller than the one that was eventually signed into law. The authors utilized a model in which it was assumed that a 1 percent increase in GDP would correspond with a 0.75 percent increase in employment; since the massive stimulus was expected to increase GDP by 3.7 percent, they calculated an increase in payroll employment from 133.9 million to 137.6 million. This allowed them to calculate that the maximum rate of U-3 unemployment would be 9 percent in the first half of 2010 before gradually returning to a stable level of 5 percent unemployment by the second quarter of 2013. But before the end of the year, it became widely recognized that the new administration's forecasts were overly optimistic, thanks primarily to a chart that purported to graphically demonstrate the difference that the Recovery Plan would have on the unemployment rate over the next five years. At the time of this writing, the BEA is reporting U-3 unemployment at 9.4 percent, more than a percentage point higher than it was expected to be with or without the so-called Recovery Plan.

The Risk to the Downside
There are ten reasons to believe the recession that began in 2008 actually marks the return of the Great Depression. Even if we are fortunate and the desperate measures of the global monetary and fiscal authorities are successful in again staving off the threatened

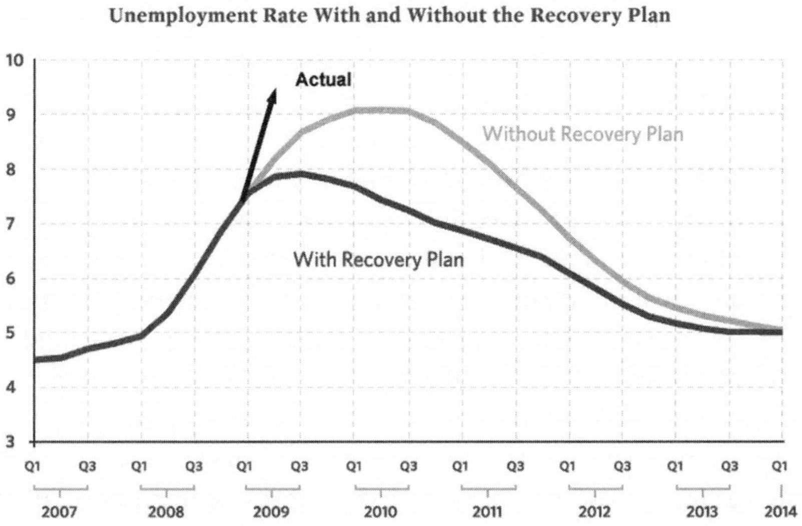

Unemployment Rate With and Without the Recovery Plan

Figure 9.8. Recovery Plan Forecast vs. Actual U.S. Unemployment[187]

financial and economic collapse, they are also reasons why any success is likely to accomplish little more than delaying the eventual day of reckoning.

1) The general investment boom leading up to 2008 was bigger and broader than 1929.

Interest rates were lower, the amount of bank credit expansion was greater, the period of the boom was longer, and booms took place in more sectors of the economy than before. Since the size and length of a contraction is expected to be of comparable magnitude to the preceding expansion, this indicates that when the Great Depression 2.0 takes place, it will be more severe than its predecessor of eighty years ago.

2) Countercyclical fiscal policy enacted on a bigger and much wider scale than in 1929

As mentioned in the previous section, both the American and European stimulus packages are larger than their historical predeces-

187. Christina Romer and Jared Bernstein, "The Job Impact of the American Recovery and Reinvestment Plan." Office of the Vice President-Elect, January 9, 2009, 2.

sors. The Asian powers are also actively pursuing expansionary fiscal policies, as Japan has doubled the size of its stimulus program to 4 percent of GDP, while China's massive stimulus will amount to 8.5 percent of GDP. Nor are the major powers alone in their efforts. "On the fiscal front, governments from the world's largest 20 economies are expected to collectively pump about $US5 trillion into their economies by the end of next year (or nearly 8 percent of global GDP since the crisis began). Altogether, the measures are the equivalent of an extraordinary and unprecedented 18 percent of global GDP."[188] If you accept the Austrian contention that countercyclical action does not work as conceived by its neo-Keynesian advocates and that the expansionary fiscal policy of Hoover and Roosevelt aggravated the Great Contraction of 1930-1933, then reason dictates that current fiscal policies will do the same in 2009. And because the expansionary fiscal measures are so much larger in scale now, the period of contraction will be correspondingly longer as well.

3) *Less margin for government action*

If you take the contrary position and believe that countercyclical action is effective, it is important to note that the portion of the various national economies already provided by the national governments is much greater than eighty years ago. Total government spending, including state and local governments, increased from $5.1 billion to $9.2 billion during FDR's first term, an increase of 80 percent. This dramatic increase was possible because government accounted for only 9 percent of GDP at the start. Government spending presently accounts for 45 percent of GDP, with federal spending representing more than half, or 28 percent. In order to match the effect of FDR's 80 percent increase in federal spending, Obama would have to spend an additional $3.2 trillion, which would raise total government spending to 50 percent of U.S. GDP even if the economy was not contracting. This is simply not possible, so even those who believe in the historical effectiveness of the New

---

188. Kevin Rudd, "Pain on the road to recovery," *The Sydney Morning Herald*, July 25, 2009.

Deal and believe that the second American stimulus should have spent more than $787 billion must recognize that the large share of the national economies presently controlled by modern governments reduces their margin for action.

In addition to the economic *lebensraum* problem, the fact that the national governments are already engaged in substantial deficit spending further reduces their future margin for action. At $11.5 trillion, the U.S. national debt is presently three times higher than it was in 1991, when Alan Greenspan believed it had limited the government's ability to deal with an economic contraction.[189]

Not all the central banks of the major economies are genuine governmental institutions, but the issue of ownership is not relevant here. The significant fact is that the various monetary authorities are even more restrained by their past actions than are the fiscal authorities. With their key interest rates now uniformly below 1 percent, far below the 6 percent at which the Federal Reserve's discount rate was set at the end of 1929, the central banks find themselves limited to a range of untested and exotic options that are of questionable effectiveness.

Table 9.9. World Budget Deficits and Interest Rates, 2009

USA	Germany[190]	UK	France	Japan
12.3%	4.4%	12.6%	7.5%	8.0%
0.18%	0.25%	0.50%	0.25%	0.10%

4) *Loan defaults expanding rapidly into other credit sectors*

While the financial media's focus is still mostly on the U.S. housing sector, where the subprime crisis has expanded to the prime market and 22 percent of homeowners now own homes that are worth less than the mortgages which secure them, an additional threat is posed by the corporate and consumer debt sectors. In the

---

189. "So much debt continued to hang over the budget that when the recession came, the administration didn't have the fiscal flexibility to address it." Greenspan, *The Age of Turbulence*, (New York: Penguin Press LLC, 2007), 119.

190. French and German interest rates are controlled by the European Central Bank. U.S. Federal Funds daily rate as of June 30, 2009; target rate is 0-0.25%.

2009 *World Economic Outlook*, the IMF reported that while corporate defaults are still below the level seen in the early 2000s after the bursting of the dot-com bubble, they are rising quickly. In May, *Moody's Default Research* reported that the global speculative-grade corporate default rate rose from 1.7 percent a year ago to 9.2 percent and projected a peak at 13.8 percent in late 2009. Europe is expected to be the hardest hit, with a default rate of 21 percent forecast for the end of the year. This exceeds the 15.4 percent U.S. default rate that marked the height of the Great Depression in 1933.[191]

U.S. credit card defaults have also risen to record highs. Presently at 10.1 percent, they are expected to rise to 11.25 percent halfway through 2010. The largest issuer, Bank of America, is already reporting a 12 percent default rate among its credit card debtors. Since credit cards and various other forms of consumer debt have been securitized in the same manner that mortgages were, an increase in the number of defaults would threaten not only the lending banks, but a much wider range of financial institutions as well.

5) *Financial necromancy maintaining zombie banks and corporations*
The bailout of the bankrupt automotive manufacturers General Motors and Chrysler is presently estimated to cost $83 billion. The nationalization and bailout of American Insurance Group, in which the U.S. government now owns a 79.9 percent stake, cost $130 billion. The nationalization of mortgage insurers Fannie Mae and Freddie Mac cost $200 billion and, according to Mises Institute contributor Don Rich, could wind up costing as much as $1.3 trillion. When pushed by former Secretary of the Treasury Henry Paulson it was sold to the American public as a $25 billion deal. And then, of course, there are the financial industry bailouts, which dwarf the rest and make up the rest of the $8.5 trillion in funds committed by the Federal Reserve, the Federal Deposit Insurance Corporation, the Treasury Department, and the Federal Housing

---

191. Edmund Conway, "Moody's predicts default rate will exceed peaks hit in Great Depression," *The Daily Telegraph*. February 26, 2009.

Administration.[192] As astonishing as these massive sums may be, the real cost of preventing these organizations from being liquidated is one of opportunity. The Japanese example has shown that using government power to abort the process of creative destruction that causes new companies to be born as old ones die, works about as well as attempting to maintain a nation's population by combining birth control with life support systems for the elderly. Ironically, as recently as 2005, it was argued that one reason America would not face a slow-motion Japanese-style bust was that the U.S. government did not prevent insolvent companies from going out of business. With the adoption of the too-big-to-fail policy by the Bush administration in 2008, the impossibility has rapidly become a probability.

6) Derivatives and the credit contraction multiplier

Keynesian economists like to refer to a multiplier effect, in which each dollar of government spending has a larger impact on GDP than its direct addition as part of the G component. In the case of the second American stimulus package, the multiplier utilized in the forecasting model is reported to be 1.5,[193] thus $787 billion in government spending would be expected to increase GDP by $1.2 trillion. Setting aside the numerous logical flaws intrinsic to this concept and the fact that the multiplier effect of World War II spending has been calculated to be only 0.8,[194] the real problem is the negative multiplier involved in the contraction of credit. This means that for every dollar of capital that is lost, the contraction of the credit that is leveraged upon it can be as large as a factor of 40. Much of this leverage factor is in the form of credit derivatives, and the full extent of the risks being taken by the financial institutions that deal in them is still unknown. While the presumption is that the institutions at risk have been taking advantage of the March

---

192. Corrected for inflation, World War II cost only $3.6 trillion. At some point, one has to wonder if it might not make more sense to simply invade Canada and sell it to China. Maybe cut a deal with France for Quebec on the side. 43°41' or fight!

193. Paul Krugman, "Stimulus arithmetic (wonkish but important)," The Conscience of a Liberal New York Times blog, January 6, 2009.

194. Robert J. Barro, "Government Spending Is No Free Lunch," The Wall Street Journal, January 22, 2009.

market rally and the massive quantities of credit being provided by the central banks to unwind their dangerous positions, some of the BIS statistics appear to indicate that, instead of extricating themselves from the derivatives market, the financial institutions are doubling down. It is impossible to calculate the probable effects of the derivatives market and the credit contraction multiplier because the full extent of the potential danger they pose is unknown, but it seems likely that it is not inconsequential.

7) *Labor inefficiency*

A conventional method of combating unemployment during a recession is to substitute underemployment for complete unemployment. This reduction of hours per worker is intended to keep wage rates high; however it has the effect of reducing efficiency and productivity by spreading the available work between multiple workers. In some respects, it amounts to inverting the division of labor that is at the heart of the capitalist system. As with the zombie banks and corporations, the problem is one of opportunity cost. Workers that would otherwise be unemployed and available to work more hours at lower wages for companies with sufficient demand to justify their employment will instead work fewer hours at higher wages for companies that already produce enough to meet the demand for their goods. While this might be acceptable to the individual worker, the negative net effect on the aggregate economy should be obvious. Maintaining wage rates was a central focus of the Hoover administration and wages were largely kept at 1929 levels through the end of 1931.[195]

Initial signs indicate that, at least in the United States, this same process is at work. Average weekly hours of non-supervisory workers has fallen from 34.2 in July 2007 to 33.1 in July 2009, while hourly earnings have risen from 17.48 to 18.56 in the same two years. Another indication is the change in the ratio between the U-5

---

195. In May, 1931, Secretary of the Treasury Andrew Mellon said: *"In this country, there has been a concerted and determined effort on the part of both government and business not only to prevent any reduction in wages, but to keep the maximum number of men employed, and thereby to increase consumption."* AGD 268.

unemployment rate and the U-6 unemployment rate. The only distinction between the two statistics is the inclusion of workers who are employed part time for economic reasons in the latter figure. Since U-5 subtracted from U-6 rose from 3.5 in June 2008 to 5.7 percent a year later, this indicates that employers are increasingly electing to under-employ workers rather than simply laying them off.[196] On an anecdotal note, the fact that the United Auto Workers union now owns 65 percent of Chrysler and 17.5 percent of General Motors suggests that the predilection to preserve wage rates will be stronger in 2010 than it was in 1930.

8) An untimely shortage of war

The idea that war is inherently stimulative to the economy has been successfully refuted many times by various economists applying Frederic Bastiat's concept of the Broken Window fallacy. When a shopkeeper's window is broken by his careless son, the six francs benefit to the glazier, which then circulates into the economy by the glazier and encourages other industries is six francs that the shopkeeper could not elect to spend on the cobbler or the bookbinder. What anti-war economists often forget, however, is that if the glazier sends his son over to the next town and has him break a shopkeeper's window there – we shall assume, for the sake of illustration, that the glazier is the closest one – and the glazier then spends his six francs repair fee in his own town, the economy of that town is measurably better off.

There is no question that war can have a distinctly stimulative effect on an economy, with one very important caveat. The war must be a victorious one, with little damage to the nation's productive capacity and it must be paid for without too much reliance on debt. Ideally, a nation should also destroy the productive capacity of nations that pose economic competition in order to create new

---

196. I should note that there is an alternative explanation for the faster pace of underemployment growth compared to unemployment. Because government regulations increase the price to the employer for full-time workers, the growing preference for part-time workers may not be indicative of corporate attempts to preserve wage rates, but rather a sign of their desire to avoid regulatory costs. Table A-12. Alternative measures of labor underutilization, Bureau of Labor Statistics, July 2, 2009.

postwar markets for capital and consumer goods. So, the 40 percent increase in Japanese GDP during the 1930s is an example of its successful war against China, while the great postwar economic expansion in the United States had far more to do with the fact that great numbers of the industrialized nations of Europe and Asia had been left in smoking ruins than it did with the economic theories in vogue at the time. Of course, the United States is presently occupying two countries it conquered in the last decade, but from the economic perspective these wars were distinctly suboptimal since neither Afghanistan nor Iraq possessed large industrial infrastructures that would require rebuilding.

I may well be speaking too soon here about a dearth of warfare. Socionomic theory states that conflict increases during economic downturns, so it is not only possible, it is probable that the longer the economic contraction continues, the more likely it is that wars will occur. From the U.S. point of view, defeating China would offer the maximum benefit, but Europe would make for a more desirable target once the expected benefits are weighed against the probable costs. And, of course, as Athens learned at Sicily, there is always the chance that the unexpected will happen and the wealthy maritime empire will be defeated.

9) *Waxman-Markey legislation*

For many years, it was supposed that the Smoot-Hawley tariff of 1930 played a major role in the economic contraction of the Great Depression. As more economists are gradually coming to realize, this was unlikely the case for several reasons. First, the 15.5 percent annual decline in exports from 1929 to 1933 was less precipitous than the pre-tariff 18.3 percent decline from 1920 to 1922. Second, because the amount of imports also fell, the net effect of the $328 million reduction in the balance of trade on the economy amounted to only 0.3 percent of 1929 GDP. Third, the balance of trade turned negative and by 1940 had increased to nearly ten times the size of the 1929 positive balance while the economy was growing.[197]

---

197. USA Colonial, Series 187-200, "Value of Exports and Imports: 1790 to 1970," 884.

At the end of June 2009, the House of Representatives passed the American Clean Energy and Security Act. While the Congressional Budget Office has calculated that the annual cost of the bill, known as Waxman-Markey, to be only $22 billion, the CBO report contains a major caveat: "The resource cost does not indicate the potential decrease in gross domestic product (GDP) that could result from the cap. The reduction in GDP would also include indirect general equilibrium effects, such as changes in the labor supply resulting from reductions in real wages and potential reductions in the productivity of capital and labor."

The Heritage Foundation has calculated that the cost of the economic effects omitted from the CBO report will cost an additional $371 billion per year, indicating that Waxman-Markey will reduce GDP by 2.8 percent per annum.[198] Since Japan and the European countries are in the process of implementing Kyoto Protocol, the global effects of climate change legislation are likely to be significantly more contractionary than the consequences of protectionist legislation in the 1930s. In an ironic echo of the past, Waxman-Markey also contains a proviso for a "border adjustment," which is a protectionist tariff on goods imported from countries that do not limit their global warming emissions. But the motive is irrelevant; a protectionist tariff in the interest of cooling the planet is no less contractionary than a protectionist tariff in the interest of defending American jobs or American markets.

10) *Socionomic patterns and the Grand Supercycle bear wave*
In his novel *War and Peace*, Russian novelist Leo Tolstoy illustrates the arrogant incompetence of human understanding and the inability of human reason to explain even the simplest of social phenomena. With unrelenting precision, Tolstoy dissects the notion that men dictate events. In one specific example, he examines, with minute detail, the four specific orders Napoleon gave to his army prior to the battle of Borodino. He then proves that none of them were, or even could have been, carried out. Tolstoy later proceeds

---

198. "CBO Grossly Underestimates Costs of Cap and Trade," The Heritage Foundation, June 22, 2009.

to abuse specific and universal historians by demonstrating how their explanations of various historical events are not only contradictory, but are often constructed on unsupportable premises. Two hundred years later, the technical analyst Robert Prechter Jr., author of *Conquer the Crash*, developed a scientific discipline called socionomics from Elliott Wave investment theory. Socionomics, which is somewhat similar to the fictional concept of psychohistory described in Isaac Asimov's Foundation novels, attempts to understand and measure the great waves of human will and emotion that Tolstoy described in order to forecast future events.

These waves of human emotion are believed to move in certain specific patterns which are replicated at various levels of magnitude, including Primary, Cycle, and Supercycle. Prechter and other Elliott Wave technicians presently believe that the United States has entered a Grand Supercycle bear market, which is one magnitude greater than the Supercycle bear market that encompassed the Great Depression. This would mark the correction of the wave that Ralph Elliott believed began around the time of the Revolutionary War. The socionomic prediction borders on the apocalyptic, as in *At the Crest of the Tidal Wave*, Prechter predicts a major war and a 90 percent decline in the Dow. But it is not quite apocalyptic, as Prechter is confident that the world will not be returning to the condition of the Dark Ages, as would have been the implication of a larger magnitude wave.[199] Both Elliott Wave theory and socionomics are controversial, but I find them interesting and it's certainly intriguing to note the ways that Prechter's socionomic theories have played out correctly, for the most part, since the Grand Supercycle peak in 2000.[200] And they are certainly

---

199. "While a Grand Supercycle bear market portends major war, which will be devastating to be sure, we can now retire any fears of an all-out global holocaust that devastates the planet and sets civilization back a thousand years, which would have been the implication of a Millennium degree bear market. Such fears will probably be intense and widespread before this Grand Supercycle bear market is over, and not without reason, as it will engender severe global tensions and armed conflict." Prechter, Robert, *At the Crest of the Tidal Wave: A Forecast for the Great Bear Market* (Gainesville: New Library Classics, 1995), 66.

200. Fans of Joseph Schumpeter can substitute Kondratieff Winter for the socionomics if they like. My grasp of long-wave cycles is insufficient to have an opinion on the matter, although Kondratieff Winter certainly hints at bad things such as white witches, no Christmas, and other unpleasantries.

in line with what Austrian economic theory informs us at the present.

Even if there are a number of unknown factors that trump the ten reasons provided above that prove me to be ultimately incorrect, there can be little doubt that sooner or later the Great Depression will return. Despite the optimistic insistence of influential men who should know better, it is never different "this time." Although they are poorly perceived and the processes that drive them are even less well understood, there are historical patterns that have played out time and time again throughout history. Societies are born, they grow, and they die. Political economy is an important part of this societal process, and just as there will never be a permanent slump, there will never be a permanent boom. The sun rises and sets, prices rise and fall, and the Invisible Hand eventually triumphs over all.

> [T]he ideas of economists and political philosophers, both when they are right and when they are wrong, are more powerful than is commonly understood. Indeed the world is ruled by little else. Practical men, who believe themselves to be quite exempt from any intellectual influences, are usually the slaves of some defunct economist.
>
> —John Maynard Keynes,
> *The General Theory of Employment, Interest, and Money*

GREAT DEPRESSION 2.0

*Nothing made me more frustrated than having to intervene
in a couple cases where wild bets threatened to bring down the
financial system. But I was not going to be the Federal Reserve
chairman who presided over the second Great Depression.
I had to hold my nose and stop those firms from failing.*
—BEN BERNANKE, *The NewsHour with Jim Lehrer*, 2009

A S THIS book is being completed during the third quarter of
2009, the consensus view is that the economic contraction of
the last eighteen months is essentially over. Federal Reserve officials have declared that the U.S. economy is in the process of stabilizing and that recovery will take place in the latter half of the year.
The Blue Chip consensus is that the peak-to-trough decline in
GDP will turn out to be 3.5 percent, and two-thirds of the 50 economists that make up the forecasting panel for the Blue Chip Economic Indicators publication presently expect the recession to
have ended before September 2009. And the chairman of the Federal Reserve recently asserted that economic growth would return
at a minimal pace before the end of the year, even if the unemployment rate does not peak until 2010.

However, as Murray Rothbard reminds us, towards the end of
1930 both the politicians and the economists were certain that
1931 would bring recovery.[201] Most of the economists presently
predicting a second half recovery in 2009 previously predicted a
second half recovery in 2008 as well. And the utility of these opti-

---

201. Rothbard, 257.

mistic predictions is questionable in any event because the same economic models that failed to predict the crisis originally are now being used to forecast the future.

Compounding the problem of determining when the recession of 2008 either comes to an end or transforms into a second Great Depression of 2008–2012 is the nebulous nature of economic contractions as measured in modern statistical terms. One of the difficulties in predicting either the extent or the duration of an economic depression is that there is no agreed-upon definition of the term. The distinction between recession and depression is a modern one; Gottfried von Haberler's *Prosperity and Depression* is a theoretical work on business cycles rather than the Steinbeckian novel suggested by the title. While the financial media usually refers to a depression as being a 10 percent decline in real GDP, this definition is merely one of the several rudimentary rules of thumb suggested by Julius Shiskin, a former Commissioner of the Bureau of Labor Statistics, to help economists determine when recessions and depressions have occurred in the past.

In practical application, most macroeconomists regard the use of strictly defined rules to determine economic contractions to be both impractical and dangerous due to the probability that policy actions based on them would be enacted at the wrong time. These concerns are not misplaced, for as Bruce Bartlett showed, this has usually been the case, at least with regards to fiscal policy actions. The GDP-based definition of is depression almost completely useless once you take into account the inherent unreliability of a statistic that is largely determined by subjective estimates and approximations multiplied by averages. While unemployment rates are often used as a rough metric of an economy's health, these statistics are arguably even less useful for attempting to determine when a depression is taking place. The U-3 and U-6 numbers from the Bureau of Labor Statistics are no more reliable than GDP, but unlike GDP, we do not possess valid historical unemployment rates to which they can be reasonably compared.

Whereas the federal government has kept annual statistics on international trade and Gross National Product since at least 1889, (and GNP is similar enough to modern GDP to be reasonably comparable), the current methodology used to collect unemployment data only goes back to 1940. The notorious 25 percent civilian unemployment rate for 1933 is nothing more than a rough estimate made well after the fact, as the "conceptual structure and techniques for measurement of current labor force data were developed during the late 1930's by the Works Projects Administration."[202]

Ronald Reagan once said "Recession is when a neighbor loses his job. Depression is when you lose yours." This is probably a more relevant definition for the average individual than any formula concocted by an economist, but it's not terribly helpful from a macroeconomic perspective. Furthermore, the very notion of attempting to precisely define the size of a national economy measured in dollars in a world where money is electronic debt, property is post-scarce, capital flows freely across economic lines, labor migrates across national borders virtually unchecked, and politicians leave the government's greatest expenses off the books has become increasingly absurd over time. Although statisticians and econometricians are prone to forget this important fact, the map is not the territory.

But the unreliability of official GDP figures and unemployment rates does not mean that we are entirely in the dark as to whether the economy is expanding or contracting. We have merely to keep two conflicting concepts in mind. The first is the Econometric Uncertainty Principle, which reflects the inevitable pressure on the measuring agency and subsequent bureaucratic manipulation of any statistic identified as a politically significant macroeconomic measure.[203] It's not a precisely accurate analogy, of course, since the act of observing changes the observation rather than the

---

202. *"However, prior to 1940, especially during the 1930's, the economically active sector was differentiated on the basis of its ability and willingness to work. Thus, most surveys during the 1930's counted as unemployed those persons not working, but "willing and able to work." Willingess and ability, however, turned out to be extremely subjective in pracitce, and since those concepts were dependent upon the attitudes of the persons involved, it was difficult to compile data on a comparable baiss from place to place and time to time.... The estimates shown here, prior to 1940, were prepared on comparable a basis as possible with the concepts used since 1940."* D 1-74 p. 121.

203. This should not be confused with Mike Shedlock's Fed Uncertainty Principle, which refers to the observer/participant feedback loop that prevents free market operations in an economy with a central bank possessing a monetary monopoly.

actual object being observed,[204] but it should serve to illustrate the point in a sufficiently pseudo-scientific manner. The second is that the truth about the state of the economy will eventually come out regardless of how much effort the government puts into concealing it. Redefinitions of the labor force and hedonic adjustments of the consumer price levels can only disguise actual unemployment and observable price changes in the short term; over time even the most obtuse individual will notice that half their neighbors are out of work and gasoline costs twice what it did the summer before.

So, the correct way to look for signs of significant economic contraction indicating a depression is to view the official GDP and unemployment figures with an educated skepticism while still taking them into account in the light of other data that is less easily subject to interpretation. International and industry statistics can be particularly useful for this purpose, because businesses and trade organizations can seldom afford to get too creative with their statistics since doing so would render them useless. Unlike politicians, for whom perception of more pressing concern than reality, most businesses are forced to deal in tangibles and so demand a greater degree of precision in their data. Of course, you still must always be careful to understand the nature of the organization producing the information; for example, the forecast of an economist working for the National Association of Realtors, whose business depends primarily upon the psychological confidence of potential homebuyers, is almost always going to be markedly more optimistic than the economist providing real estate projections to lumberyards, whose activity relies upon the real material demand for their products by the homebuilders.

Six Scenarios

There are six economics scenarios describing the next decade which I consider to be worth contemplating. Some of them are widely believed to be more probable than they actually are, others are still considered to be well outside the realm of reasonable possibility by

---

204. Or, in the case of an observer possessed of an overabundance of integrity, a change in the employment status of the observer himself.

most observers despite the fact that events have laid the necessary groundwork for them to take place. In each case, I have attempted to find the strongest arguments made on behalf of the scenario, considered the assumptions being made to justify them, and made a determination of how likely the scenario is to come to pass. Being a good Austrian, I see no point in assigning a fictional mathematical probability to each scenario merely to create an illusion of accuracy, but I have attempted to make it very clear which scenarios are more probable than others, and why I believe this to be the case.

Scenario 1: Saint Bernanke and the Green Shoots

Also known as the "V-shaped recession" or an "immaculate recovery," this is the most optimistic scenario and involves the perilous assumption that the economic experts and financial media seen on television are the most likely to correctly forecast events and tell the truth. It rests on the idea of the U.S. economy recovering and returning to positive growth in the second half of 2009 and is at present the most popular scenario among economists and financial analysts. It is mostly based on a combination of hope, belief in the effectiveness of contracyclical fiscal policy, and faith in the U.S. stock market rally which has seen the S&P 500 rise 50 percent in six months, and tends to be focused on the U.S. rather than the global economy. If this scenario turns out to be correct and the "green shoots" detected by the Federal Reserve chairman truly are in the process of growing into a bountiful harvest, even his most skeptical critics will be forced to conclude that Ben Bernanke merits a place in economic history as the greatest central banker since Benjamin Strong and Nouriel Roubini was correct to dub him "The Great Preventer."[205]

Adherents to this scenario include the aforementioned Blue Chip consensus, the economists of the International Monetary Fund, who believe that a "darker scenario seems to have been avoided"

---

205. "Both the conventional and unconventional decisions made by this scholar of the Great Depression prevented the Great Recession of 2008-2009 from turning into the Great Depression 2.0." Nouriel Roubini, "The Great Preventer." *The New York Times*, July 27, 2009.

because of "strong economic policy effort" while projecting robust GDP growth across the OECD averaging 2.75 percent per year starting in 2011. Other subscribing to the Green Shoots concept include the Federal Reserve Chairman himself, of course, who expects the U.S. economy to average 1 percent growth in the second half of 2009, and the irrepressibly optimistic Jim Cramer, who declared the recession already over in the second quarter. Macroeconomist Robert Gordon from the elite Business Cycle Dating Committee of the National Bureau of Economic Analysis has also declared the bottom of the recession to have passed based on a peak in claims for unemployment benefits, while Donald Luskin expects the bottom to have been marked in May or June 2009. Analysts from the major financial institutions uniformly subscribe to this scenario, although they are presently divided into two camps, as those from Moody's, JP Morgan, Credit Suisse, Goldman Sachs, Barclays, Bank of America, Alliance Bernstein, Fannie Mae, UBS, IHS Global Insight, Morgan Stanley see recovery taking place in the third quarter, while Deutsche Bank and Capital Economics expect it to occur in the fourth quarter instead.[206]

However, the lack of confidence of most members of the Green Shoots school have in their forecasts, and the extent to which the scenario is based on hope rather than reason, is evident in Larry Kudlow's declaration of definite hope on his CNBC show.

> "I sincerely hope that the leading indicators are giving us the right message, it's very, very important. If that's true, then not only is this stock market completely for real, but the earnings picture is going to get better and better as we get into the second half of the year and into 2010. And we will get a recovery! Maybe two percent, maybe three percent, but it sure is better than what we had until now."
>
> —Larry Kudlow, *The Kudlow Report*, July 20, 2009

---

206. These forecasts for recovery, from July 2009, are slightly more optimistic than those of February 2009. At that time, the same analysts held more divergent opinions. Q2 2009: Alliance Bernstein, UBS. Q3 2009: Moody's, JP Morgan, Credit Suisse, Goldman Sachs, Barclays, Bank of America. Q4 2009: S&P, Morgan Stanley, Deutsche Bank, IHS Global Insight. Q1 2010 or beyond: Capital Economics, Fannie Mae.

Conclusion: The probability of a V-shaped recovery, especially one capable of leading into a genuine stock market bull and another New Economy is nil. This scenario is based on finance, not economics, and consists of little more than happy talk, wishful thinking, and billions of digital credit dollars being injected into the U.S. stock market by the Federal Reserve via Goldman Sachs. On a technical note, the rapid pace of the stock advance from March far more indicative of a major bear market rally correcting the previous decline prior to another, larger decline than it is of the start of a bull market preceding a long period of economic growth. Those of a more historical bent may find it worth noting that the Dow recovered 52 percent in the five months following the November 1929 low, which indicates that rapid stock market recoveries should probably not be considered a reliable indicator of economic recovery. Although the monetary and fiscal authorities will work very hard to create an illusion that this scenario is playing out, I consider it to be the least likely of the six scenarios over the course of the next decade.

Scenario 2: The Jobless Recovery
This scenario is a little more nebulous than the first scenario and is more pessimistic as well. The precise timing of the recovery is unknown, and little in the way of future growth estimates are provided. Jobless Recovery expects a longer U-shaped recovery that is in peril of turning into a W-shaped "double-dip recession" should another unforeseen shock to the system occur. This scenario tends to be favored by economists with a more global perspective, who are aware of the extent to which the economic contractions in countries across Europe and Asia have exceeded the recession to date in the United States, and who pay attention to the broader economic statistics that seldom appear in the headlines. Most of the Jobless Recovery adherents are, like their Green Shoots counterparts, conventional neo-Keynesian economists, but due to their concerns about the unexpectedly high unemployment rates, the uncertain state of foreign export markets, and the way in which the Obama stimulus plan has not generated the predicted results,

they are less sanguine about the prospects for economic growth in the near future. They also believe that whatever growth does occur will be insufficient to have a significant effect on the labor markets, so unemployment will remain higher than normal. In general, they don't think the U.S. economy can truly recover until the global economy does, and while they believe in the effectiveness of monetary and fiscal policy, they don't believe that the second stimulus package was large enough to accomplish its goals.

Those who subscribe to variants of the jobless recovery scenario include Paul Krugman, who has said the U.S. is heading for for a prolonged jobless recovery barring a second round of government stimulus money from the Obama administration. Others include Nobel laureate Joseph Stiglitz, the excellent economics blog Calculated Risk, Brad Delong of U.C. Berkeley, Andy Xie and Nouriel Roubini. There are some small signs that this could be the correct scenario, for as Calculated Risk pointed out, in June there were slight upticks in total housing starts, light vehicle sales, and new home sales that provided "a little sunshine" to those looking for signs of incipient growth in the statistical jungle. But despite these positive indicators that the two statistical engines primarily required to drive the U.S. economy out of recession, consumer spending and residential investment, are showing signs of improvement, both remain under pressure and could collapse again without providing much in the way of notice.

> "I see a one percent growth in the economy in the next few years. There will also be 11 percent unemployment next year and the recovery is going to be slow. It's going to feel like a recession even when it ends. We may be out of a freefall for the financial system. We have seen the worst in that sense. But in my view there is a sluggish U shaped recovery that might go into a W double dip if we don't fix the problems in the economy."
> —Nouriel Roubini, "Roubini Statement on the
> U.S. Economic Outlook," July 16, 2009

Conclusion: This is a superficially more credible scenario than Green Shoots, but it is still fundamentally based upon the same incorrect economic model and the same underlying assumptions about the way the economy works. While Jobless Recovery takes into account the international aspect of the crisis and properly discounts the significance of the stock market rally, it requires ignoring numerous historical warning signs, such as astronomical price/earnings ratios, the amount of total credit market debt, the increasing number of consumer bankruptcies and mortgage defaults, and the unknown impact of potential factors such as a series of large bank failures rendering the FDIC insolvent, the bankruptcy of a U.S. State, or a crash in the derivatives market. It also assumes the harmlessness of the increase in the national deficit to around $4 trillion and that if the gigantic increase in the money supply by the Federal Reserve proves to be successful, it can be safely drained off without an inflationary explosion. I believe that the consensus scenario will gradually transform from Green Shoots into Jobless Recovery, which will remain the mainstream consensus until it begins to become apparent in the autumn of 2010 that even Jobless Recovery is too optimistic. I consider this to be the fourth most likely scenario, ahead of only the first and sixth scenarios.

Scenario 3: Whiskey Zulu India
This is the inflation scenario, which foresees Bernanke and his famous printing press forcing the United States to follow the hyperinflationary lead of Germany's failed Weimar Republic and Robert Mugabe's Zimbabwe in a futile attempt to reinflate one more asset bubble. It is popular among many of the most-respected economic contrarians, including Jim Rogers, Marc Faber, Peter Schiff, the Mogambo Guru, Jim Sinclair, David Bruckner, Bill Fleckenstein, and a small horde of the metal investors known as gold bugs. These contrarians tend to be investors rather than economists, and they place less credence in aggregate statistics published by the various governments than they do in the actions of the central banks in aggressively injecting vast quantities of liquidity into the markets, the increase in federal intervention represented by the banking bailouts, the automotive bailouts, and the proposed national health

care program, and the difficulty that various national governments are beginning to experience in selling their debt.

The inflationists primarily show the influence of Austrian School and Classical economics; most are openly contemptuous of neo-Keynesianism and suspicious about the validity of most government-published data. Unlike those who subscribe to the first two scenarios, most of the Whiskey Zulu adherents did correctly anticipate both the financial crisis and recession. In fact, better-known individuals such as Peter Schiff and Jim Rogers had been vociferously warning of the structural weaknesses in the system, especially related to the credit and housing markets, for several years prior to the 2008 meltdown.

> "[W]e'll wind up with higher rates at a time when we are very dependent on *massive* stimulus and *extremely* low rates. Perversely, an improved economy could trigger an ugly outcome sooner, as higher rates could really wreak havoc in the housing market and all the debt outstanding. That will slow the economy, and then we'll lapse into recession. We saw a variation of this stop-go economic action in the 1970s – and wound up dealing with a whole lot of inflation. The bottom line is, we are in a box because we had a mania."
>
> —Bill Fleckenstein, "All Roads Lead to Inflation,"
> November 17, 2003

Of course, Fleckenstein clearly expected that instead of doing what responsible central bankers had previously done and taking the punch bowl away from the party,[207] Alan Greenspan would decide to spike the punch with 80 proof monetary policy, thus delaying the day of reckoning while ensuring it would be even more bitter. The Whiskey Zulu scenario assumes that because Greenspan failed to end the party by raising interest rates, the central banks of the world now have no choice but to engage in rapid inflation. They will have to fire up the printing presses because there is other way that the national governments they nominally serve can rea-

---

207. The primary responsibility of the central banker is "to take away the punch bowl just as the party gets going." William McChesney Martin, Jr., 9th Chairman of the Board of Governors of the Federal Reserve.

sonably hope to continue to pay interest on the massive public debts they have accrued, debts that are now growing faster than ever thanks to the record budgetary deficits being run. They see the recent stock market rise is nothing more than the same sort of central bank-created asset inflation that generated the previous stock market and housing bubbles, and view the collapse in the U.S. dollar index as evidence that the dollar is in rapid decline and will eventually go the way of the Papiermark and the Zimbabwean dollar, which last year had 12 zeroes from it as a consequence of that currency's 9 million percent inflation rate. Of particular concern as well is the fact that nothing fundamental has changed about the structure of the U.S. financial system despite its near-death experience.

> "I think we had a crisis and nothing has been solved. If you look at how the system works, the derivatives market, how banks operate, the profits at Goldman Sachs... usually, a major crisis like we had should clean the system. And nothing has been cleaned, it's gotten worse. Politically, the linkage between the politicians in America, and the Federal Reserve, and the Treasury Department, and Wall Street and so forth. The big crisis will yet come. It will be huge, it will be a total collapse. A total collapse!"[208]
>
> —Marc Faber, CNBC, July 20, 2009

Conclusion: I believe Whiskey Zulu is correct in many of the essentials with the significant exception of one specific element, which unfortunately happens to be the vital one. While the overall economic and financial picture have largely played out according to this scenario, prices in the commodities markets have plunged, which is precisely the opposite of what was expected to happen. Of

---

208. It should be noted that according to a Reuters report dated three days before the quoted CNBC broadcast, Faber – the original Dr. Doom – said he expects the stock market rally from the March intermediate low to last between 12 and 18 months, and that the ultimate crisis would take place sometime after that. This would indicate another stock market collapse leading to a deeper contraction sometime after the spring of 2010. Faber is definitely an inflationist, as he asserts 100 percent certainty that hyperinflation will take place. In February he told CNBC's *Asia Squawk Box:* "In the U.S., we have a totally new school, and it's called the Zimbabwe school....And that is the monetary policy the U.S. is pursuing."

particular concern is the price of gold; while it has risen threefold since 2002 when it was around $270, it has not taken off to the extent that everyone was expecting given the very loose monetary policy around the world and oversized increase in the various money supplies. I was biased towards the inflationist perspective for quite some time myself, and while I still have a high regard for many of these bold, contrarian analysts, the way in which events simply have not followed the path projected by the inflationary model to date causes me to doubt that we will see the rise in prices and the divergence between positive nominal GDP and negative real GDP projected by this scenario. I therefore consider this to be the third most likely scenario of the six; if the price of gold exceeds $1,500 per ounce by the end of 2010, this will be a strong indicator that the Whiskey Zulu scenario is unfolding.

Scenario 4: The Great Recession
This scenario is more of a range of loosely related scenarios than a singular one per se, and encompasses a variety of negative expectations that involve neither short-term economic recovery nor rampant inflation. As you might expect, those who subscribe to it are an eclectic lot, and include both respected establishment economists as well as star investment analysts. Most are not iconoclasts like their Whiskey Zulu counterparts, and unlike the inflationists they are more likely to utilize conventional economic theory. However, their opinions tend to be marked by an informed skepticism in the structure of the global financial system and an inability to believe that a brief dose of economic contraction will prove sufficient to get the global economy back on its previous track. The recurring theme tends to be one of a new economy, not in the sense of the Greenspan-era New Economy where computers and increased productivity meant that the old economic rules of scarcity no longer applied, but the end of an unsustainable period of widespread prosperity to which the industrialized economies of the West cannot expect to return.

Great Recessionists include the eminent Morgan Stanley economist Stephen Roach, bond kingpin Bill Gross, former U.S. Secretary of Labor Robert Reich, Hugh Hendry, David Rosenberg, and Meredith Whitney, whose frightening Halloween 2007 report on Citigroup correctly presaged the collapse of the banking sector. While most of these observers don't expect the economic contraction to reach the levels of the Great Depression, they don't see any recovery on the horizon either in any letter of the alphabet, including V, U, and L. Robert Reich, for example, has written that the economy can't recover because it can't return to what it was before the crash, while Whitney believes that the U.S. economy requires rebuilding from the ground up.

> "Our unbalanced world is now in the midst of a painful but necessary rebalancing what with the U.S. consumer most likely in the early stages of a multi-year contraction and the fact that there is no other consumer group to fill the void. As such, a post crisis global economy is likely to struggle for years to come."
> —Stephen Roach, "After the Era of Excess," March 5, 2009

Conclusion: What is noticeably missing from the various Great Recession scenarios, as expressed by those who adhere to one or another of the variants, is an appreciation for the continuing risks posed to the financial institutions, the multinational corporations, and even national governments by the incredible quantities of debt in which the global financial system is now awash. I also suspect their difficulty in picturing a more severe, if not longer-lasting scenario, is primarily due to the fact that most of them still lend credence to official government statistics. Despite these shortcomings, I consider the Great Recession to be the second most likely scenario to come to pass, as even if we are fortunate enough to avoid both hyperinflation and double-digit economic contraction through good fortune, God's grace, or flawless neo-Keynesian governance, there are still a long list of factors suggesting that the pre-2008 global economy remains unsustainable.

Scenario 5: Great Depression 2.0
As should surprise no one at this point, the return of the Great Depression is the scenario which I have seen developing since 2002.

Others saw this even earlier. Robert Prechter saw 2000 as the peak of the Grand Supercycle wave and went on record accordingly in his book *Conquer the Crash*. Immanuel Wallerstein, the venerable historian who has a far wider perspective than most, sees the present depression as part of a much larger systemic collapse caused by a chronic debt crisis that began in Poland in 1980. Others who view the future through a lens darkly include Paul Volcker,[209] Mike Shedlock, John J. Xenakis of Generational Dynamics, Steve Keen, John Williams of Shadowstats, and Barry Eichengreen, who, in partnership with Kevin Rourke, has created a series of illuminating charts that graphically demonstrate the way in which the present contraction exceeds the Great Depression on a global basis.[210]

> "The parallels between the Great Depression of the 1930s and our current Great Recession have been widely remarked upon .... This and most other commentary contrasting the two episodes compares America then and now. This, however, is a misleading picture. The Great Depression was a global phenomenon. Even if it originated, in some sense, in the US, it was transmitted internationally by trade flows, capital flows and commodity prices.... To sum up, globally we are tracking or doing even worse than the Great Depression, whether the metric is industrial production, exports or equity valuations. Focusing on the US causes one to minimize this alarming fact. The 'Great Recession' label may turn out to be too optimistic. This is a Depression-sized event."
> —Barry Eichengreen and Kevin H. O'Rourke,
> *A Tale of Two Depressions*, April 6, 2009

In the previous chapter, I delineated ten major reasons why the Great Depression 2.0 would be worse than its predecessor. And while Eichengreen's graphs are an excellent illustration of the greater

---

209. "One year ago, we would have said things were tough in the United States, but the rest of the world was holding up. The rest of the world has not held up. I don't remember any time, maybe even the Great Depression, when things went down quite so fast." Paul Volcker, February 20, 2009.

210. Barry Eichengreen and Kevin H. O'Rourke, "A Tale of Two Depressions," June 4, 2009. http://www.voxeu.org/index.php?q=node/3421.

magnitude of the current situation, the fact that the world stock markets have fallen faster, that the volume of world trade has contracted faster, and that the decline in world industrial output is roughly tracking the historical decline are all merely symptoms of the causal factor, which is the fact that most of the perceived economic growth that has taken place in recent decades was nothing more than debt-based consumption, it did not reflect an actual increase in global wealth. The ability to spend tomorrow's money today does not create any wealth, and to the extent that tomorrow's money is spent in a manner that serves to divert resources away from what otherwise would have been wealth-creating activities, it will reduce tomorrow's wealth despite the increase in consumption. And once tomorrow's money is spent, it becomes harder to find those who will accept payment in the day after tomorrow's money, and even harder to find those who will accept next week's money. Eventually, the system becomes unsustainable.

This increasing inability to spend next week's money today is exactly what is now beginning to be observed in the Treasury auctions around the world, as more and more national governments are finding it difficult to sell the debt that underlies their currencies. Even the market for U.S. debt is beginning to show signs of reaching the limits of its demand for it, and at a rather inopportune time considering that the federal government has announced its need to borrow significantly more money over the next decade by running ten years of deficits *conservatively* estimated to amount to $11.1 trillion. There is, of course, little chance that the actual deficits will not be even larger; the previous federal budget anticipated a $407 billion deficit in 2009, not the $1,845 billion one currently projected.

But the global debt problem is far from being solely a matter of national government debt. For example, the U.S. national debt of $11 trillion is less than a quarter of the $53 trillion in debt currently owed by U.S. households, corporations, and the various levels of government.

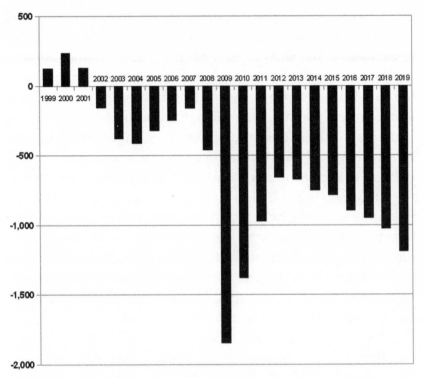

Figure 10.1. U.S. federal budget deficits, 1999–2019[211]

Table 10.2. Total Credit Market Debt by Sector, 2009 ($ millions)

Sector	Debt Owed	Debt Held	Credit Market Net
Household	13,748,485	4,263,533	-9,484,952
Financial	17,014,701	38,603,945	21,589,244
Corporate Non-financial	7,217,124	139,735	-7,077,389
State & Local Governments	2,262,454	1,404,718	-857,736
Federal Government[212]	6,826,945	443,720	-6,383,225

---

211. In billions. 1999 to 2008 are actual, 2009 to 2019 are projected. Source: "A Preliminary Analysis of the President's Budget and an Update of CBO's Budget and Economic Outlook," Congressional Budget Office, March 2009.

212. $4.6 trillion in U.S. Treasuries are held by various federal agencies, about half by the Federal Old-Age and Survivors Insurance Trust Fund. This accounts for difference between the $11 trillion national debt figure and the $6.8 trillion in outstanding credit market debt owed by the federal government.

These figures mark a significant change from the post-World War II period. While non-financial corporations and governments have long been debtors, the household sector has devolved from a 21 percent creditor position to one that is 69 percent debtor. The financial sector remains a net creditor, naturally, but its ratio of credit market debt held to credit market debt owed has fallen from 31.4 to 2.3. Furthermore, the financial sector's credit market debt held figure assumes that the various mortgages and credit card balances owned are actually worth their book value; due to the rising rate of foreclosures and bankruptcies we already know this cannot possibly be the case. So, it is possible that the entire financial sector is, like every other major sector of the U.S. economy, also facing net debtor status, and that total U.S. credit market debt is not 375 percent of GDP, but is actually approaching 400 percent.

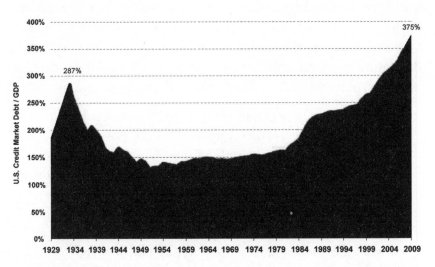

Figure 10.3: U.S. Credit Market Debt/GDP, 1929–2009[213]

There is more to the severe economic threat posed by these excessive debt levels than is suggested by mere historical pattern recognition. This has to do with the distinction between the inflationists

213. Source: Morgan Stanley, The Daily Reckoning, Federal Reserve Statistical Release Z.1: Flow of Funds Accounts of the United States, June 11, 2009.

and the deflationists. While much of the Great Depression scenario is clearly recognized by the Whiskey Zulu adherents as being
relevant to it, the major distinction between the hyperinflation
scenario and Great Depression 2.0 is the inflationist belief in the ability of the central banks to create sufficient money to repay the outstanding debt. However, since modern "paper" money is actually
debt, this creates a tautological dilemma. Debt can be devalued by
paper, but debt cannot be devalued by debt. It must be delever-
aged; Australian economist Steven Keen has noted that the initial
deleveraging process in Australia has already begun at a faster pace
than it did in the 1930s; it has not even started yet in the United
States where debt to GDP is still rising. But it will. And though it's
true that a printing press can print unlimited quantities of dollar
bills, not even Ben Bernanke's magical printing press is capable of
printing buyers of U.S. Treasuries. Robert Prechter explains both
the nature of the debt-money problem as well as its eventual outcome; while he frames his analysis in terms of Elliott Wave theory,
that is irrelevant to the economic case he is making with regards to
the nature of credit inflation and the way in which it renders inherently vulnerable any economy that is dependent upon it.

> "The tremendous inflation of the past 76 years has occurred
> primarily by way of instruments of credit, not banknotes.
> Credit can implode. The only monetary outcome that will
> make sense of the Elliott wave structure is for the market
> value of dollar-denominated credit to shrink by over 90 per-
> cent. Given the eroded state of capital goods in the U.S. and
> the depletion of manufacturing capacity, it is not hard to see
> why all these IOUs have a deteriorating basis of repayment.
> The future has already been fully mortgaged; it's time to pay.
> But there is no money to pay, only more IOUs, which cannot
> be paid either. So the credit supply (after a brief respite) will
> continue to shrink, which means that wealth, and therefore
> purchasing power, will disappear along with it.... I expect
> that the final implosion in credit value will be so swift that
> the authorities will not act in time to counter it. They will
> continue to try to maintain the fictions of full face value for

IOUs until they fail spectacularly to keep up the scam. Then
they will start to scramble, but it will be too late."
—Robert Prechter, *The Elliott Wave Theorist*, April 18, 2009

Conclusion: The Great Depression 2.0 is what is presently developing, although due to a reactive wave of positive social mood, statistical obfuscation, and understandable denial, it will take about a
year for the consensus opinion to cycle through the various scenarios in descending order of optimism before the grim reality
finally becomes apparent to even the casual observer.

Fallout 4 Live
It sounds both absurd and extreme to seriously consider a dooms-
day scenario that encompasses not only a metaphorical economic
Armageddon, but a genuine global catastrophe involving the collapse of national governments, widespread famine, large scale military conflict, and a significant reduction in the human population.
Aside from the global warming profiteers and Christian eschatolo-
gists keeping a wary eye out for the Antichrist, no economist even
pretends to subscribe to this scenario, although Robert Prechter admitted that there was a time when he was concerned that the Elliott
waves were on the verge of predicting a Millennium bear wave
rather than a downturn of mere Grand Supercycle magnitude.

The good news about the catastrophic scenario is that at least
we can be confident that the global youth are adequately prepared
for it, having been in training for literal decades since the release
of *Gamma World* by TSR in 1978. Considering the widespread
popularity of post-apocalyptic survival games such as the *Resident
Evil*, *Fallout*, and *Left 4 Dead* series, we can be confident that the
surviving remnants of humanity will be more than a match for
any number of rampaging zombies, radioactive mutants, or hyper-
intelligent killer cockroaches.

"They're going to need the more practical skills, like how to
build a shelter from abandoned cars or how to find drinking
water by collecting the morning dew in human skulls. That's

the type of knowledge these kids are going to need when their world has been turned into a brutal Hellscape."

—Ted Levinson, *In The Know with Clifford Barnes*, February 25, 2009[214]

Conclusion: This is the second-least likely scenario, ahead of only the highly improbable immaculate recovery leading to the halcyon days of recent yore. It's still very unlikely, though, and I would no more lose any sleep over it than I would borrow money to invest in a triple-leveraged ETF focused on banking stocks. Unfortunately, I find it more probable that Iran will purchase a few nukes from North Korea or Pakistan and set them off in shipping containers near the Port of Haifa and Manhattan Island, or that China will decide to rid itself of its excess male population by launching an invasion of Taiwan, than worldwide fiscal and monetary stimulus will prove able to fix the global economic problems caused by too much government spending and too much debt.

Calculating the Great Depression 2.0

I made my first attempt to calculate the extent and length of the current contraction in a *WorldNetDaily* column published in November 2008. It is reproduced here, in its entirety:

> It's remarkable to see how quickly mainstream economists have gone from declaring a new age of permanent global prosperity to apocalyptic predictions of doom, gloom and financial Ragnarok. However, it's important to remember that no matter what the politicians, bankers and CNBC commentators would like us to believe, the Dow does not make up the entirety of the U.S. economy and even if Manhattan and Washington, D.C., were to vanish tomorrow, the rest of the country would continue to exist.

---

214. On the other hand, it must be noted that analyst David Barrowdale is pessimistic about the actual quality of that training. On the panel which addressed the vital question "Are violent video games adequately preparing children for the apocalypse?" he complained: "The games make it all seem deceptively simple. I mean, in the future a kid's not going to be able to kill a six-foot long irradiated beetle just by pressing a few buttons. He's going to have to get in there with an axe, and hack, and hack, and hack!"

One can even make a reasonable case that it would be much better off in the long run. But I digress.

While notable liberals such as Paul Krugman and Tom Friedman are already crying "Code Red" and banging the drum for a second and larger New Deal, it should be noted that according to Austrian economic theory, complete panic is not necessarily in order. This is important, because unlike the Neo-Keynesianism to which the mainstream economists and columnists adhere, Austrian theory correctly predicted the present crisis. And unlike Neo-Keynesian theory, Austrian economics provides a heuristic device to roughly estimate how bad the economic contraction is likely to be.

Because the debt-inflated economic boom was the problem, creating as it did the sort of resource misallocations that are presently being corrected by the ongoing layoffs, foreclosures and bankruptcies, we know that the magnitude of the correction should be approximately the size of the expansion. And since we already know the extent of the historical contraction and expansion, this means we can compare that relationship to the recent expansion to calculate how much the economy is likely to contract in the near future.

The Great War caused U.S. GDP to bottom out in 1914. In the 15 years through 1929, the U.S. economy grew 184 percent, during which time total local, state and federal government spending increased 234 percent. Following the recession of the early 1990s, the 15 years from 1993 through 2008 (est) saw the U.S. economy grow 118 percent, with a concomitant increase in total government spending of 116.5 percent. As impressive has the recent long boom has been, it is actually smaller in percentage terms than its historical antecedent.

Why does the recent expansion seem so much larger? Why do things seem so much more out of hand? There are at least two reasons: First, the equity markets expanded at an even faster rate than the 1920s economy did; the Dow rose 320 percent from October 1992 to October 2007. But, as has already been noted, the stock market is not the economy. Second, the expansion from the most recent recession, in 2001, is of strikingly similar size to the historical expansion subsequent to the 1921 recession.

1922–1929: 41.4 percent GDP growth and 25.8 percent increase total spending

2002–2008: 42.3 percent GDP growth and 42.9 percent increase total spending

The important question, then, is which point in time should the beginning of the expansion be traced. Since the Federal Reserve has been cutting interest rates and attempting to stave off economic contraction since the dot com bubble burst in 2000, I think the longer period is probably the more relevant. A comparison of the two 15-year expansions indicates a projected contraction that would be expected to hit its nadir at 64 percent of the contraction during the Great Depression. Since GDP declined by 45.6 percent from 1929 to 1933, this would indicate a 29.2 percent contraction to a GDP of $10.14 trillion in 2013.

Combined with the expected population growth, this points to a GDP per capita of $29,920, which would certainly mean a palpable reduction in the American standard of living but not mass poverty of the sort that would trigger total social chaos, much less a return to caves and grass huts. A depression of these proportions would be expected to drive up the unemployment level to around 17 percent, and require waiting until 2018 for the economy to return to current levels.

Of course, there is a panoply of reasons why these projections could be completely incorrect. Government statistics are notoriously inaccurate, and given the understated inflation of the last eight years, it's entirely possible that the economy has actually been in contraction for the entirety of 2008. No one knows the full extent of the derivatives debacle or how its unwinding is likely to exacerbate the ongoing crisis. Constrained by George Bush's spending and its own left-wing ideology, the Obama administration may not be able to either increase spending or slash upper income taxes as much as its academic allies would advise.

> But, one can only work with the numbers with which one is provided. And regardless of how the scenario plays out, it should be eminently clear that these are perilous financial times that demand prudence of every responsible man.
>
> —"Calculating the Next Depression,"
> *WorldNetDaily*, November 24, 2008

However, I now believe that this perspective is a little too optimistic due to a number of factors, many of which were previously mentioned. First, in the column I made use of the commonly cited nominal GDP figures which were exaggerated by the deflation of the Great Contraction period from 1929 to 1933. Second, in addition to the huge and ineffective second stimulus plan, the continued leveraging of the U.S. economy, the global trade statistics, worldwide contracyclical policy measures and the rising unemployment rates, other factors such as dividend yields, bond yield/stock yield ratios, and the Dow/gold ratio all indicate that the equity markets are trading in ranges more akin to market tops than market bottoms.[215] Moreover, the unreliability of GDP, especially when one considers the amount of statistical revision that has taken place over the last eight decades, means that it is probably a mistake to place too much emphasis on the comparative size of the 1914-1929 and the 1993-2008 expansions as measured in GDP.

Therefore, I have concluded that the next depression will not be smaller than its predecessor, but larger and longer. Utilizing total credit market debt as a proxy for the relative size of the contractions, I estimate that Great Depression 2.0 will be approximately one-third worse than the Great Depression. This indicates a 35 percent decline in real GDP over a five-year period, indicating a nadir of 9,455 sometime between the end of 2012 and the middle of 2013. This calculation is necessarily somewhat vague because the National Bureau of Economic Research dates the beginning of the contraction to December 2007, while the Bureau of Economic Analysis shows the peak in nominal GDP to have been 14,546.7 in

---

215. Andrew Lunstad, *Attractive Bottoms*. Lewisburg: Bucknell University Press, 1991. 41.

the third quarter of 2008 and the peak in real GDP (chained 2005 dollars) to have been 13,415.3 in the *second* quarter of 2008.[216]

Four quarters of contraction have wiped out $522 billion in real dollars; four more years would see the elimination of another $4.2 trillion, thus implying an approximate doubling in the rate of contraction from what has been seen to date. With an estimated U.S. population of 327,368,017 in 2012, this suggests a GDP per capita of $28,914, which is roughly that of modern Israel. Difficult, to be sure, but again hardly something to suggest mass cannibalism. However, a lengthy contraction of this proportion will be enough to devastate the financial markets and probably to destroy the U.S. dollar, at least in its current manifestation as a Federal Reserve Note. I expect the Dow/Gold ratio to drop to around 1.25; it is presently at 9.56.[217] Barring a hyperinflation scenario that sees the price of gold rise above the $5,000 mark, this implies a series of market crashes that will take the Dow below 1,500.

Since the stock markets tend to be a leading indicator, it can be useful to know what to look for in a major market bottom that would precede the economy's eventual rebound. Two primary measures are price/earnings ratios from 5-7 and dividend yields in excess of 10 percent. As of July 31, 2009, the P/E ratio of the S&P 500 was 17.6 and the dividend yield was 1.96 percent. Note that these time frames only mark the estimated bottoms and it will take much longer for GDP and other related statistics to return to their 2008 values. Since the Great Depression lasted seven years when measured in real terms, it will probably be 2018 before U.S. GDP again exceeds $14.4 trillion in 2009 dollars, and sometime in the 2020s before whatever passes for the Dow Jones Industrial Average – which may not survive the ravaging of Wall Street – exceeds 14,000 again.

Obviously, these estimates will prove to be ludicrously inaccurate if it turns out that a new bull market began in March 2009 or

---

216. I have calculated the real decline from the nominal figure, since that's the one that is widely reported. If one takes the real $13.4 trillion figure as a starting point, this would provide an estimated bottom of $8.7 trillion.

217. It is perhaps worth noting that this is 52 percent below the *1929* high and 77 percent below the 1999 peak. The 1932 Dow/Gold low was 2.14.

if the hyperinflation scenario takes place. But, when one considers the sixty percent plus price declines during 2008 in every commodity market from cotton and corn to copper and oil at a time when it seemed as if every financial expert in the world was warning of peak oil, imminent inflation, and food shortages, it seems fairly evident that the debt-deflation of the 1930s and the return of the Great Depression is nigh.

WHAT CAN BE DONE?

In truth, because of the continued profligacy of the government
and Federal Reserve, the imbalances that caused the current
recession have actually worsened. We are now in an even deeper
hole than when the crisis began. Rather than wrapping up a
recession, we are actually sinking into a depression. If things look
better now, it's just because we are in the eye of the storm.... In
order to lay the foundation for real and lasting recovery, market
forces must be allowed to repair the damage. However,
current policy is counterproductive to this end.

—PETER SCHIFF, "Happy Days Aren't Here Again,"
August 1, 2009

T HE FIRST, and most important, thing that every economic
actor inhabiting the wealthy, industrialized economies needs
to understand and accept is that there is no easy, magical solution
to a situation that has taken decades to come to fruition. Regardless of whether one traces the roots of the problem back to the
1971 creation of the "full faith and credit" debt-dollar, the 1933
abandonment of the gold standard, or the 1913 establishment of
the Federal Reserve, this is not a crisis that developed overnight
and it will not sort itself out quickly either. The short answer to
the question posed by the title of this chapter is nothing. The car
has already hit the tree and the bumper is already in the process of
buckling inward, so there is no time to turn the wheel or fasten
seatbelts. It is too late to do anything but scream.

Economies do not turn on a dime and when they do turn, they
usually provide a panoply of indicators suggesting that change is

coming. The absence of these indicators, both statistical and anecdotal, is why most of the economic contrarians who correctly
anticipated the present crisis are so confident that it is not over.
While mainstream economists look at charts that compare the
declines in real GDP from their previous peak and conclude that
because, at 4 percent, it was worse than the ten previous U.S.
recessions since 1947 and therefore must be over, this is simply an
artifact of their overreliance on an increasingly irrelevant statistical measure. The main reason that the economic situation currently looks as if the pace of contraction has slowed is because
GDP is primarily a measure of spending, which through the black
magic of debt issuance can continue to take place even when there
is no increase in anything productive. Moreover, due to the specific
formula involved, a decline in spending on imports actually counts
as an increase in domestic consumption; the only positive components in the improvement from the -6.4 percent contraction of the
first quarter of 2009 to the -1.0 contraction of the second quarter
were increased government spending and decreased spending on
imports.[218] That the government spending $35 billion in money it
manifestly does not have while the American people are spending
$72 billion *less* on imported goods and services[219] is supposed to
indicate the economy is *growing* is about as complete a condemna-
tion of GDP as a statistical measure as should be required to justify
its abandonment.

Imagine if Americans completely stopped buying the $2 trillion
in imports they purchase every year, but without a corresponding
increase in the number of domestic goods sold. No more Nin-
tendos, no more Sonys, no more German cars or cheap Chinese
clothes. Would anyone believe this complete absence of economic

---

218. "The decrease in real GDP in the second quarter primarily reflected negative contributions
from nonresidential fixed investment, personal consumption expenditures (PCE), residential
fixed investment, private inventory investment, and exports that were partly offset by positive
contributions from federal government spending and state and local government spending.
Imports, which are a subtraction in the calculation of GDP, decreased." "National Income and
Product Accounts, Gross Domestic Product: Second Quarter 2009 (Advance estimate),"
Bureau of Economic Analysis, July 31, 2009.

219. It's not as if the decline in imports meant an increase in exports either. American exports
declined $26 billion in the second quarter of 2009.

activity to be a genuine sign that the American economy was healthy and growing? Of course not! And yet, under the present statistical regime, this would be reported as a veritable economic miracle! Whereas in reality, removing these two "positive" contributions from the most recent GDP indicates that the economy was shrinking at an annual rate more than four times faster than reported in the second quarter of 2009. If you take into account the $55 billion increase in government debt-spending and the $398 billion decline in American imports since the recession began,[220] then the present peak-to-trough contraction is 7.3 percent in real terms, which is nearly twice that reported and much closer to the 5.7 percent cumulative contraction reported in the U.K. and the 7 percent contraction reported in Japan for the last two quarters alone. This is fast approaching the ten percent territory that is sometimes used as a crude indicator of modern economic depression.

Returning to the question of what can be done, the longer answer requires division into the tactical and strategic perspectives. At the tactical level, there are a number of practical policies that can be implemented at the present level of economic understanding, much of which is even compatible with the mainstream economic paradigm. These policies are unlikely to make things better in the short run, in fact, they may well make things look worse initially by stripping away some comforting illusions, but they will at least ensure that the situation is not actively exacerbated by the fiscal and monetary authorities. Ten immediate measures that would help bring about economic recovery sooner rather than later are as follows:

1. Stop pouring gasoline on the fire. The Federal Reserve must raise interest rates and permit deflation to accelerate the deleveraging process. The sooner it's over, the sooner real economic growth can begin.

---

220. These are chained 2005 real dollars, as per Table 3B. Real Gross Domestic Product and Related Measures from the Q2 2009 Advance report. The second quarter of 2008 presently marks the peak GDP figure in real terms, at $13,415.3 billion in 2005 dollars. The peak in nominal GDP occurred one quarter later, at $14,546.7 billion. Removing the decrease in imports and the increase in government spending over the last four quarters would reduce real GDP to $12,438.9 billion.

2. No more financial necromancy. No more bailouts. An organization that is too big to fail is too big to be permitted to exist in its bloated, risk-laden form. Financial institutions which are insolvent and only survive thanks to life support provided by the Fed and the U.S. Treasury must be permitted to go bankrupt so that their useful deposits and assets can be acquired by more productive owners. This applies to non-banking corporations as well.

3. Cut state and federal income taxes in half. Federal tax receipts have already fallen significantly on a year-on-year basis, 27.3 percent for individual income and 89.6 percent for corporate as of April 2009, so the only way to increase the forty percent of GDP that is personal consumption is going to be permitting consumers to keep more of their money. C not only possesses a higher multiple than G, but is more efficient as well. This will also help the deleveraging process by enabling consumers to more quickly extricate themselves from debt.

4. Eliminate all federal spending that cannot be supported by a supermajority in both the House and Senate. Yes, every Congressman and Senator will hate this idea, but they're even less likely to enjoy their fates should the nation and the economy continue on their present trajectory. California would not be on the verge of bankruptcy today if its legislators had been forced to reign in state spending in the same manner they were forced to limit state tax rates. A third U.S. stimulus plan should be absolutely out of the question, given the failure of the first two.

5. Audit the Federal Reserve. The chances are high that there are some ugly truths yet to be discovered in the central bank's books and it is absurd for Fed officials to hide behind their "independence" as an excuse to keep their records from the public. Every American corporation and individual is subject to having their records audited by various government agencies and this doesn't make them any less independent or any more intrinsically part of the federal government than the Federal Reserve System.

6. Repeal the Gramm-Leach-Bliley Act of 1999, the Garn-St. Germain Depository Institutions Act of 1982, and elements of the Depository Institutions Deregulation and Monetary Control Act of 1980. Partial deregulation combined with the nationalization of losses is much more dangerous in terms of the systemic risk it creates than either full nationalization or full deregulation. Also, the SEC's power to license and regulate stock exchanges should be curtailed. The Madoff scheme showed the uselessness of the SEC as a fraud police while the very concept of a conventional stock exchange is technologically outmoded. Forcing entrepreneurs to work through investment banks in order to access capital markets is one of the primary brakes on entrepreneurial and technological development today.

7. Withdraw American troops from Afghanistan, Iraq, South Korea, Europe, and most of the dozens of countries around the world where they are stationed. Wars are expensive and a nation that is deeply in debt while facing economic depression cannot afford the expense of fighting unnecessary ones. Because major economic downturns are often accompanied by significant military conflicts, it is vital to save military resources for when they are absolutely required rather than expending them on missions that are tangential at best to the national interest.

8. Halt immigration and provide significant financial incentive for married women with children to raise them at home. Throughout the 1960s, when GDP growth was at its highest during the post-war period, only 37 percent of the U.S. population was employed. After a decade of no net job creation, 46.5 percent of the population is employed. Immigration and a doubling of the female labor force are why average weekly wages are lower in 2009 than their peak in 1973. If one examines the pattern in the Bureau of Labor Statistics figures, it's readily apparent that young women, including married mothers, are forced to work so that men over the age of 55 can collect retirement and play

golf.[221] This is not the hallmark of a functioning economy in a sustainable society.

9. Ban banking bonuses and put hard caps on compensation for all banking employees, including executives. Nothing has undermined the confidence in the system more than for the American people to see their taxes shoveled to the banks under the guise of an emergency, then seeing those banks pay out ludicrous sums of money to their employees. In 2008, Goldman Sachs, Morgan Stanley, JP Morgan Chase, Citigroup, and Merrill Lynch received $100 billion in bailout money, *lost* $44.4 billion, and paid out $27 billion in bonuses.[222] It's time to call the banks on their threat that their best employees will find employment elsewhere; where, one wonders, do they expect they will make similar money? And considering the havoc they have wreaked on the American economy, wouldn't it be in the best interest of the American people to encourage them to do so?

10. End the federal monetary monopoly. Removing the Federal Reserve's charter would be a reasonable start, and indeed, may become a political necessity sooner than anyone believes, but the problem stems more from the government-granted monopoly on money than it does the particular form this latest monopolistic establishment happens to take. The three previous central bank monopolies weren't ended because they worked so well, after all. As with everything else, the benefit of monetary decentralization is that when a currency fails, as every currency in the history of mankind has been eventually known to do, at least its failure will only financially ruin a limited number of users. As the global financial crisis is now demonstrating in real-time, the more widely held the currency, the more people that will be negatively effected by its ultimate failure.

---

221. Since 1950, the percentage of women 25-34 in the labor force has increased from 34 percent to an estimated 81 percent in 2010. The participation rate of Men 55+ is estimated to have declined from 66 percent to 42 percent. Mitra Toosi, "A century of change: the U.S. labor force, 1950–2050," *Monthly Labor Review*, May 2002. Pp. 15-28.
222. Andrew M. Cuomo, "No Rhyme or Reason: The 'Heads I Win, Tails You Lose' Bank Bonus," July 30, 2009.

There is very little chance that any of these practical policies will be adopted. The Federal Reserve and the SEC will probably be given more power, not less. If American troops are removed from Iraq, it will probably be in order to send them to Afghanistan or Iran. State and federal taxes will be raised, banks will be pressured to provide more credit, and the Obama administration will probably attempt at least two further rounds of economic stimulus before finally, like the Roosevelt administration, giving up in despair. However, the social mood of the nation after eight years of desultory war and economic stagnation is such that it appears unlikely Obama will be given eight more years to try to bring about economic recovery, international stability, and full employment. And the fact that his experts are equipped with the wrong theoretical tools all but ensures that no amount of effort or audacious hope will bring about success.

> [M]any of the more ambitious and impatient students of these problems refuse to recognize these limitations to our possible knowledge, and possible power of prediction, and therefore also of our possible power of control.... It seems to me more and more that the immense efforts which during the great popularity of macroeconomics over the last thirty or forty years have been devoted to it, were largely misspent.
> —F.A. Hayek, "Coping with Ignorance," 1978

The particular danger of the present crisis is that its global nature not only threatens the end of the United States Federal Reserve Note as the world's reserve currency, but U.S. national sovereignty as well. For the last sixty years, the usual response of global policymakers around the world to economic crises has been to address them with organizational solutions that involve multiple layers of international bureaucracy combined with increased centralization. The United Nations, the World Bank, and the International Monetary Fund are only three of the hundreds of international organizations with aspirations towards global governance. In 1988, the *Economist* published a piece entitled "Get Ready for the Phoenix" in which it made the case for an international currency and a global

Federal Reserve.[223] Given the increasing probability that there will be economic ashes for this phoenix to rise from, the projected introductory date of 2018 appears rather more plausible than it did twenty-one years ago.

More recently, the *Economist* had something pertinent to say about the strategic implications of the global economic crisis for the science of economics. "[T]wo central parts of the discipline— macroeconomics and financial economics—are now, rightly, being severely re-examined. There are three main critiques: that macro and financial economists helped cause the crisis, that they failed to spot it, and that they have no idea how to fix it."[224] As can be seen with regards to the unreliability of GDP, one of the first things we need is better statistical measures, which means that we need to rethink the basic assumptions of both macroeconomics and financial economics. Conventional macroeconomics, with its long record of predictive failure and scientific irrelevance, needs to be abandoned along with the aggregate-focused general theory that supports it. Financial economics is ahead of macroeconomics on this score, as the uselessness of the random walk and efficient market theories is already widely recognized. Fortunately, we already have a pretty good idea of where we can find reasonable foundations for rebuilding our understanding of aspects of the discipline.

The combination of Austrian business cycle theory and praxeology with behavioral economics offers a much sounder logical and empirical basis for macroeconomics than the theoretical shambles of neo-Keynesian econometrics that serve as economic orthodoxy today. The socionomic theory of finance markets is far less well-established, but it is already more scientifically coherent

---

223. "The phoenix zone would impose tight constraints on national governments. There would be no such thing, for instance, as a national monetary policy. The world phoenix supply would be fixed by a new central bank, descended perhaps from the IMF. The world inflation rate – and hence, within narrow margins, each national inflation rate – would be in its charge. Each country could use taxes and public spending to offset temporary falls in demand, but it would have to borrow rather than print money to finance its budget deficit. With no recourse to the inflation tax, governments and their creditors would be forced to judge their borrowing and lending plans more carefully than they do today. This means a big loss of economic sovereignty, but the trends that make the phoenix so appealing are taking that sovereignty away in any case." "Get Ready for the Phoenix," *Economist*. September 1, 1988.

224. "What went wrong with economics," *Economist*. July 16, 2009.

and credible than the efficient market hypothesis, the random walk theory, or the M3 amalgamation of Minsky, Maxwell and Mandlebrot and is the most credible candidate on the financial economics side. While Austrian economics and socionomics cannot bring about an end to the present crisis, they may help us comprehend what is happening as the crisis continues to unfold in the interest of avoiding similar crises in the future.

Although we can expect to eventually improve our understanding of both human events and human action, it must always be kept in mind that when it comes to human nature, there is nothing new under the sun. Because economics is a social science and cannot be separated from human nature, one should always be deeply skeptical of any economic theory which claims to replace long-established economics laws or serves as a justification to allow one man to dispose of the property of another. The "New Economy" of Alan Greenspan was never more than a mirage and the outmoded "New Economics" of John Maynard Keynes will not rescue the world from a second Great Depression that it neither predicted nor prevented.

We have been very fortunate to live through a unique time in human history where literal billions have enjoyed the benefit of what most of our ancestors would have regarded as unbelievable prosperity. That prosperity has not necessarily come to an end, but it is at risk in a manner in which it has not been for decades. Demagogues will appear, promising the public those old lies of free lunches and something for nothing that have seduced so many over the centuries. The death of capitalism and the free market will be pronounced again and again, while politicians sacrifice economic liberty on the altar of economic security and in doing so lose both. New theories with new names will be offered as new justifications for preserving the failed status quo and further expanding the power of those who already wield it. There will be wars and rumors of wars, as governments and nations fall. And the people of the world will be increasingly called upon to accept centralized, authoritarian government by an unelected technocratic elite. For the nature of Man is such that there are always would-be rulers who wait with great anticipation for difficult times such as these.

Depressions have been times of crisis, chaos, conflict and change for most of human history. The terrible depression of the late third century[225] was not only contemporaneous with great structural changes to the Roman Empire, but bore witness to the first voluntary abdication of an emperor. The Great Depression wrought tremendous changes in American society and the American people that still echo today. Eighty years later, the return of the Great Depression will surely inspire changes of similar magnitude, but we must dare to hope that this time, Americans and the people of other nations around the world will discover that the solution will not be found in more government control over society, but through an increase in human liberty and freedom for the individual economic actor.

---

225. "When Diocletian came to the throne in 284, he found three great problems before him...The third and hardest was mainly economic – to restore the dwindled agriculture, commerce, and population of the Empire. On this Diocletian and Constantine went wrong together. They not only failed to cure the evil, but greatly increased it. Not much was gained by remitting taxes that could not be paid, and settling barbarian colonists and barbarian serfs in the wasted provinces. Serious economic difficulties have moral causes, and there was no radical cure short of a complete change in the temper of society. Yet much might have been done by a permanent reduction of taxation and a reform of its incidence and of the methods of collection. Instead of this, the machinery of government (and its expense) was greatly increased. The army had to be held in check by courts of Oriental splendour and a vast establishment of corrupt officials. We can see the growth of officialism even in the language, if we compare the Latin words in Athanasius with those in the New Testament. So heavier taxes had to be levied from a smaller and poorer population. Taxation under the Empire had never been light ; in the third century it grew heavy, under Diocletian it was crushing, and in the later years of Constantine the burden was further increased by the enormous expenditure which built up the new capital like the city in a fairy tale. We are within sight of the time when the whole policy of the government was dictated by dire financial need." J.B. Bury, ed. *The Cambridge Medieval History, Vol. I.* Cambridge: Cambridge University Press, 1911. 20.

An Infernal Economy

Canto I

In a dark woodland I espied a bear
Vicious, hirsute, with a low, evil brow.
His stinking breath befouled the forest air;
A roar, and animal spirits somehow
Vanished, like ghosts dissipating in mist,
Taking with them fully half from the Dow.
I knew not how I should hope to resist
This great beast, when before me then appeared
A genius, albeit one much dismissed,
For espousing truths both exact and feared
By men parsimonious in wisdom.
"No man, yet I act," said him I revered,
"To spare thee much needless pain have I come!"
Then he raised a gleaming sword of pure gold
Before which the terrible beast did succumb
And turn away. Thus inspired I made bold
To inquire of insights he might convey.
"No, I shall not teach, instead shall I scold.
Come, thou shalt witness how ends the soiree!"
We found ourselves before a wide Abyss
From which came moans and cries of great dismay,
The regrets of men who'd been so remiss
As to believe markets will always rise.
"Speak, damned broker," I said with a hiss,
To a wretched shade with dark, haunted eyes,

All naked but for his well-tattered suit.
"Every long-term chart showed we were wise."
He protested, his contrition acute.
"Dollar-cost averaging, interest compound,
We thought they invested risk free, absolute!"
My Guide laughed, it was a cold, hollow sound
Of scorn for innocence so misplaced.
"That which goes up must finally come down,
And asset inflation will be retraced.
For growth cannot last indefinitely
When debt is rising and money debased."
Behind us we left that sad misery,
Weeping and wailing under the cliff's edge,
Descending down to the second degree.
There we encountered the god of the pledge,
Visa, the Master of living and dead.
Who sneered at my Guide: "From whence didst thou dredge
This old fossil, academic unread
By my countless servants, my serfs, my slaves?
He shall not enter, but for thee, instead
I'll offer a card that actually saves
Thee five percent even as thou doth spend!"
Temptation rushed o'er me, enticing waves,
Cast by the fat goblin off'ring to lend
Me all that I wanted, and more beside!
"Stand fast, man, and do not think thou shalt bend!"
So spoke my Guardian, the consummate Guide,
Who, bare-handed, tore that false god in half!
"His day is done, comest thou alongside.
Seest the shades blown like wheat amidst chaff?"
Throughout the depths blew a most fearsome wind
Hurling poor souls around, all the riff-raff
In mighty numbers, those fools who had sinned,
Caught up in the feverish gluttony
Of consumption, and now, too late, chagrined.
They tumbled through clouds of fiat money,

Faith rendered faithless in one mad moment,
Then came a pair still in matrimony
Bound. They shrieked and fought for they did resent
The ties that held them linked close together
In bitter rage and mutual dissent.
The woman cried, clawing at her tether.
Impoverished, angry, seeking divorce,
And falling for the netherest nether
They plunged to the depths like a Russian bourse.
"New house, new clothes, new car financed with debt
They married for better, but found the worst,"
Said the Master without sounding upset.
"So now, they can't even pay for a split!"
Such countless horrors no one could forget,
Happily did I that fell mirk acquit.
But new torments I saw, new terrors. I found
Myself standing in the midst of a pit,
Where an icy rain came tumbling down
Upon the unjust, and the unjust alone,
For there the just in their absence abound.
Suffering journalists wept to atone
For lying deceits practiced on the crowd.
While above towered three heads overgrown
From one horrid shape better disavowed,
Kudlow and Cramer and Bartiromo.
Three slavering heads drooled and barked aloud:
"Buy with both hands, this is doubtless the low!"
All the while snapping and snarfing up dirt.
Souls sold for nothing, not even a show,
No newspaperman had so much as a shirt
As hatless, shoeless, they froze in the rain,
Lamenting the truth they'd tried to pervert.
Shivering, I asked to depart this plane
A request to which my Guide acceded.
Thus we abandoned the media's bane,
The encroaching ice quickly receded.

235

Before us there stood rows of mighty stones
And behind each a small man proceeded
To push it back and forth, with moans and groans,
Across the dismal field of outsized dreams.
"Economists," I heard the amused tones
Of the Guide, "and duly damned for their schemes
That served as the key to open the door
For terrible tax-and-spending regimes."
I spared but a brief sigh for Nobel's whore
As we fell to a field of sepulchers
Uncovered and belching forth with a roar
Crimson flames that seared those entrepreneurs
Of finance, gamblers, investment bankers
Who played games with exotic wire transfers.
Those who had been for their banks anchors
Howled in unending agony, the fire
Fueled by derivatives, lethal cankers
Of financial cunning that now require
Unthinkable time to fully unwind.
Until then, each screams in his stone pyre.
No more could I bear, horror smote my mind,
I reeled before sights I could not forget.
And then my adviser did me remind
We'd yet to meet the political set.

Canto II

At the peak of a lofty precipice
A noisome stench wafted high in the air,
And yet my guide commenced to reminisce
As if there was no mirksome foulness there.
It was ever so at the cycle's peak,
He said with a rueful shake of despair.
Greed, whispered words, and an air of mystique
Brings the innocent lambs to the slaughter.
They hope to catch on to the winning streak,

Doomed, from the start, come Hell or high water.
But justice they'll have, for here it is found,
Payback for each duplicitious fraudster.
He showed me a path that led further down,
Deeper into that corpse-scented chasm.
O Guide, do warn me what we'll find here bound,
What sort of odoriferous phantasm?
I know not how I shall hope to bear this.
For I much feared an internal spasm.
Was imminent, given the foul abyss.
But I soon forgot my sense of affliction
As we looked upon the flowers of Dis.
For there was planted without restriction
An orchard such as none have ever seen,
Nor will see outside of Hell's jurisdiction.
Displayed in a manner beyond obscene
The bodies of men, dead, yet living still.
Everywhere faces of treacherous mien
Staring at us with palpable ill-will,
Flippers of mortgages, sellers of stocks,
Feeders of hedge funds, and then, the great shill.
I saw the mastermind, Ponzi's fox
Buried to his waist in the stinking mire,
His skin all covered by a weeping pox.
Is that who I think it is, my good sire?
Indeed, acceded the wise with grim smile,
Be glad we pass when the tide is higher
You would not fain see beneath the muck vile
Below is where the worms him devour.
We walked over stones along the defile,
Dark was the sky and late was the hour.
We passed chasms filled with human debris
Hearing screams of those in evil's power,
And still I shed no tear of sympathy
Nor did the Master once slacken his stride.
Who could ever feel any empathy

For those accursed with such towering pride?
Beyond we saw a great red-golden glow
Downward we strode and downward did we slide
Towards a gleaming pit through which there flow'd
The river of Midas in full advance.
Bubbling, boiling, burning, and so
Scalding the servants of debt and finance
That they shrieked, and wept, and shamelessly cried.
The archaic current took its vengeance
On politicians from every side.
A fitting reward I had to admit
For the predicament they'd caused worldwide.
In silence we walked on past the dread pit
Sublime, it was, verily to behold,
And prodigious heat did it emit.
Leaving behind that great river of gold.
Beneath my feet was no more stone, but ice,
Darkness descended and also the cold.
I shivered and hoped the Guide would suffice
To ensure we were permitted to pass
This Fimbul-winter of devils' device
That Zero Kelvin would barely surpass.
Then I saw two shades held in ice confined
A frozen embrace thus holding them fast.
Their eyes, tormented, showed madness of mind
And snow on the beard of one could be seen
Their arms were locked and their fates intertwined.
As none could hope to ever intervene.
Freezing though I was, colder my blood ran
Upon realizing that icy scene
Was Ben Bernanke and Alan Greenspan.
Entrapped in cruel bonds of hard liquidity,
My Guide gestured round with expansive hand.
They damned themselves by their cupidity.
Live by the target, then die by the rate,
This is the the consequence, naturally.

They sold for credit the soul of the state.
Finance First and Foremost was their belief
Thus they encouraged assets to inflate
While withholding from the public relief.
Then we left the Maestro and the Scholar
In ongoing committee of boundless brief.
Not far now was the King of the Dollar
Toward him, my Guide urged. If your eyes avail
To espy him, go and see the squalor
Ere the Last Trump and the epic fail
Of the King of the kingdom of Despair
And out of the ice, at such mighty scale
I saw a giant beyond all compare.
His ghastly visages were thricely florid,
Although mayhap they were once passing fair
Afore his constitution fell morbid.
Entrapped was he, by that which held the two,
Central bankers caught on that plain horrid,
Liquid flowed down causing ice to accrue
And held that monster fast about the waist.
Each of his three mouths endeavored to chew
What turned out to be an awful repaste.
Three great sinners now great evil endured.
The first called Schoolmaster, now in poor taste,
His legs dangled as his head was tortured.
The second was once a president too,
Twelve long years a thief, his fate was assured.
The third morsel managed to so construe
A crisis as to hold nations hostage,
Arrogance such as the world never knew.
Look well on them, for this is the knowledge,
The fruit of the tree of economy
Which will in the end human action judge.
Man is not born into man's slavery
Nor may he be ruled, even in defeat,
Through the will of another's knavery.

Ergo the reliance upon deceit
By those who dare think to control the land,
Theirs is no more than the fatal conceit,
Oft shattered by the Invisible Hand.

GLOSSARY

Austrian School: An economic ideology based on the theories of Carl Menger, Eugen von Böhm-Bawerk, Ludwig von Mises, and F.A. Hayek. Primarily known for its business cycle theory and a preference for logical analysis over statistical empiricism.

BEA: The Bureau of Economic Analysis. Responsible for tracking and reporting GDP, CPI, and other important macroeconomic statistics.

BLS: The Bureau of Labor Statistics. Responsible for tracking and reporting the labor force and unemployment rates.

BOJ: The Bank of Japan. The Japanese central bank.

Boom: A period of economic expansion, especially rapid economic expansion. It can refer to either an economy as a whole, an economic sector, or even a specific asset class.

Bubble: A rapid increase in prices driven by speculation or bank credit inflation in an asset class.

Business cycle: An economy's tendency to transition between expansionary and contractionary phases.

Bust: A period of economic contraction or a rapid post-bubble decline in prices in an economic sector or asset class.

Central Bank: The financial organization given legal monopoly power over money by a sovereign government; can be a private institution or a national one. Usually responsible for setting interest rate targets and controlling the growth of the money supply. In the United States, the Federal Reserve System also assumes some responsibility for regulating the financial system, encouraging GDP growth, and maintaining asset price levels.

Credit Inflation: An increase in the amount of debt.

CPI: The Consumer Price Index. A statistical measure of monetary inflation computed by tracking the prices of a basket of goods and services. There are several variants reported by the BEA.

Contraction: A decrease in the value of the sum total of economic activity in a given economy. In macroeconomic terms, this is defined as a decline in real GDP.

Contracyclical: Against the business cycle. An expansionary monetary policy enacted in times of economic contraction is "contracyclical."

Deflation: A general decrease in the money supply. Often confused with its primary symptom, a decrease in the general level of prices.

Depression: A generic term for any economic contraction. Today, it is more typically regarded as an economic contraction that is more severe than a recession and features a reduction in real GDP of 10 percent or more.

Economy: An abstract concept encompassing all of the value-related human action in a geographic region or by a specific group of people. The Oxford English Dictionary describes it as "the state of a country or region in terms of the production and consumption of goods and services and the supply of money."

Economics: The study of value. Conventionally, the scientific discipline concerned with the production, consumption, and transfer of wealth.

Expansion: An increase in the value of the sum total of economic activity in a given economy. In macroeconomic terms this is considered to be synonymous with an increase in real GDP.

FDIC: Federal Deposit Insurance Corporation. The government agency that insures American bank deposits for up to $250,000 and is responsible for seizing and distributing the assets of insolvent banks.

Federal Reserve: The 4th and current central bank of the United States.

Federal Reserve Note: Paper liabilities of the Federal Reserve Banks issued as currency and backed by the credit of the U.S. government. More commonly known as "U.S. dollars."

Federal Funds Rate: The important interest rate at which the Federal Reserve targets for unsecured loans of reserves belonging to one bank which loaned to another bank, usually overnight. Because these reserves are held at the Federal Reserve Banks, they are called "federal funds."

Fiat: That which holds value solely through the declaration of the political authorities. Most modern currencies are currently "fiat money" because they possess no intrinsic value, unlike a gold Roman *solidus* or even a copper penny, which will retain its value long after the government that issued it is gone.

Fiscal Policy: Government taxing and spending. To lower taxes and increase spending is considered expansionary, to raise taxes and reduce spending is considered contractionary.

Gaijin: Foreigner, non-Japanese.

GDP: Gross Domestic Product. The primary macroeconomic measure of a geographically defined national economy, defined by the BEA as a measure of the market value of goods, services, and structures produced in the economy during a particular period. Reported on a quarterly basis, GDP consists of a basic formula involving C (private consumption) + I (private domestic investment) + G (government spending and investment) +((X–M) eXports – iMports). An aggregate statistical measure developed from Keynesian general theory; it is often utilized as a practical synonym for "the economy."

GNP: Gross National Product. Similar to GDP, but adds the economic activity of a country's nationals regardless of where they are resident while subtracting the activity of foreign nationals resident in the country.

Great Depression: The worldwide economic downturn of the 1930s. The Encyclopedia Britannica defines it as lasting from 1929 to 1939, but the depth and extent varied from country to country. In the United States, it lasted from 1929 to 1936 in real terms, but did not end in terms of nominal GDP until 1941.

Heisei Boom: The Japanese investment boom of the 1980s that came to an end in the first year of the reign of the Heisei Emperor, Akihito.

IMF: The International Monetary Fund. An international bank that oversees the global financial system, tracks macroeconomic data, offers loans to national governments, and manages a basket currency called Special Drawing Rights. The most likely candidate for a global central bank.

Inflation: A general increase in the money supply. Often confused with its primary symptom, an increase in the general level of prices. CPI is the primary statistical measure of the latter.

Interest rate: The price of borrowing money.

Invisible Hand: Adam Smith's famous term for the forces of the free market.

Keiretsu: A Japanese business group with interlocking ownership centered around a major bank.

Keynesianism: An economic ideology based on the general theory of John Maynard Keynes. Formerly known as "The New Economics." Best known for its contracyclical policy prescriptions, it became the dominant economic theory after World War II and provided the primary theoretical basis for modern macroeconomics.

M0-M3: Different measures of the money supply, or the amount of money circulating in an economic system. M0 is the most strictly defined, M3 is the broadest.

Macroeconomics: The branch of economics encompassing theories, models, and statistical measures that relate to the aggregate economy rather than individual actors.

Malinvestment: Investment being directed into unproductive economic sectors, usually as a result of false market signals created by bank credit inflation. An important Austrian School concept.

Microeconomics: The branch of economics concerned with the behavior of unitary economic actors, such as individuals, households and organizations.

Monetarism: An economic ideology based on the monetary theories of Milton Friedman. Also known as "The Chicago School" of economics. It is a theoretical off-shoot of Keynesianism that regards the variation in the size of the money supply as the most important economic variable.

Monetary Policy: The central bank's official position on interest rate targets and the growth rate of the money supply. Expansionary monetary policy indicates low interest rates and faster growth of the money supply, contractionary policy is high interest rates and a reduction of the money supply.

Neo-Keynesianism: An economic ideology which makes use of Keynesian concepts, contracyclical policy prescriptions and aggregate statistical measures without accepting their theoretical bases in Keynesian general theory. It is sometimes described as a synthesis of Keynesian general theory with neo-classical economic models or microeconomics.

Nominal: Uncorrected for changes in monetary value. GDP is reported in both nominal and real terms.

N-body: A variable number of bodies, N representing a numerical value.

OECD: The Organisation for Economic Co-operation and Development. Founded to administer the post-WWII Marshall Plan, member states are: Austria, Belgium, Canada, Denmark, France, Germany, Greece, Iceland, Ireland, Italy, Luxembourg, Netherlands,

Norway, Portugal, Spain, Sweden, Switzerland, Turkey, United Kingdom, United States, Japan, Finland, Australia, New Zealand, Mexico, Czech Republic, South Korea, Hungary, Poland, Slovakia. Publishes *The World Economic Outlook*.

Praxeology: The science of human action. A core concept of the Austrian School.

Real: Corrected for changes in monetary value. In order to accurately compare two time periods, it is necessary to account for the inflation or the deflation of the money supply from the previous period to the more recent one. A 2 percent gain in nominal GDP combined with 2 percent inflation indicates no change in real GDP.

Recession: A mild to moderate economic contraction indicated by a decline in real GDP. A decline in two consecutive quarters is usually considered a recession.

Securitization: The packaging and selling of debt to third party investors. A debt-based investment product is known as a "security."

Socionomics: The neo-science of mass human social mood.

Stagflation: Simultaneous inflation and high unemployment combined with low-to-negative GDP growth. This was considered to be a theoretical impossibility by the Neo-Keynesians prior to the American stagflation of the 1970s.

Wall Street: Slang term encompassing the American financial sector, as many important financial institutions have their headquarters located on the Manhattan street of this name, which also hosts the New York Stock Exchange.

BANK FAILURES
1930–2009

Year	Banks	Total	% Fail	Failed Deposits	Total Deposits	% Fail	Failed Deposits ($2009)
1930	1,350	21,717	6.2%	837,096	50,711,000	1.65%	10,811,721
1931	2,293	20,367	11.3%	160,232	46,974,000	0.34%	2,273,744
1932	1,453	18,074	8.0%	706,188	35,484,000	1.99%	11,118,234
1933	2,666	17,796	14.9%	2,729,698	31,911,000	8.55%	45,290,519
2008	25	8,534	0.3%	234,321,715	7,300,600,000	3.21%	234,746,166
2009	81	8,195	1.0%	73,142,835	7,566,800,000	0.97%	73,142,835 YTD

It should be noted that the 2009 figures only cover January through August 2009. Since the rate of bank failure has been increasing, from 25 in all of 2008 to 45 in the first half of 2009 alone, total deposits in failed banks for 2009 will likely be in excess of $105 billion and 1.4% of total deposits held by U.S. depository institutions. These failures have severely depleted the FDIC's Deposit Insurance Fund, which was on pace to run out before the end of the year were it not for the establishment of a $500 billion line of credit from the federal government in May.

247

BIBLIOGRAPHY

Asher, David L. "What became of the Japanese 'miracle,'" *ORBIS*. (Spring, 1996).

Bernanke, Ben S. *Essays on The Great Depression*. Princeton: Princeton University Press, 2000.

Böhm-Bawerk, Eugen. *Karl Marx and the Close of His System*.

Bury, J.B., ed. *The Cambridge Medieval History, Vol. I*. Cambridge: Cambridge University Press, 1911.

Carlson, Mark. *A Brief History of the 1987 Stock Market Crash with a Discussion of the Federal Reserve Response*. New York: Board of Governors of the Federal Reserve. November 2008.

Colander, David, et al. "The Financial Crisis and the Systemic Failure of Academic Economics," Kiel Institute for the World Economy. No. 1489 February 2009.

Connant, Charles A. *The Principles of Money and Banking*. New York: Harper & Brothers Publishers, 1905.

Cooper, George. *The Origin of Financial Crises: Central Banks, Credit Bubbles and the Efficient Market Fallacy*. New York: Vintage Books, 2008.

Eichengreen, Barry. "The Origins and Nature of the Great Slump Revisited," *The Economic History Review*, New Series, Volume 45, Issue 2 (May, 1992), 213-239.

Epstein, Edward Jay. "What Was Lost (and Found) in Japan's Lost Decade," *Vanity Fair*. 17 Feb. 2009.

Fixler, Dennis J. and Bruce T. Grimm. "The Reliability of the GDP and GDI Estimates." Survey of Current Business. Feb. 2008, 16-32.

Friedman, Milton, *Capitalism & Freedom*. Chicago: The University of Chicago Press, 1962.

——. *Essays in Positive Economics*. Chicago: The University of Chicago Press, 1953.

——. *The Optimum Quantity of Money and Other Essays*. Chicago: Aldine Publishing Company, 1970.

——. *Money Mischief*. Orlando: Harcourt Brace, 1992.

——. "The Role of Monetary Policy," *The American Economic Review*, Vol. 58, No. 1. (Mar., 1968), pp. 1-17.

Friedman, Milton and Rose Friedman. *Free to Choose: A Personal Statement*. Orlando: Harcourt Books, 1990.

Friedman, Milton and Anna Jacobson Schwartz. *A Monetary History of the United States, 1857-1960*. Princeton: Princeton University Press, 1993.

Getter, Darryl E. et al. "Financial Crisis? The Liquidity Crunch of August 2007" *CRS Report for Congress*, September 21, 2007.

Greenlees, John S. and Robert B. McClelland. "Misconceptions about the CPI," *Monthly Labor Review*. August 2008. pp. 3-17.

Greenspan, Alan. *The Age of Turbulence: Adventures in a New World*. New York: Penguin Books, 2008.

Hazlitt, Henry. *The Failure of the "New Economics": An Analysis of the Keynesian Fallacies*. Princeton: D. Van Nostrand Company, 1959.

Hazlitt, Henry, ed. *The Critics of Keynesian Economics*. Irvington-on-Hudson: The Foundation for Economic Education, 1995.

Hayek, F.A. *The Collected Works of F.A. Hayek Volume IX: Contra Keynes and Cambridge: Essays, Correspondence*. Edited by Bruce Caldwell. Chicago: University of Chicago Press, 1995.

Holcome, Randall G., ed. *15 Great Austrian Economists*. Auburn: Ludwig Von Mises Institute, 1999.

Hülsmann, Jörg Guido. *Deflation and Liberty*. Auburn: Ludwig Von Mises Institute, 2008.

International Monetary Fund. *World Economic Outlook April 2009: Crisis and Recovery*. Washington, DC: International Monetary Fund, 2009.

———. *World Economic Outlook October 2008: Financial Stress, Downturns, and Recoveries*. Washington, DC: International Monetary Fund, 2008.

———. *World Economic Outlook April 2008: Housing and the Business Cycle*. Washington, DC: International Monetary Fund, 2008.

———. *World Economic Outlook October 2007: Globalization and Inequality*. Washington, DC: International Monetary Fund, 2007.

———. *World Economic Outlook April 2007: Spillovers and Cycles in the Global Economy*. Washington, DC: International Monetary Fund, 2007.

———. *World Economic Outlook October 2006: Financial Systems and Economic Cycles*. Washington, DC: International Monetary Fund, 2006.

———. *World Economic Outlook April 2006: Globalization and Inflation*. Washington, DC: International Monetary Fund, 2006.

Keynes, John Maynard. *The General Theory of Employment, Interest, and Money*. Hamburg: Management Laboratory Press, 2009.

———. *A Tract on Monetary Reform*. BN Publishing, 2008.

———. *The Economic Consequences of the Peace*. 1919.

Kindleberger, Charles P. and Robert Aliber. *Manics, Panics, and Crashes: A History of Financial Crises*. Hoboken: John Wiley & Sons, 2005.

Koo, Richard C. *The Holy Grail of Macroeconomics: Lessons From Japan's Great Recession*. Singapore: John Wiley & Sons (Asia), 2008.

Krugman, Paul. *The Return of Depression Economics*. London: Penguin Books, 1999.

———. *The Return of Depression Economics and the Crisis of 2008*. New York: W.W. Norton & Company, 2009.

——. *The Accidental Theorist*. London: Penguin Books, 1999.

——. *The Great Unravelling: Losing Our Way in the New Century*. New York: W.W. Norton & Company, 2004

Lunstad, Andrew. *Attractive Bottoms*. Lewisburg: Bucknell University Press, 1991.

Mises, Ludwig von. *Human Action: A Treatise on Economics*. Auburn: The Ludwig von Mises Institute, 1998.

Miyashita, Kenichi and David Russell. *Keiretsu: Inside the Hidden Japanese Conglomerates*. New York: McGraw-Hill, 1994.

Morita, Akio and Shintaro Ishihara. *The Japan That Can Say No*. Unauthorized translation, 1989.

Newton, Isaac. *The Principia: Mathematical Principles of Natural Philosophy*. Translated by I. Bernard Cohen and Anne Whitman. Berkeley: The University of California Press, 1999.

O'Rourke, P.J. *On The Wealth of Nations*. New York: Atlantic Monthly Press, 2007.

Pinsky, Robert. *The Inferno of Dante*. New York: Farrar, Straus, and Giroux, 1997.

Prechter, Robert Jr. and A.J. Frost. *Elliott Wave Principle*. Gainesville: New Classics Library, 2001.

Prechter, Robert J. and Wayne D. Parker. "The Financial/Economic Dichotomy in Social Behavioral Dynamics: The Socionomic Perspective," *The Journal of Behavioral Finance*, Vol. 8, No. 2. 2007.

Prechter, Robert Jr. *The Wave Principle of Human Social Behavior and the New Science of Socionomics*. Gainesville: New Classics Library, 2002.

——. *Pioneering Studies in Socionomics*. Gainesville: New Classics Library, 2003.

Ricardo, David. *The Principles of Political Economy and Taxation*. Mineola: Dover Publications, 2004.

Rothbard, Murray N. *A History of Money and Banking in the United States: The Colonial Era to World War II*. Auburn: The Ludwig von Mises Institute, 2002.

———. *America's Great Depression*. Auburn: The Ludwig von Mises Institute, 2000.

Runkle, David E. "Revisionist History: How Data Revisions Distort Economic Policy Research," *Federal Reserve Bank of Minneapolis Quarterly Review*, Vol. 22, No. 4, Fall 1998, pp. 3–12.

Samuelson, Paul A. *Economics: An Introductory Analysis*. New York: McGraw-Hill Book Company, 1948.

Saxonhouse, Gary R. and Robert M. Stern, ed. *Japan's Lost Decade: Origins, Consequences, and Prospects for Recovery*. Malden: Blackwell Publishing, 2004.

Schumpeter, Joseph A. *Capitalism, Socialism, and Democracy*. New York: Harper Colophon, 1975.

———. *History of Economic Analysis*. London: George Allen & Unwin Ltd, 1963.

———. *The Theory of Economic Development*. New York: Oxford University Press, 1961.

Smith, Adam. *The Wealth of Nations*. New York: Bantam Dell, 2003.

Steil, Benn, "Lessons of the Financial Crisis." *Council Special Report No. 45*. Center for Geoeconomic Studies, Council on Foreign Relations. March 2009.

Stiglitz, Joseph E., et al, ed. *The Economist's Voice: Top Economists Take on Today's Problems*. New York: Columbia University Press, 2008.

Summers, Lawrence. "Planning for the Next Financial Crisis." *Macroeconomic Consequences of Financial Crises*. 135-157.

U.S. Bureau of the Census. *Historical Statistics of the United States: Colonial Times to 1970, Bicentennial Edition, Part 1*. Washington D.C.: 1975.

———. *Historical Statistics of the United States: Colonial Times to 1970, Bicentennial Edition, Part 2*. Washington D.C.: 1975.

Woods, Thomas. *Meltdown: A Free-Market Look at Why the Stock Market Collapsed, the Economy Tanked, and Government Bailouts Will Make Things Worse*. Washington D.C.: Regnery Press, 2009.

Wynne, Mark A. "Core Inflation: A Review of Some Conceptual Issues." *Federal Reserve Bank of St. Louis Review.* May/June 2008, (Part 2), pp. 205-228.

INDEX